FEARLESS

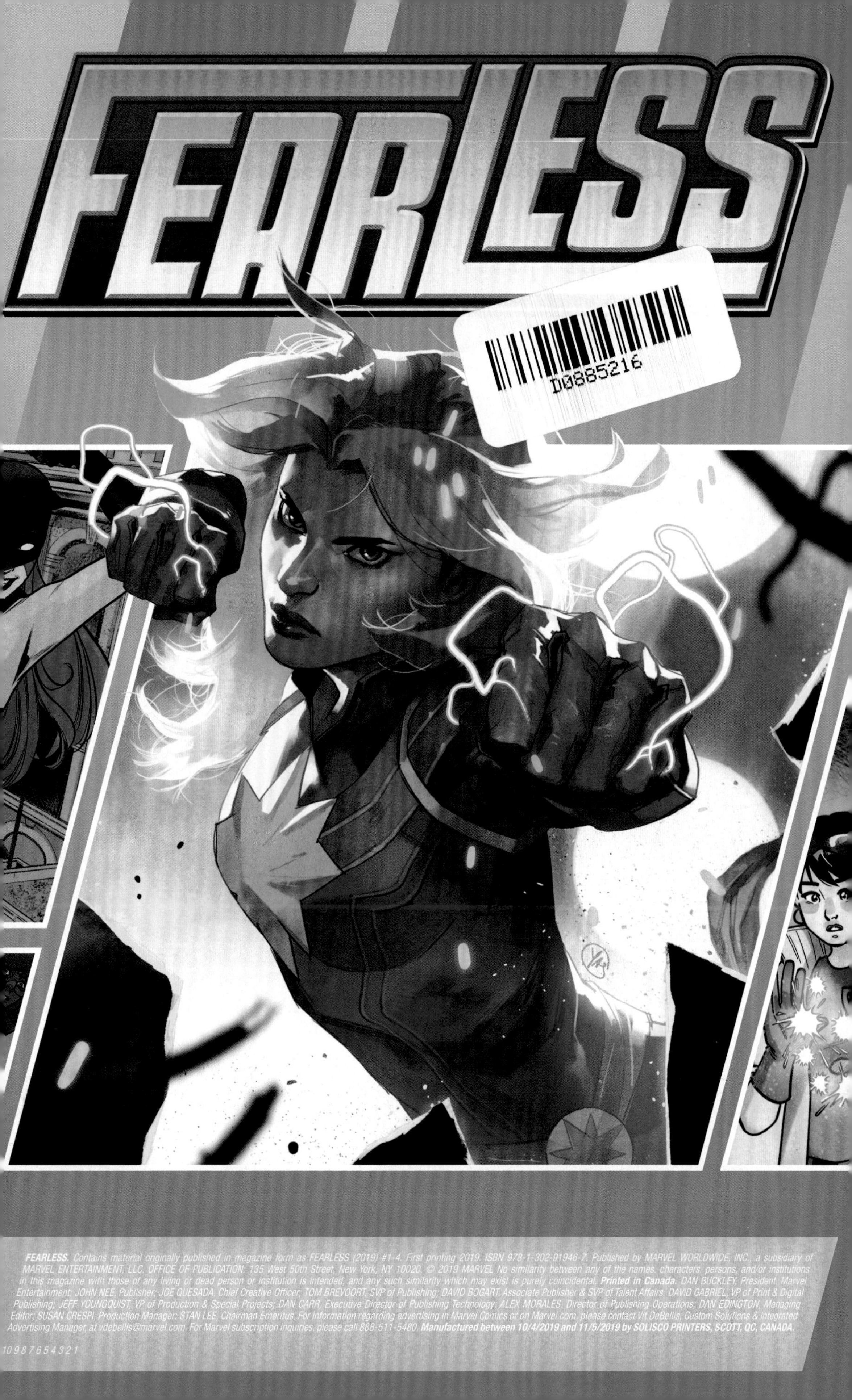

FEARLESS. Contains material originally published in magazine form as FEARLESS (2019) #1-4. First printing 2019. ISBN 978-1-302-91946-7. Published by MARVEL WORLDWIDE, INC., a subsidiary of MARVEL ENTERTAINMENT, LLC. OFFICE OF PUBLICATION: 135 West 50th Street, New York, NY 10020. © 2019 MARVEL No similarity between any of the names, characters, persons, and/or institutions in this magazine with those of any living or dead person or institution is intended, and any such similarity which may exist is purely coincidental. **Printed in Canada.** DAN BUCKLEY, President, Marvel Entertainment; JOHN NEE, Publisher; JOE QUESADA, Chief Creative Officer; TOM BREVOORT, SVP of Publishing; DAVID BOGART, Associate Publisher & SVP of Talent Affairs; DAVID GABRIEL, VP of Print & Digital Publishing; JEFF YOUNGQUIST, VP of Production & Special Projects; DAN CARR, Executive Director of Publishing Technology; ALEX MORALES, Director of Publishing Operations; DAN EDINGTON, Managing Editor; SUSAN CRESPI, Production Manager; STAN LEE, Chairman Emeritus. For information regarding advertising in Marvel Comics or on Marvel.com, please contact Vit DeBellis, Custom Solutions & Integrated Advertising Manager, at vdebellis@marvel.com. For Marvel subscription inquiries, please call 888-511-5480. **Manufactured between 10/4/2019 and 11/5/2019 by SOLISCO PRINTERS, SCOTT, QC, CANADA.**

10 9 8 7 6 5 4 3 2 1

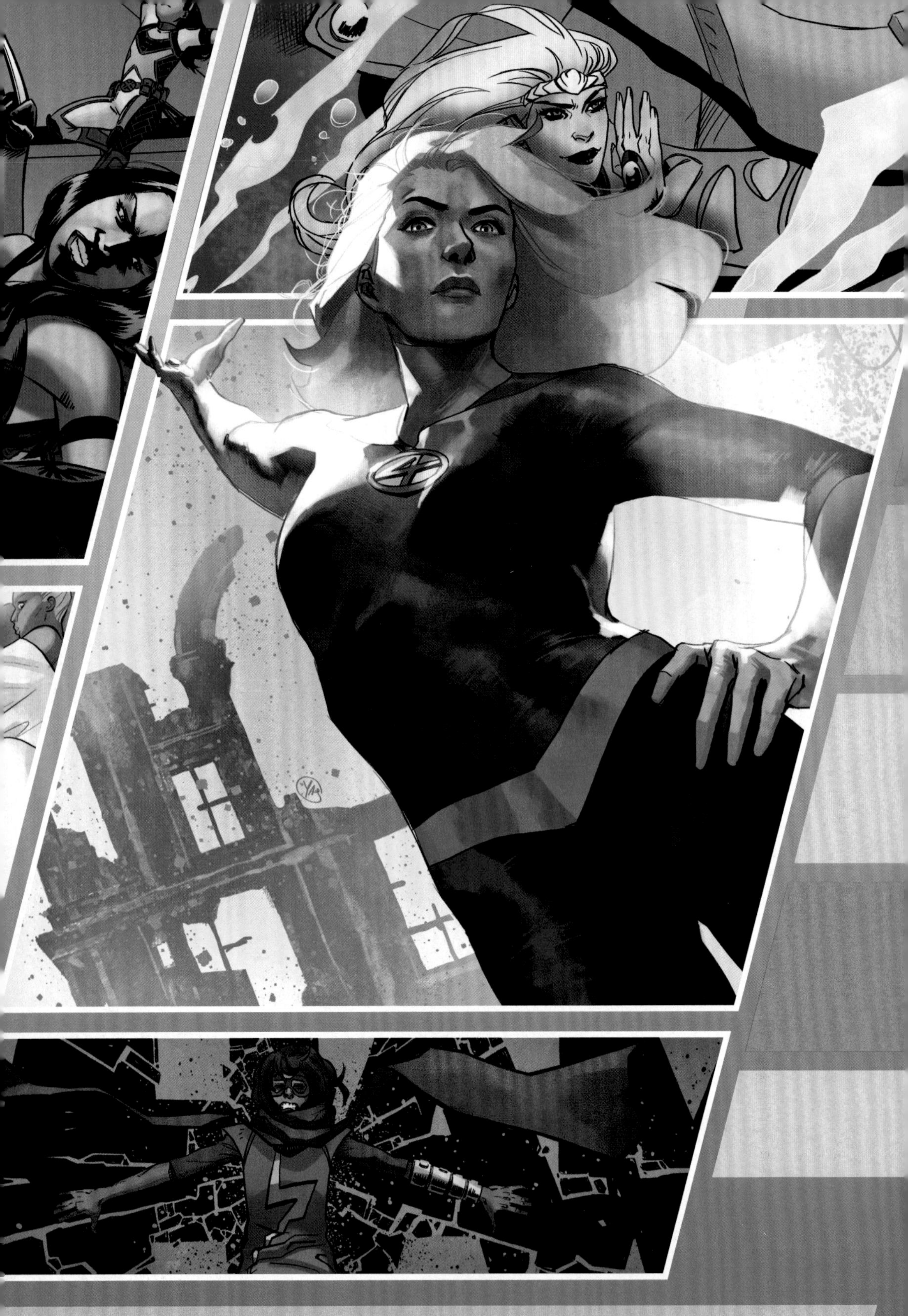

COLLECTION EDITOR: **JENNIFER GRÜNWALD**
ASSISTANT EDITOR: **CAITLIN O'CONNELL**
ASSOCIATE MANAGING EDITOR: **KATERI WOODY**
EDITOR, SPECIAL PROJECTS: **MARK D. BEAZLEY**
VP PRODUCTION & SPECIAL PROJECTS: **JEFF YOUNGQUIST**
BOOK DESIGNER: **STACIE ZUCKER**

SVP PRINT, SALES & MARKETING: **DAVID GABRIEL**
DIRECTOR, LICENSED PUBLISHING: **SVEN LARSEN**
EDITOR IN CHIEF: **C.B. CEBULSKI**
CHIEF CREATIVE OFFICER: **JOE QUESADA**
PRESIDENT: **DAN BUCKLEY**
EXECUTIVE PRODUCER: **ALAN FINE**

"CAMPFIRE SONG"
WRITER **SEANAN McGUIRE**
ARTIST **CLAIRE ROE**
COLOR ARTIST **RACHELLE ROSENBERG**

"STYLE HIGH CLUB"
WRITER **LEAH WILLIAMS**
ARTIST **NINA VAKUEVA**
COLOR ARTIST **RACHELLE ROSENBERG**

"UNUSUAL SUSPECTS"
WRITER **KELLY THOMPSON**
ARTIST **CARMEN CARNERO**
COLOR ARTIST **TAMRA BONVILLAIN**

"NIGHT NURSE: A CAPE OF HER OWN"
WRITER **KARLA PACHECO**
ARTIST **IOLANDA ZANFARDINO**
COLOR ARTIST **RACHELLE ROSENBERG**

"X-23"
WRITER **EVE L. EWING**
ARTIST **ALITHA E. MARTINEZ**
COLOR ARTIST **RACHELLE ROSENBERG**

"COPYCAT"
WRITER **ZOË QUINN**
ARTIST **MARIKA CRESTA**
COLOR ARTIST **IRMA KNIIVILA**

"JUBILATION"
WRITER **ALYSSA WONG**
ARTIST **ALTI FIRMANSYAH**
COLOR ARTIST **RACHELLE ROSENBERG**

"ATMOSPHERIA"
WRITER **TINI HOWARD**
ARTIST **ROSI KÄMPE**
COLOR ARTIST **MUNTSA VICENTE**

"GOLDEN GIRLS" & **"TWO GALS EATING ICE CREAM"**
WRITER **TRINA ROBBINS** ARTIST **MARGUERITE SAUVAGE**

LETTERERS: J̶ ̶ ̶ ̶ ̶ ̶ ̶ ̶AL RAE (#2-4)
COVER ART: YA̶ ̶ ̶ ̶
EDITORS: **LAUR̶E̶N̶ ̶ ̶ ̶ ̶ ̶ ̶ ̶ ̶, ̶ ̶ ̶ ̶ ̶ ̶ ̶, SARAH BRUNSTAD,**
ALANNA SMITH & **KATHLEEN WISNESKI**

SPECIAL THANKS TO **SHANNON ANDREWS BALLESTEROS** & **LINDSEY COHICK**

70301940

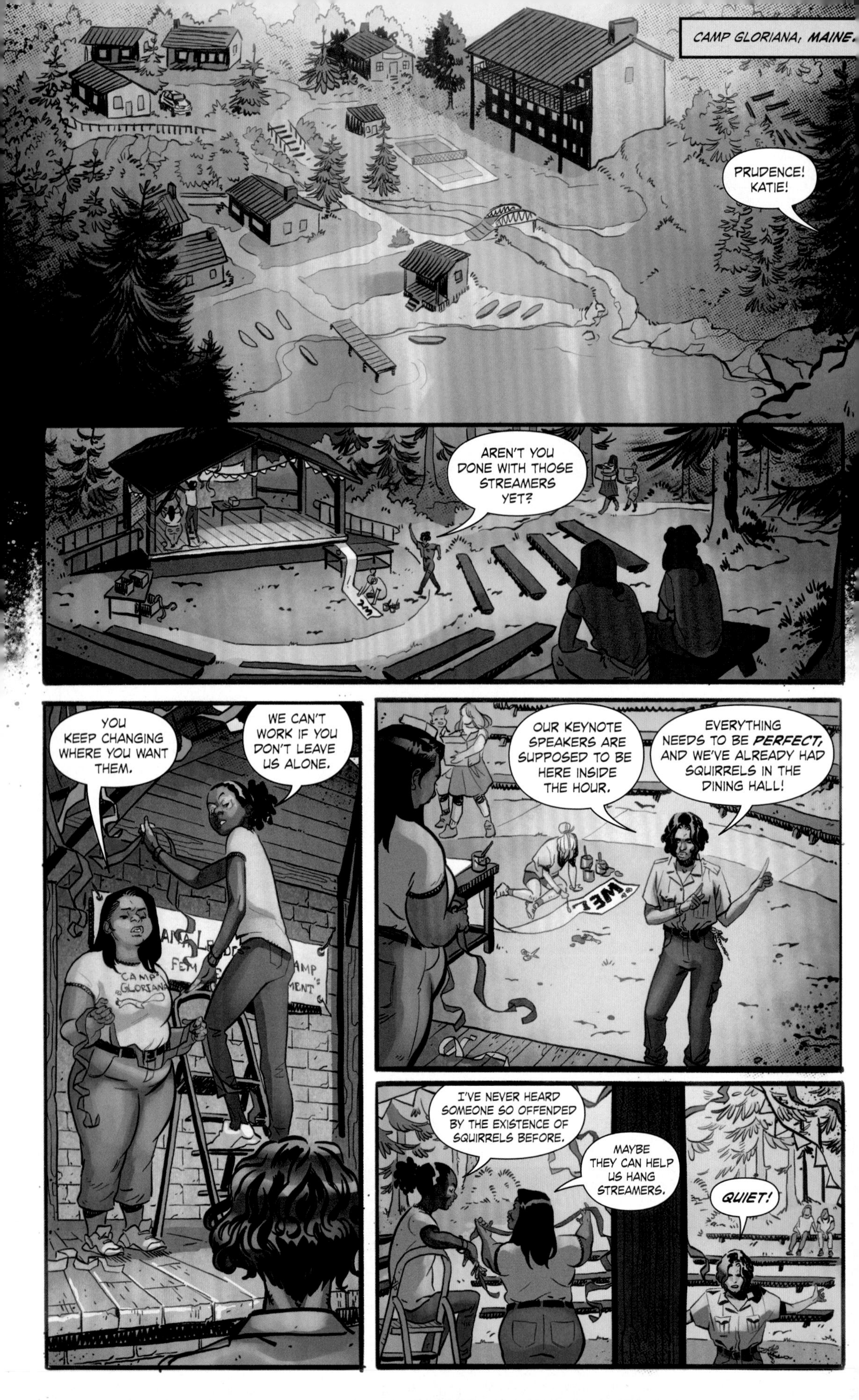
CAMP GLORIANA, MAINE.
PRUDENCE! KATIE!
AREN'T YOU DONE WITH THOSE STREAMERS YET?
YOU KEEP CHANGING WHERE YOU WANT THEM.
WE CAN'T WORK IF YOU DON'T LEAVE US ALONE.
OUR KEYNOTE SPEAKERS ARE SUPPOSED TO BE HERE INSIDE THE HOUR.
EVERYTHING NEEDS TO BE PERFECT, AND WE'VE ALREADY HAD SQUIRRELS IN THE DINING HALL!
I'VE NEVER HEARD SOMEONE SO OFFENDED BY THE EXISTENCE OF SQUIRRELS BEFORE.
MAYBE THEY CAN HELP US HANG STREAMERS.
QUIET!

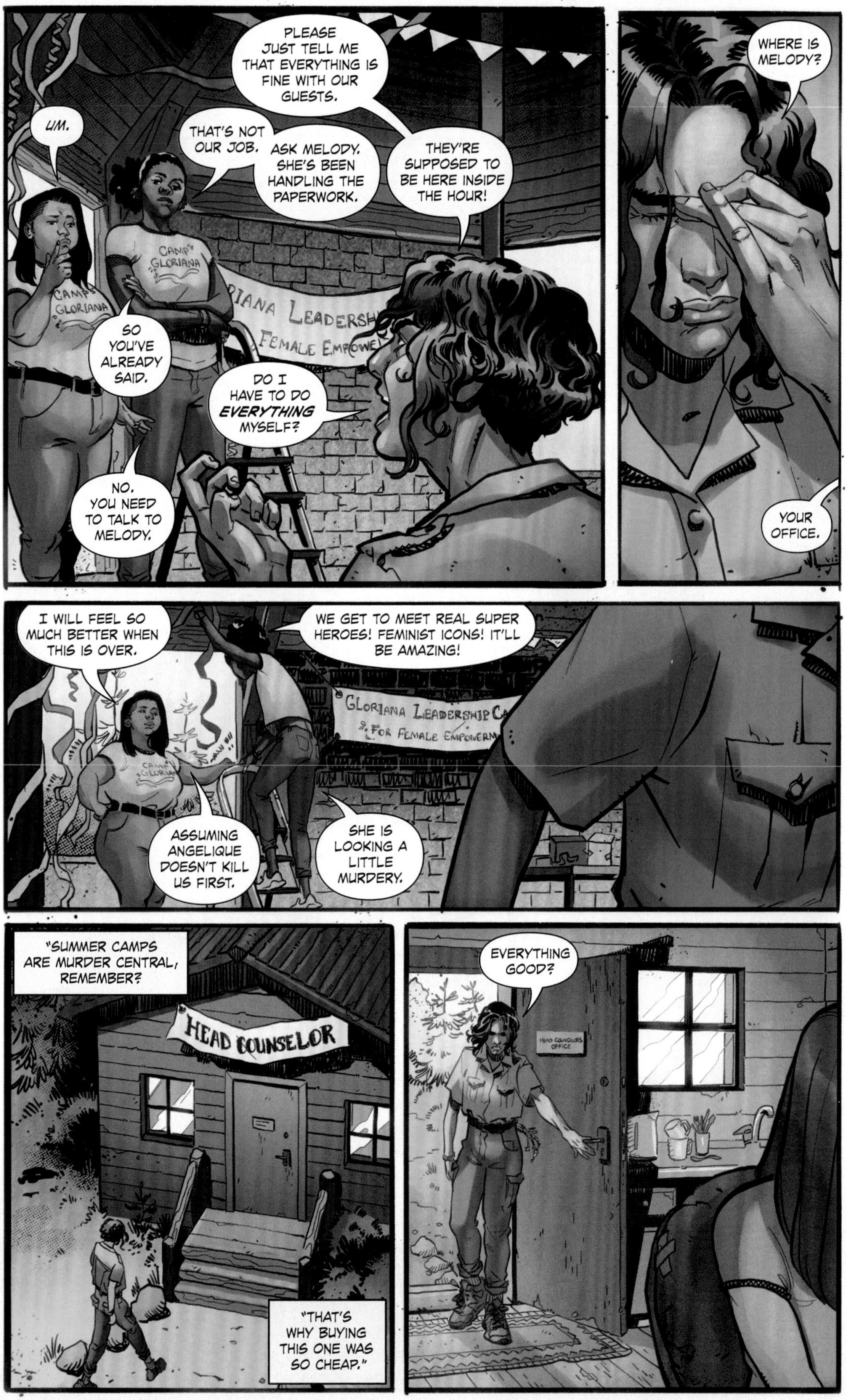
PLEASE JUST TELL ME THAT EVERYTHING IS FINE WITH OUR GUESTS.
UM.
THAT'S NOT OUR JOB.
ASK MELODY. SHE'S BEEN HANDLING THE PAPERWORK.
THEY'RE SUPPOSED TO BE HERE INSIDE THE HOUR!
CAMP GLORIANA
CAMP GLORIANA
RIANA LEADERSH
FEMALE EMPOWE
SO YOU'VE ALREADY SAID.
DO I HAVE TO DO EVERYTHING MYSELF?
NO. YOU NEED TO TALK TO MELODY.
WHERE IS MELODY?
YOUR OFFICE.
I WILL FEEL SO MUCH BETTER WHEN THIS IS OVER.
WE GET TO MEET REAL SUPER HEROES! FEMINIST ICONS! IT'LL BE AMAZING!
GLORIANA LEADERSHIP CA
FOR FEMALE EMPOWERM
CAMP GLORIANA
ASSUMING ANGELIQUE DOESN'T KILL US FIRST.
SHE IS LOOKING A LITTLE MURDERY.
"SUMMER CAMPS ARE MURDER CENTRAL, REMEMBER?
HEAD COUNSELOR
"THAT'S WHY BUYING THIS ONE WAS SO CHEAP."
EVERYTHING GOOD?

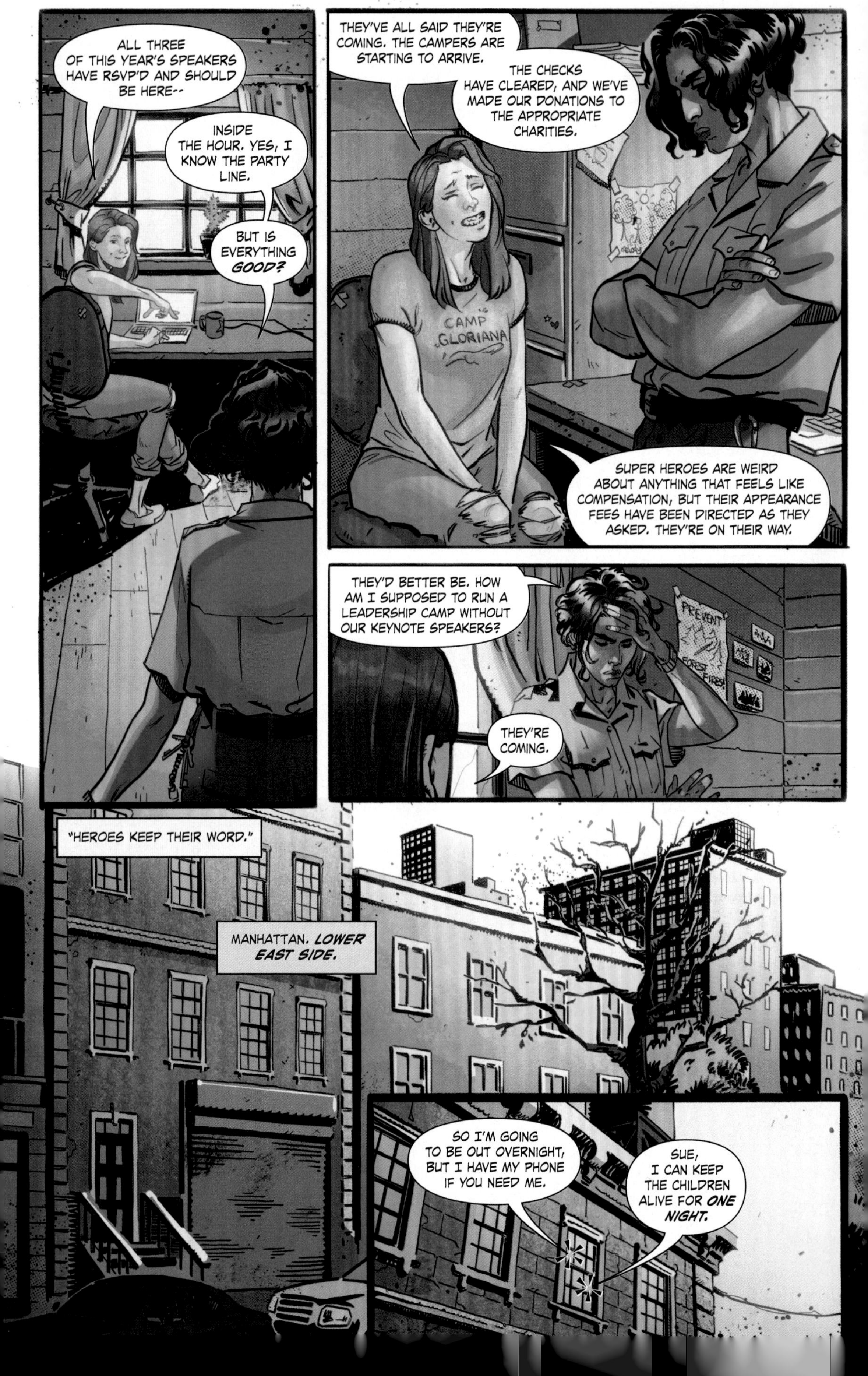
ALL THREE OF THIS YEAR'S SPEAKERS HAVE RSVP'D AND SHOULD BE HERE--
INSIDE THE HOUR. YES, I KNOW THE PARTY LINE.
BUT IS EVERYTHING *GOOD?*
THEY'VE ALL SAID THEY'RE COMING. THE CAMPERS ARE STARTING TO ARRIVE.
THE CHECKS HAVE CLEARED, AND WE'VE MADE OUR DONATIONS TO THE APPROPRIATE CHARITIES.
CAMP GLORIANA
SUPER HEROES ARE WEIRD ABOUT ANYTHING THAT FEELS LIKE COMPENSATION, BUT THEIR APPEARANCE FEES HAVE BEEN DIRECTED AS THEY ASKED. THEY'RE ON THEIR WAY.
THEY'D BETTER BE. HOW AM I SUPPOSED TO RUN A LEADERSHIP CAMP WITHOUT OUR KEYNOTE SPEAKERS?
PREVENT FOREST FIRES!
THEY'RE COMING.
"HEROES KEEP THEIR WORD."
MANHATTAN. *LOWER EAST SIDE.*
SO I'M GOING TO BE OUT OVERNIGHT, BUT I HAVE MY PHONE IF YOU NEED ME.
SUE, I CAN KEEP THE CHILDREN ALIVE FOR *ONE NIGHT.*

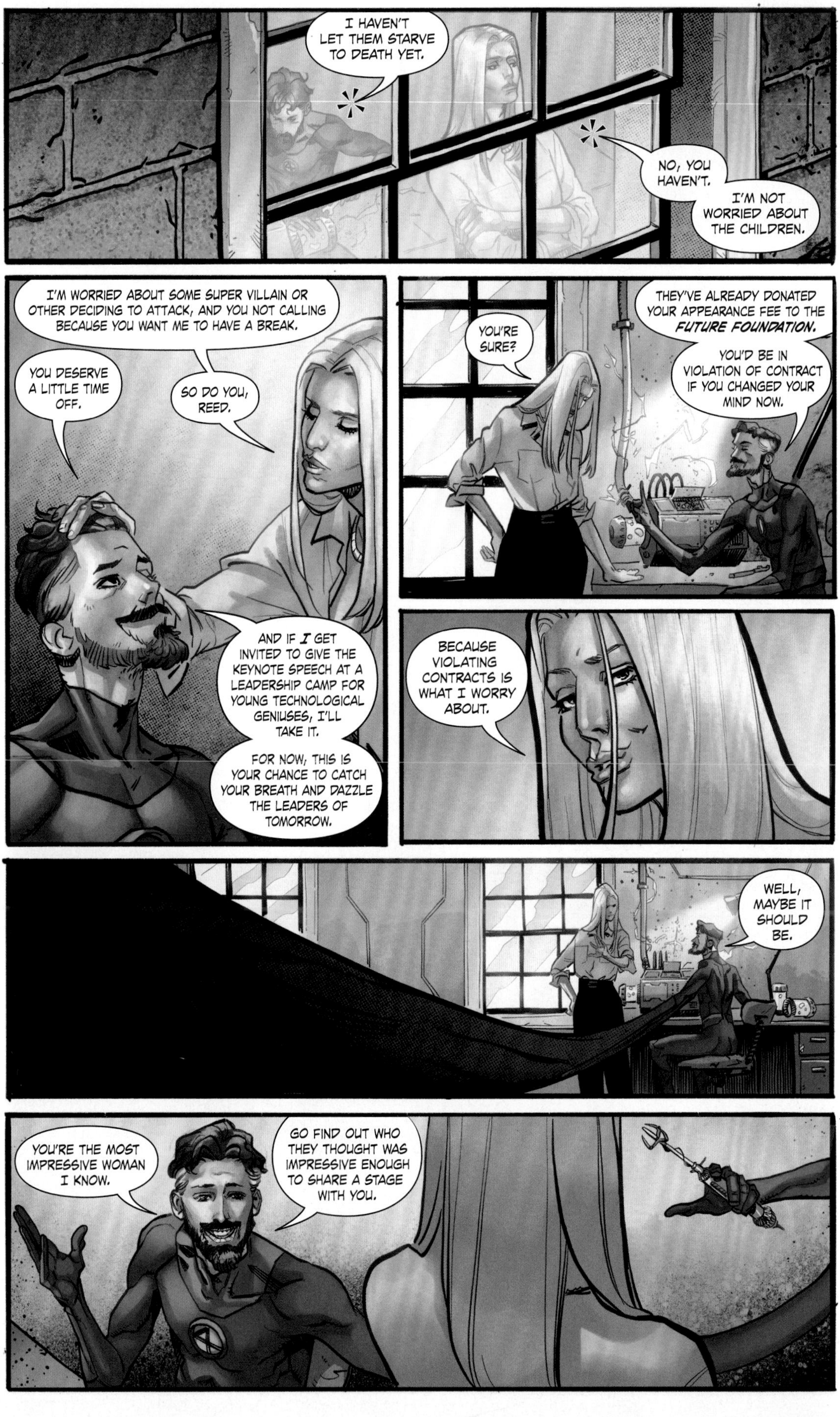
I HAVEN'T LET THEM STARVE TO DEATH YET.
NO, YOU HAVEN'T.
I'M NOT WORRIED ABOUT THE CHILDREN.
I'M WORRIED ABOUT SOME SUPER VILLAIN OR OTHER DECIDING TO ATTACK, AND YOU NOT CALLING BECAUSE YOU WANT ME TO HAVE A BREAK.
YOU DESERVE A LITTLE TIME OFF.
SO DO YOU, REED.
AND IF I GET INVITED TO GIVE THE KEYNOTE SPEECH AT A LEADERSHIP CAMP FOR YOUNG TECHNOLOGICAL GENIUSES, I'LL TAKE IT.
FOR NOW, THIS IS YOUR CHANCE TO CATCH YOUR BREATH AND DAZZLE THE LEADERS OF TOMORROW.
THEY'VE ALREADY DONATED YOUR APPEARANCE FEE TO THE FUTURE FOUNDATION.
YOU'RE SURE?
YOU'D BE IN VIOLATION OF CONTRACT IF YOU CHANGED YOUR MIND NOW.
BECAUSE VIOLATING CONTRACTS IS WHAT I WORRY ABOUT.
WELL, MAYBE IT SHOULD BE.
YOU'RE THE MOST IMPRESSIVE WOMAN I KNOW.
GO FIND OUT WHO THEY THOUGHT WAS IMPRESSIVE ENOUGH TO SHARE A STAGE WITH YOU.

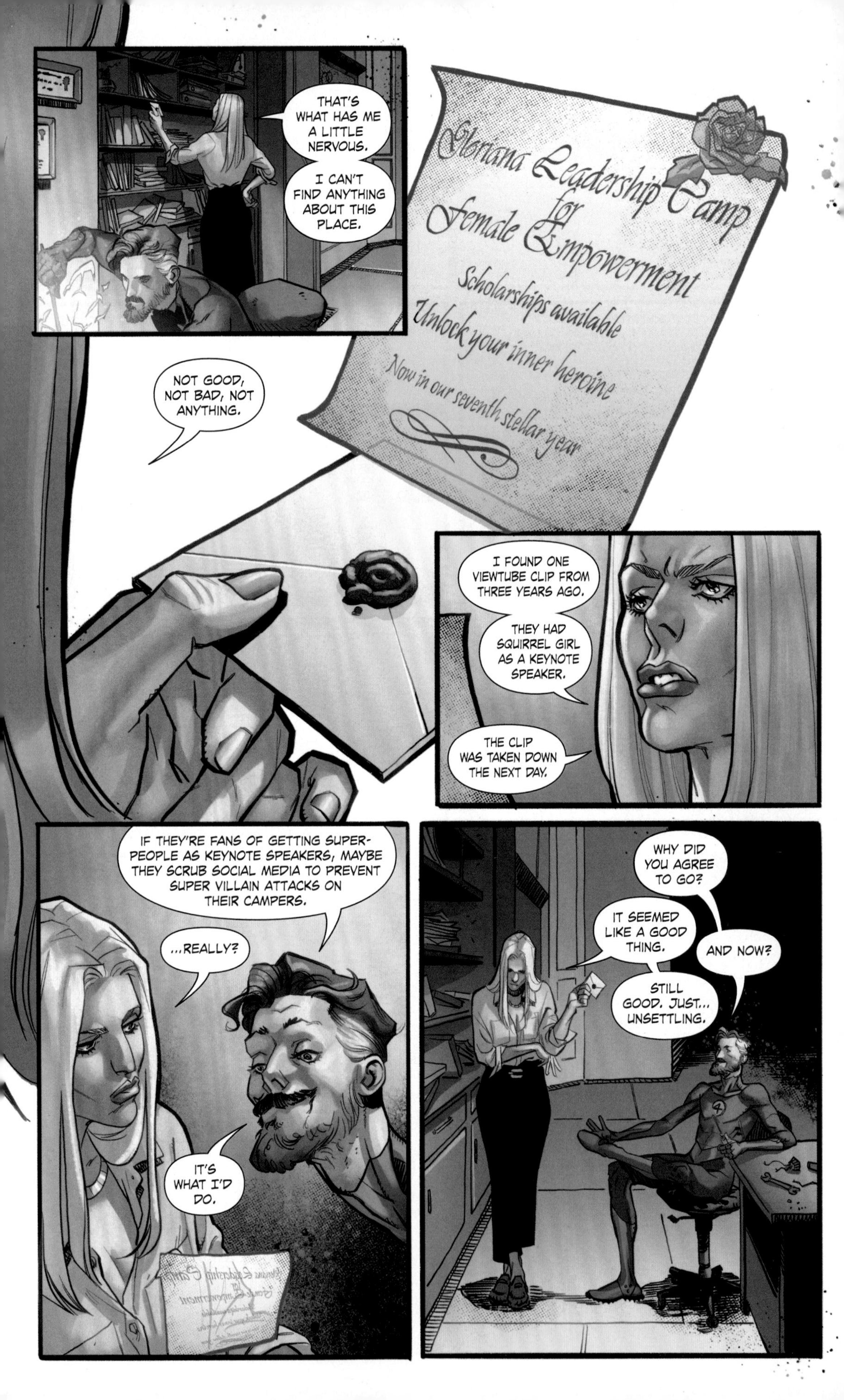
THAT'S WHAT HAS ME A LITTLE NERVOUS.
I CAN'T FIND ANYTHING ABOUT THIS PLACE.
Gloriana Leadership Camp for Female Empowerment
Scholarships available
Unlock your inner heroine
Now in our seventh stellar year
NOT GOOD, NOT BAD, NOT ANYTHING.
I FOUND ONE VIEWTUBE CLIP FROM THREE YEARS AGO.
THEY HAD SQUIRREL GIRL AS A KEYNOTE SPEAKER.
THE CLIP WAS TAKEN DOWN THE NEXT DAY.
IF THEY'RE FANS OF GETTING SUPER-PEOPLE AS KEYNOTE SPEAKERS, MAYBE THEY SCRUB SOCIAL MEDIA TO PREVENT SUPER VILLAIN ATTACKS ON THEIR CAMPERS.
...REALLY?
IT'S WHAT I'D DO.
WHY DID YOU AGREE TO GO?
IT SEEMED LIKE A GOOD THING.
AND NOW?
STILL GOOD. JUST... UNSETTLING.

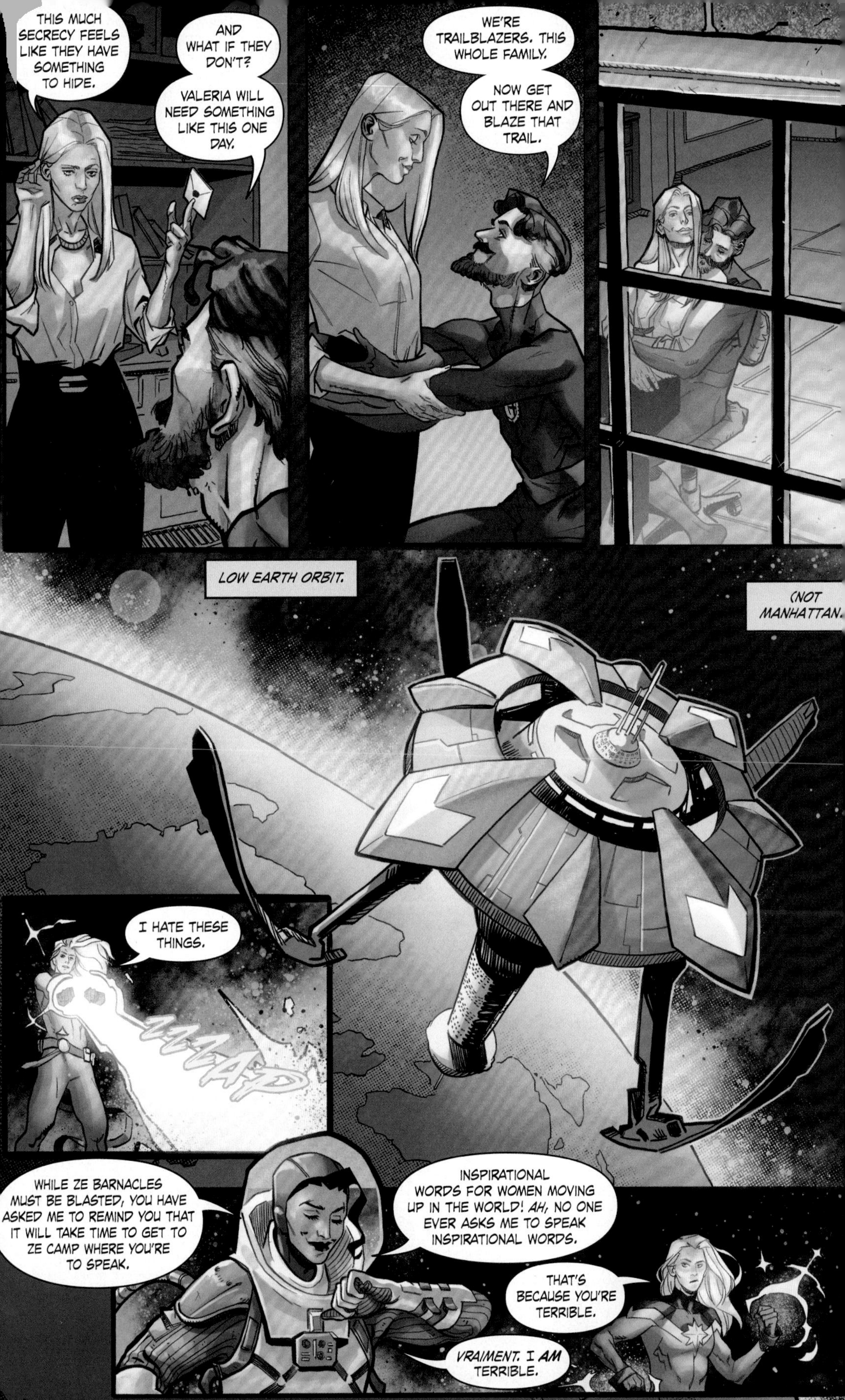
THIS MUCH SECRECY FEELS LIKE THEY HAVE SOMETHING TO HIDE.
AND WHAT IF THEY DON'T?
VALERIA WILL NEED SOMETHING LIKE THIS ONE DAY.
WE'RE TRAILBLAZERS. THIS WHOLE FAMILY.
NOW GET OUT THERE AND BLAZE THAT TRAIL.
LOW EARTH ORBIT.
(NOT MANHATTAN.
I HATE THESE THINGS.
WHILE ZE BARNACLES MUST BE BLASTED, YOU HAVE ASKED ME TO REMIND YOU THAT IT WILL TAKE TIME TO GET TO ZE CAMP WHERE YOU'RE TO SPEAK.
INSPIRATIONAL WORDS FOR WOMEN MOVING UP IN THE WORLD! AH, NO ONE EVER ASKS ME TO SPEAK INSPIRATIONAL WORDS.
THAT'S BECAUSE YOU'RE TERRIBLE.
VRAIMENT. I AM TERRIBLE.

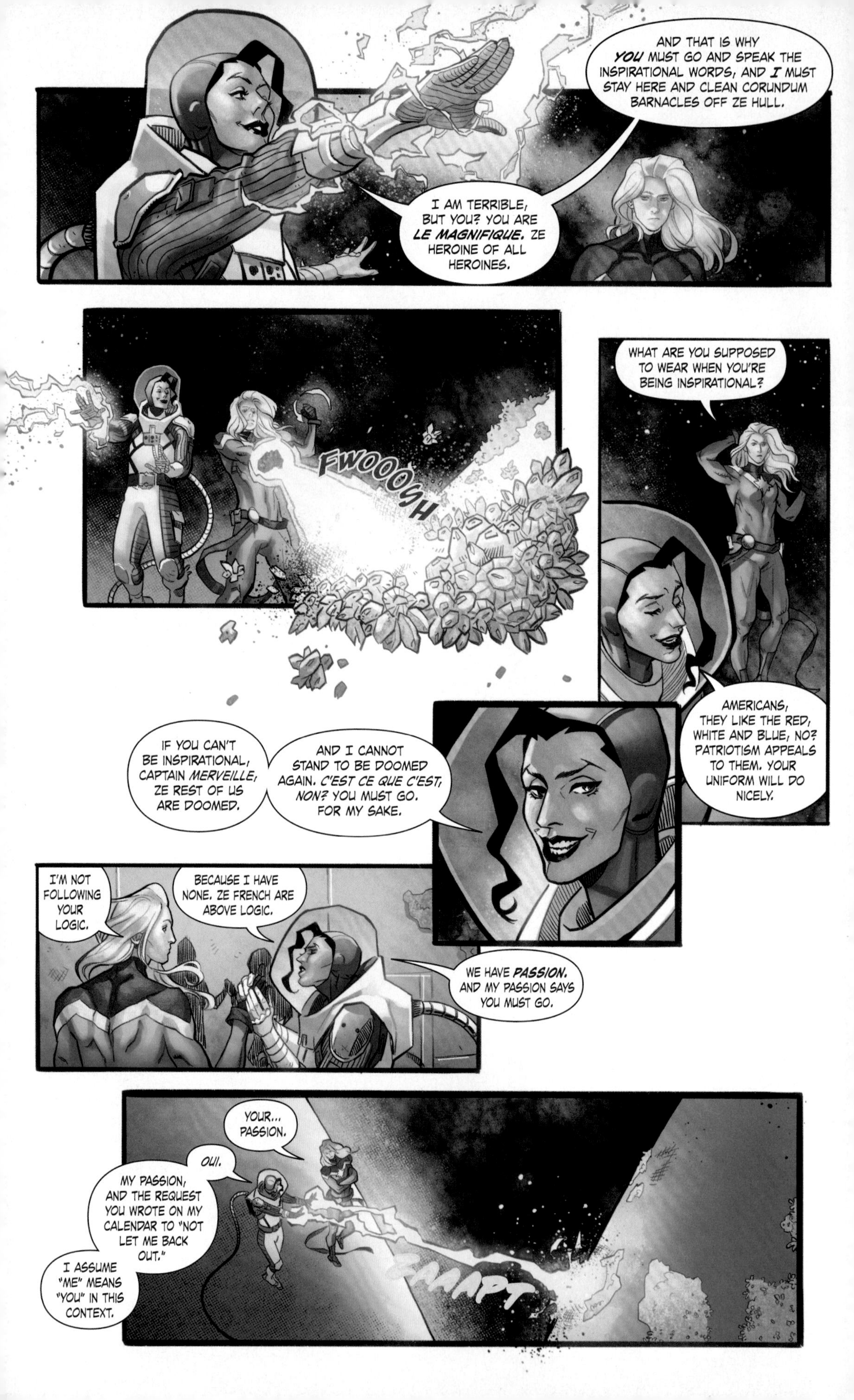
AND THAT IS WHY YOU MUST GO AND SPEAK THE INSPIRATIONAL WORDS, AND I MUST STAY HERE AND CLEAN CORUNDUM BARNACLES OFF ZE HULL.
I AM TERRIBLE, BUT YOU? YOU ARE LE MAGNIFIQUE. ZE HEROINE OF ALL HEROINES.
FWOOOSH
WHAT ARE YOU SUPPOSED TO WEAR WHEN YOU'RE BEING INSPIRATIONAL?
AMERICANS, THEY LIKE THE RED, WHITE AND BLUE, NO? PATRIOTISM APPEALS TO THEM. YOUR UNIFORM WILL DO NICELY.
IF YOU CAN'T BE INSPIRATIONAL, CAPTAIN MERVEILLE, ZE REST OF US ARE DOOMED.
AND I CANNOT STAND TO BE DOOMED AGAIN. C'EST CE QUE C'EST, NON? YOU MUST GO. FOR MY SAKE.
I'M NOT FOLLOWING YOUR LOGIC.
BECAUSE I HAVE NONE. ZE FRENCH ARE ABOVE LOGIC.
WE HAVE PASSION. AND MY PASSION SAYS YOU MUST GO.
YOUR... PASSION.
OUI.
MY PASSION, AND THE REQUEST YOU WROTE ON MY CALENDAR TO "NOT LET ME BACK OUT."
I ASSUME "ME" MEANS "YOU" IN THIS CONTEXT.

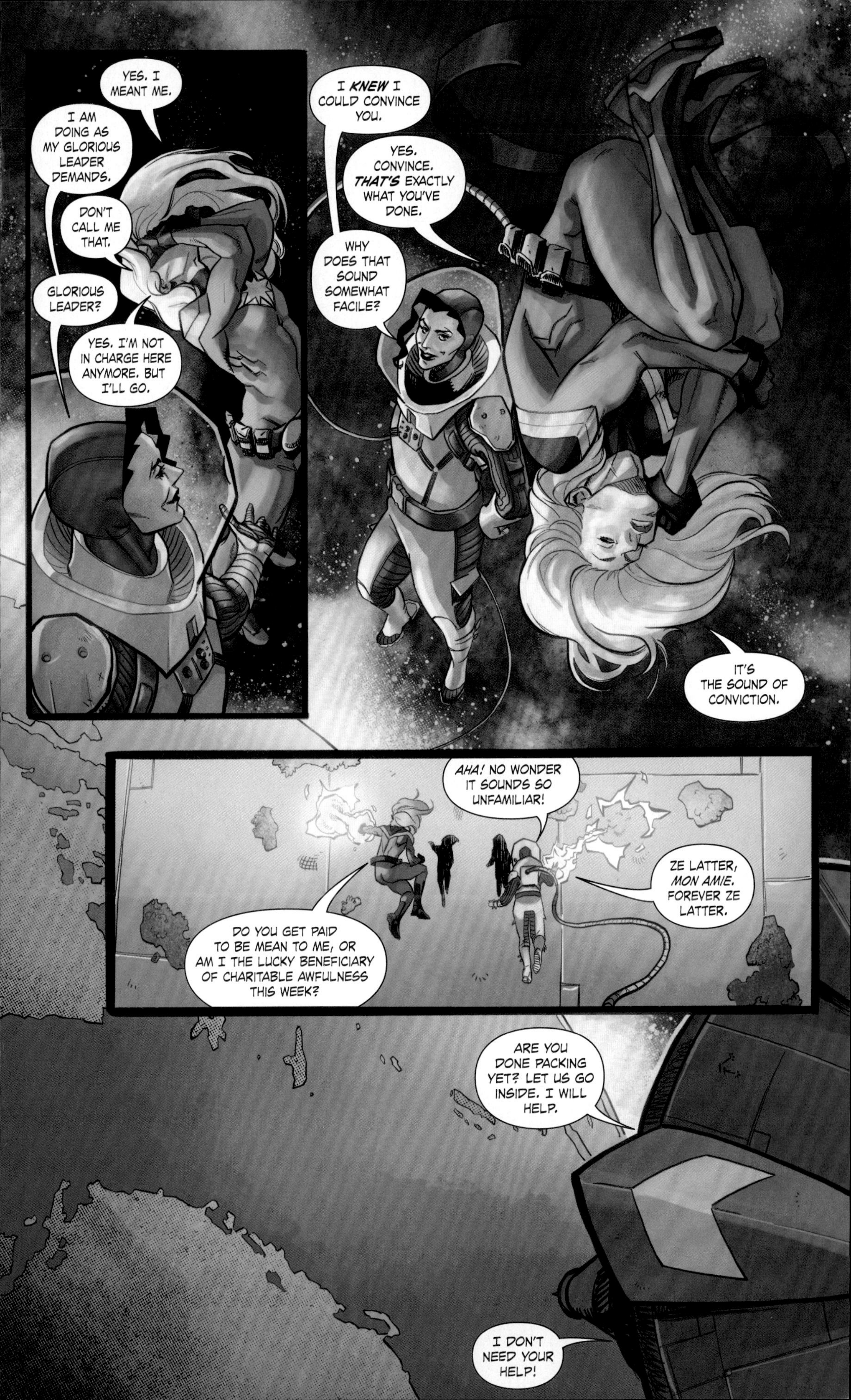

YES. I MEANT ME.
I AM DOING AS MY GLORIOUS LEADER DEMANDS.
DON'T CALL ME THAT.
GLORIOUS LEADER?
YES. I'M NOT IN CHARGE HERE ANYMORE. BUT I'LL GO.
I *KNEW* I COULD CONVINCE YOU.
YES. CONVINCE. *THAT'S* EXACTLY WHAT YOU'VE DONE.
WHY DOES THAT SOUND SOMEWHAT FACILE?
IT'S THE SOUND OF CONVICTION.
AHA! NO WONDER IT SOUNDS SO UNFAMILIAR!
DO YOU GET PAID TO BE MEAN TO ME, OR AM I THE LUCKY BENEFICIARY OF CHARITABLE AWFULNESS THIS WEEK?
ZE LATTER, *MON AMIE*. FOREVER ZE LATTER.
ARE YOU DONE PACKING YET? LET US GO INSIDE. I WILL HELP.
I DON'T NEED YOUR HELP!

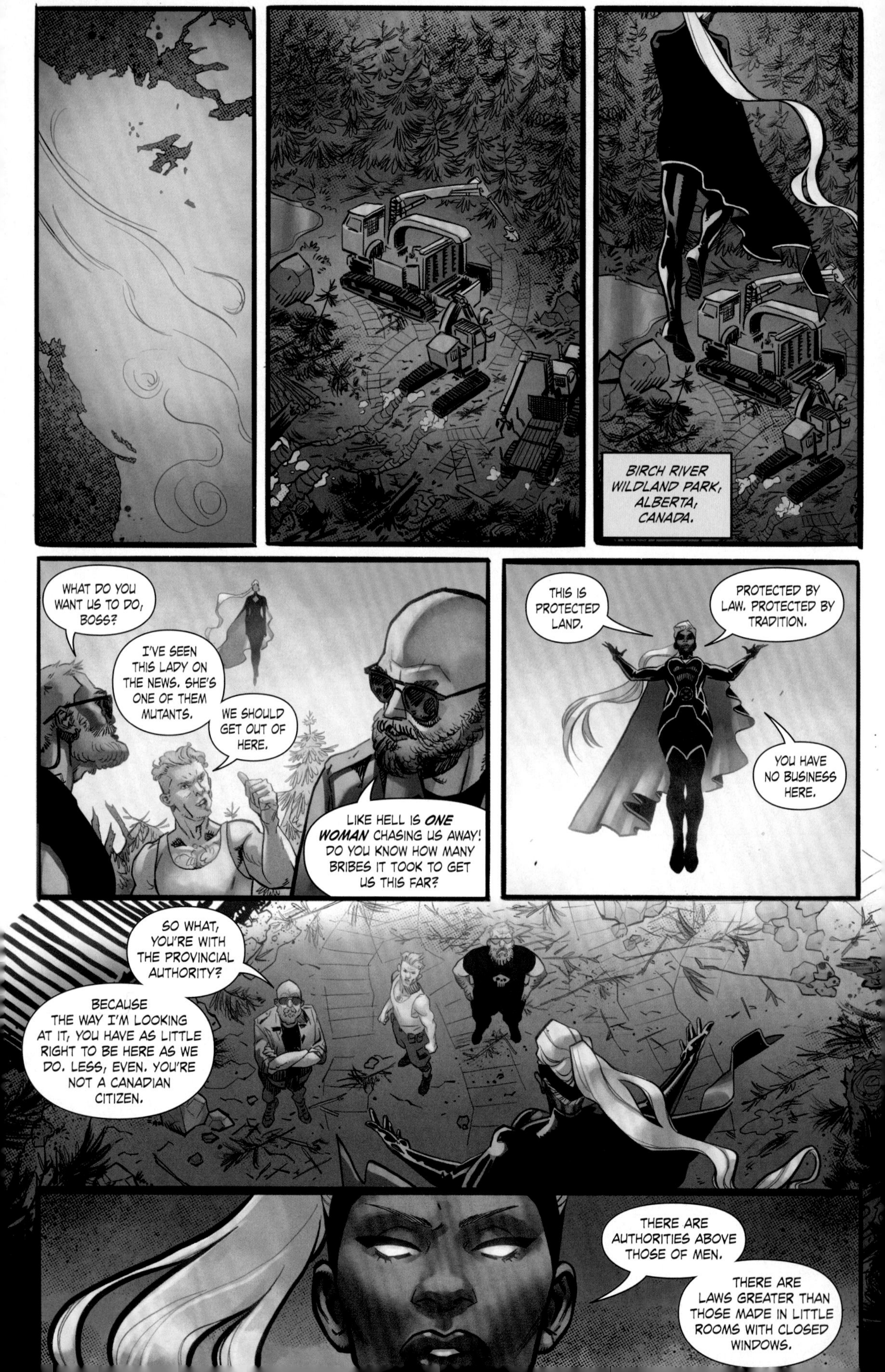
BIRCH RIVER WILDLAND PARK, ALBERTA, CANADA.
WHAT DO YOU WANT US TO DO, BOSS?
I'VE SEEN THIS LADY ON THE NEWS. SHE'S ONE OF THEM MUTANTS.
WE SHOULD GET OUT OF HERE.
LIKE HELL IS *ONE WOMAN* CHASING US AWAY! DO YOU KNOW HOW MANY BRIBES IT TOOK TO GET US THIS FAR?
THIS IS PROTECTED LAND.
PROTECTED BY LAW. PROTECTED BY TRADITION.
YOU HAVE NO BUSINESS HERE.
SO WHAT, YOU'RE WITH THE PROVINCIAL AUTHORITY?
BECAUSE THE WAY I'M LOOKING AT IT, YOU HAVE AS LITTLE RIGHT TO BE HERE AS WE DO. LESS, EVEN. YOU'RE NOT A CANADIAN CITIZEN.
THERE ARE AUTHORITIES ABOVE THOSE OF MEN.
THERE ARE LAWS GREATER THAN THOSE MADE IN LITTLE ROOMS WITH CLOSED WINDOWS.

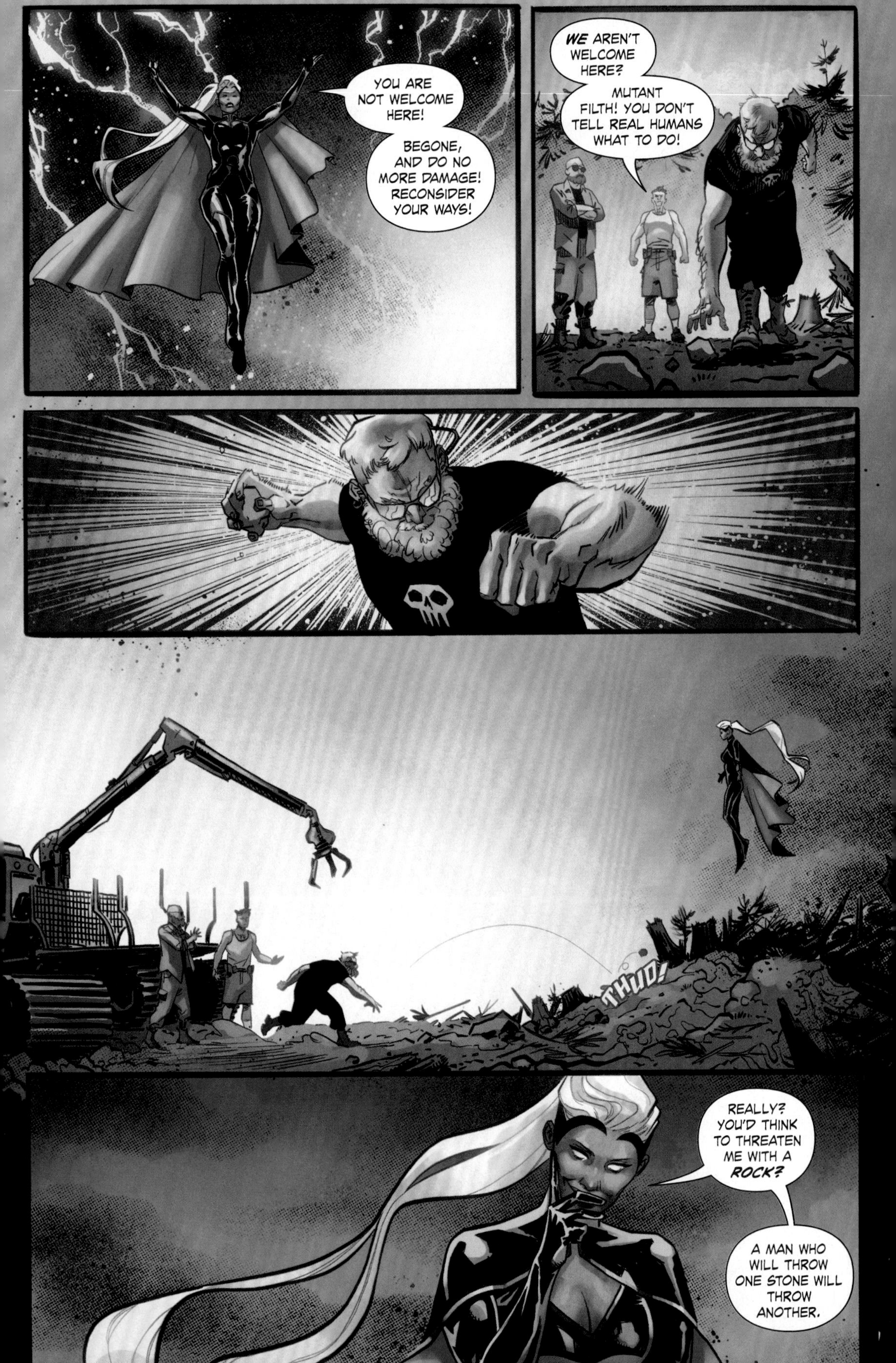
YOU ARE NOT WELCOME HERE!
BEGONE, AND DO NO MORE DAMAGE! RECONSIDER YOUR WAYS!
WE AREN'T WELCOME HERE?
MUTANT FILTH! YOU DON'T TELL REAL HUMANS WHAT TO DO!
THUD!
REALLY? YOU'D THINK TO THREATEN ME WITH A ROCK?
A MAN WHO WILL THROW ONE STONE WILL THROW ANOTHER.

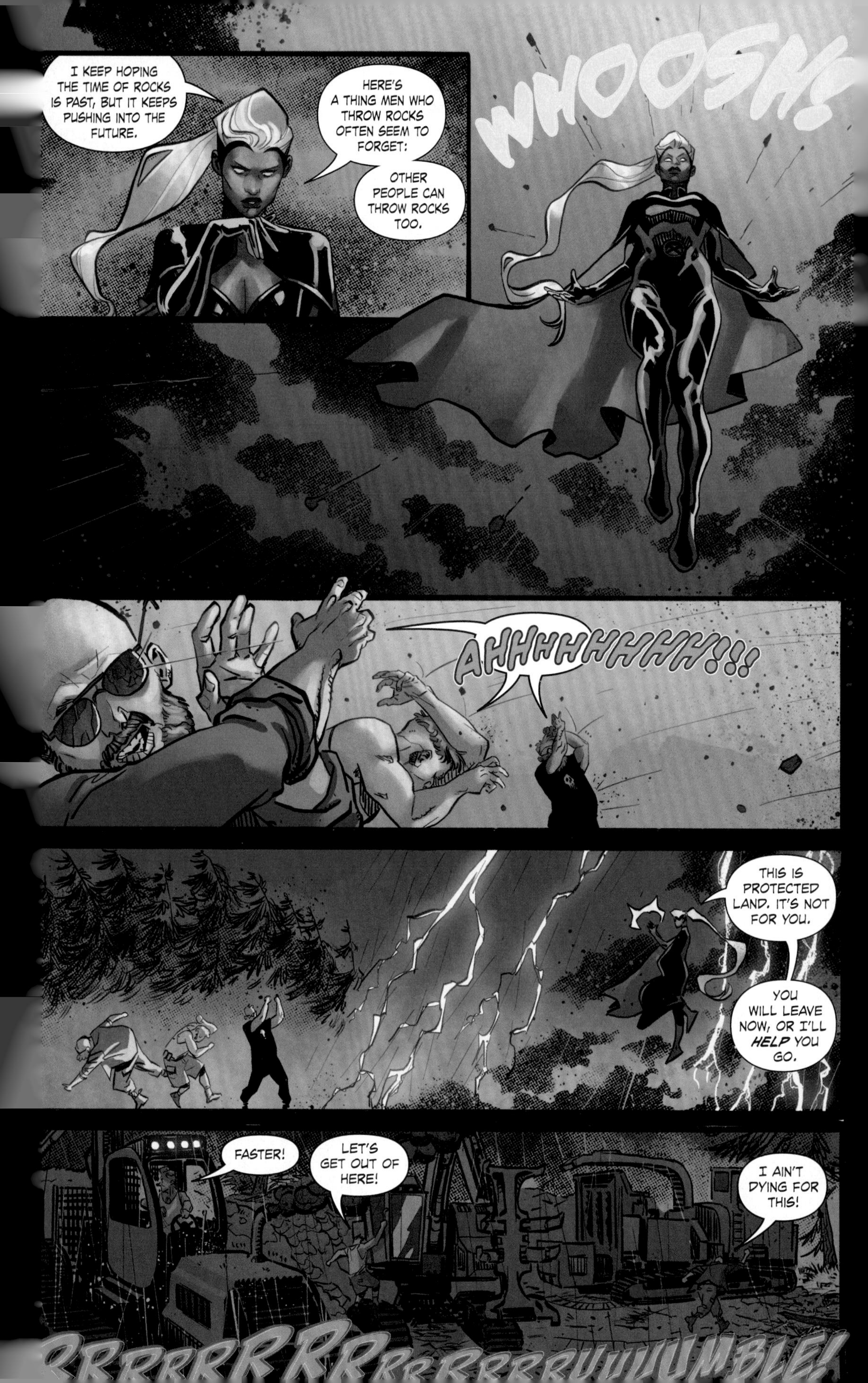
I KEEP HOPING THE TIME OF ROCKS IS PAST, BUT IT KEEPS PUSHING INTO THE FUTURE.
HERE'S A THING MEN WHO THROW ROCKS OFTEN SEEM TO FORGET:
OTHER PEOPLE CAN THROW ROCKS TOO.
WHOOSH!
AHHHHHHHH!!!
THIS IS PROTECTED LAND. IT'S NOT FOR YOU.
YOU WILL LEAVE NOW, OR I'LL *HELP* YOU GO.
FASTER!
LET'S GET OUT OF HERE!
I AIN'T DYING FOR THIS!
RRRRRRRRRrrrrrrrrRUUUUMBLE!

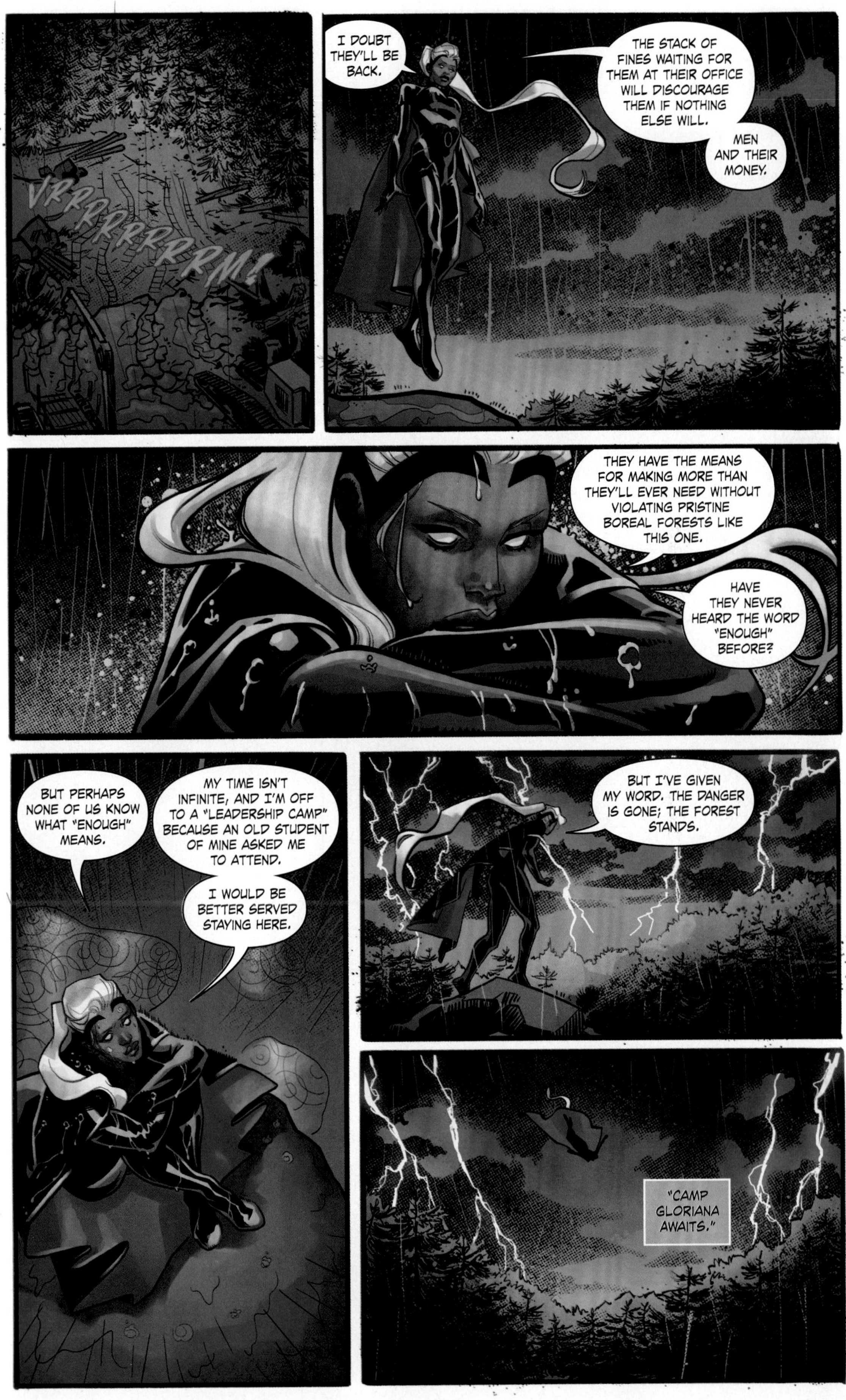
VRRRRRRRRRM!
I DOUBT THEY'LL BE BACK.
THE STACK OF FINES WAITING FOR THEM AT THEIR OFFICE WILL DISCOURAGE THEM IF NOTHING ELSE WILL.
MEN AND THEIR MONEY.
THEY HAVE THE MEANS FOR MAKING MORE THAN THEY'LL EVER NEED WITHOUT VIOLATING PRISTINE BOREAL FORESTS LIKE THIS ONE.
HAVE THEY NEVER HEARD THE WORD "ENOUGH" BEFORE?
BUT PERHAPS NONE OF US KNOW WHAT "ENOUGH" MEANS.
MY TIME ISN'T INFINITE, AND I'M OFF TO A "LEADERSHIP CAMP" BECAUSE AN OLD STUDENT OF MINE ASKED ME TO ATTEND.
I WOULD BE BETTER SERVED STAYING HERE.
BUT I'VE GIVEN MY WORD. THE DANGER IS GONE; THE FOREST STANDS.
"CAMP GLORIANA AWAITS."

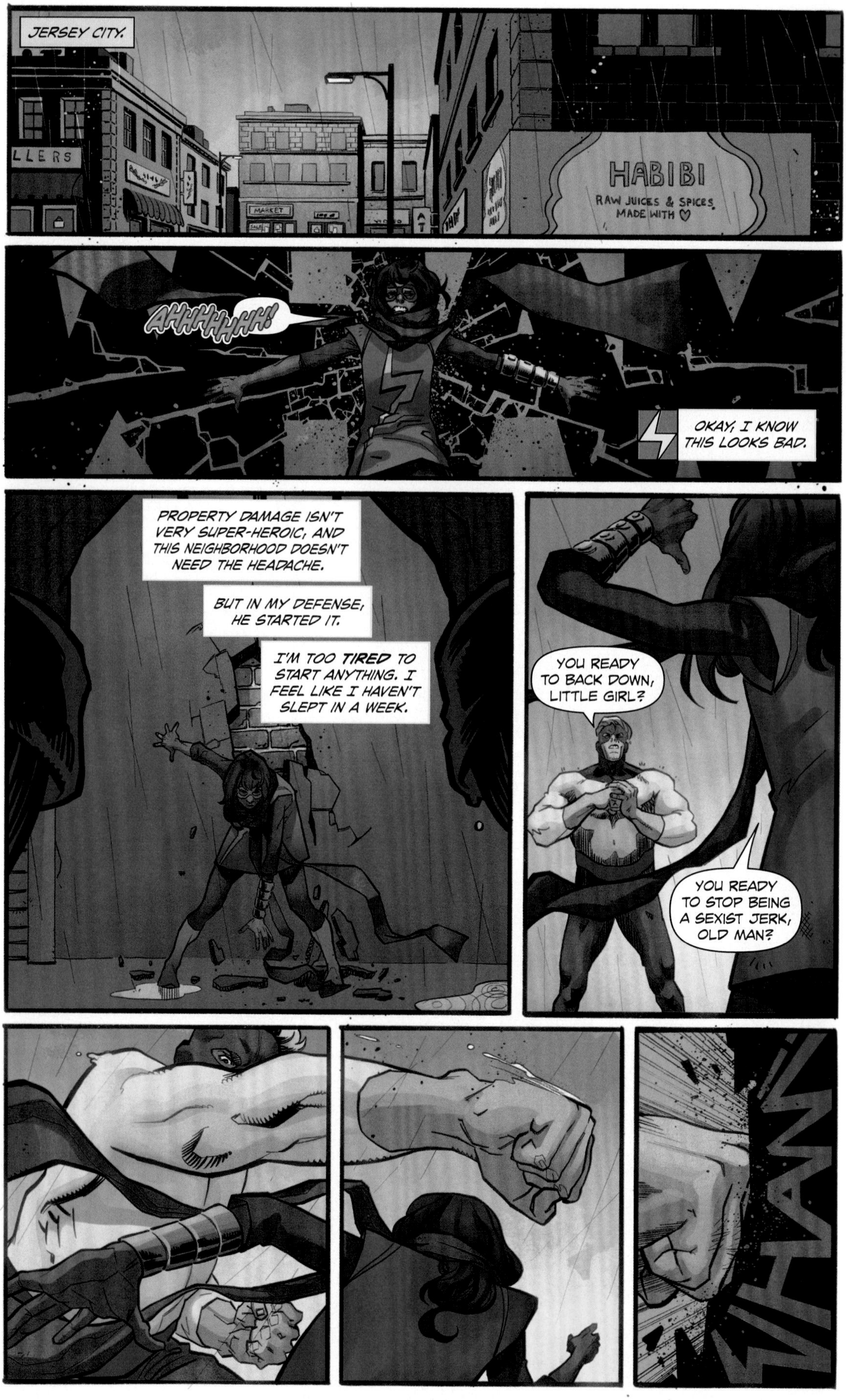
JERSEY CITY.
HABIBI
RAW JUICES & SPICES MADE WITH ♡
MARKET
AHHHHHHH!
OKAY, I KNOW THIS LOOKS BAD.
PROPERTY DAMAGE ISN'T VERY SUPER-HEROIC, AND THIS NEIGHBORHOOD DOESN'T NEED THE HEADACHE.
BUT IN MY DEFENSE, HE STARTED IT.
I'M TOO TIRED TO START ANYTHING. I FEEL LIKE I HAVEN'T SLEPT IN A WEEK.
YOU READY TO BACK DOWN, LITTLE GIRL?
YOU READY TO STOP BEING A SEXIST JERK, OLD MAN?
WHAM

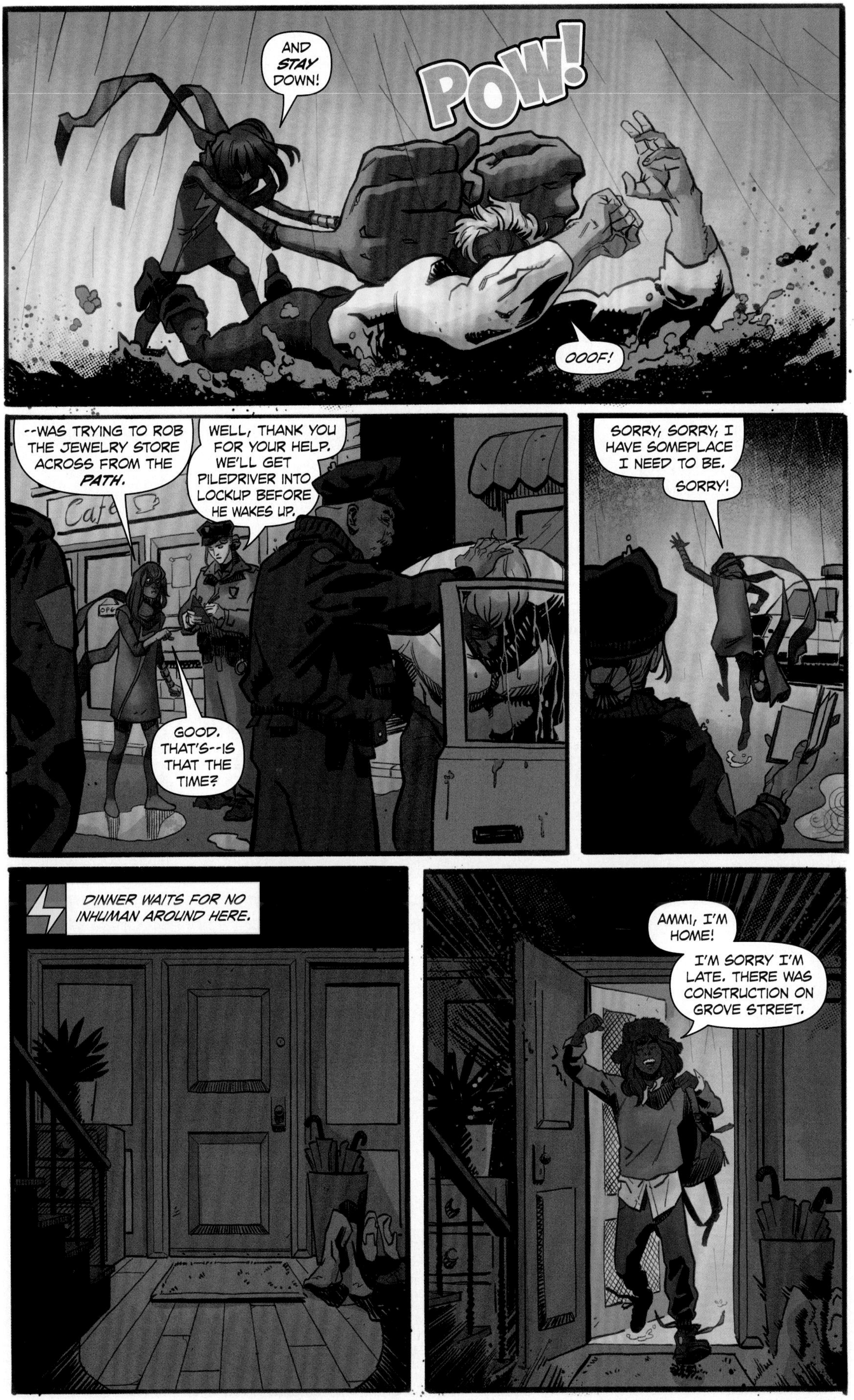
AND STAY DOWN!
POW!
OOOF!
--WAS TRYING TO ROB THE JEWELRY STORE ACROSS FROM THE PATH.
WELL, THANK YOU FOR YOUR HELP. WE'LL GET PILEDRIVER INTO LOCKUP BEFORE HE WAKES UP.
GOOD. THAT'S--IS THAT THE TIME?
SORRY, SORRY, I HAVE SOMEPLACE I NEED TO BE.
SORRY!
DINNER WAITS FOR NO INHUMAN AROUND HERE.
AMMI, I'M HOME!
I'M SORRY I'M LATE. THERE WAS CONSTRUCTION ON GROVE STREET.

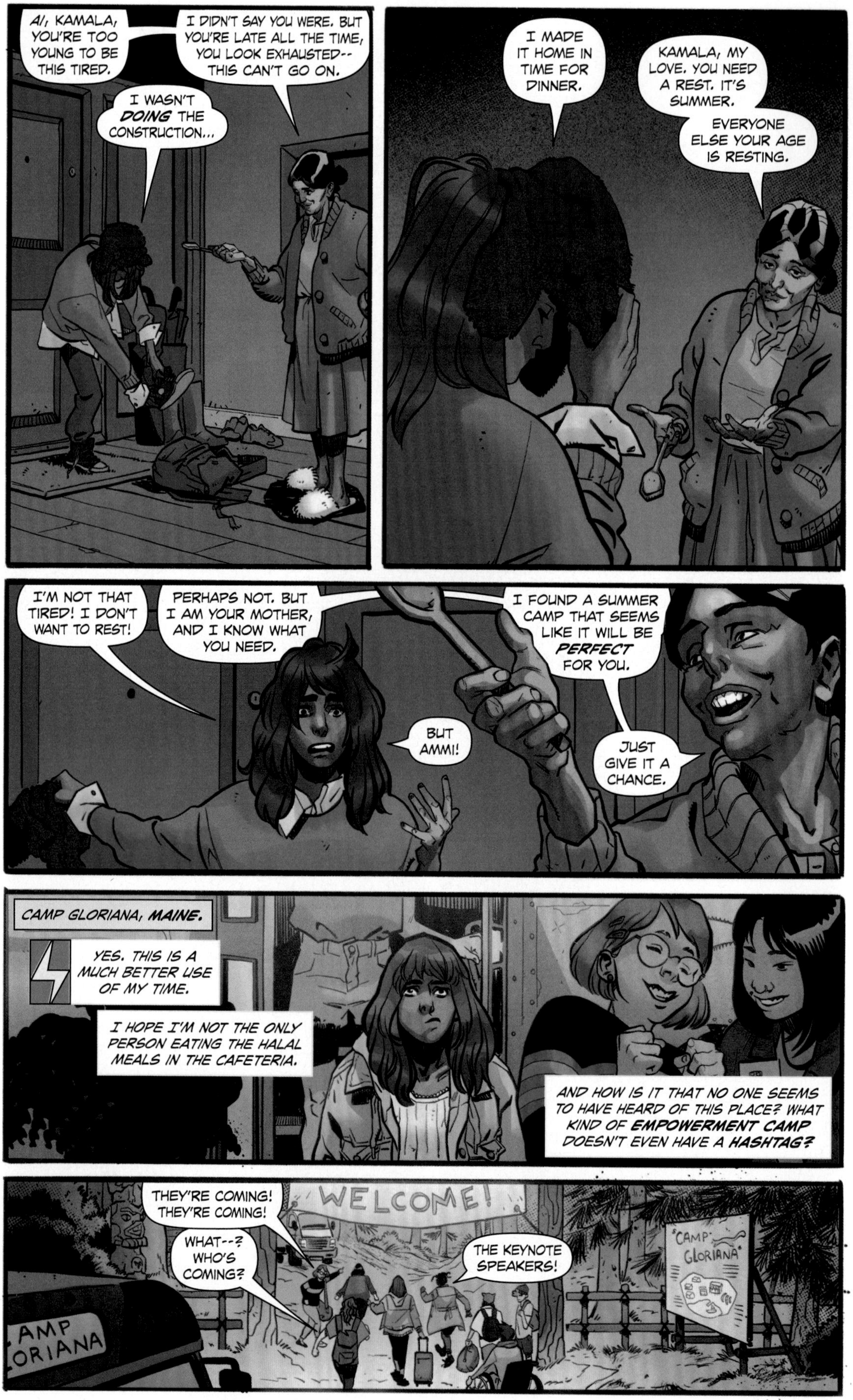
AI, KAMALA, YOU'RE TOO YOUNG TO BE THIS TIRED.
I WASN'T DOING THE CONSTRUCTION...
I DIDN'T SAY YOU WERE. BUT YOU'RE LATE ALL THE TIME, YOU LOOK EXHAUSTED-- THIS CAN'T GO ON.
I MADE IT HOME IN TIME FOR DINNER.
KAMALA, MY LOVE. YOU NEED A REST. IT'S SUMMER.
EVERYONE ELSE YOUR AGE IS RESTING.
I'M NOT THAT TIRED! I DON'T WANT TO REST!
PERHAPS NOT. BUT I AM YOUR MOTHER, AND I KNOW WHAT YOU NEED.
I FOUND A SUMMER CAMP THAT SEEMS LIKE IT WILL BE PERFECT FOR YOU.
BUT AMMI!
JUST GIVE IT A CHANCE.
CAMP GLORIANA, MAINE.
YES. THIS IS A MUCH BETTER USE OF MY TIME.
I HOPE I'M NOT THE ONLY PERSON EATING THE HALAL MEALS IN THE CAFETERIA.
AND HOW IS IT THAT NO ONE SEEMS TO HAVE HEARD OF THIS PLACE? WHAT KIND OF EMPOWERMENT CAMP DOESN'T EVEN HAVE A HASHTAG?
WELCOME!
THEY'RE COMING! THEY'RE COMING!
WHAT--? WHO'S COMING?
THE KEYNOTE SPEAKERS!
CAMP GLORIANA
CAMP GLORIANA

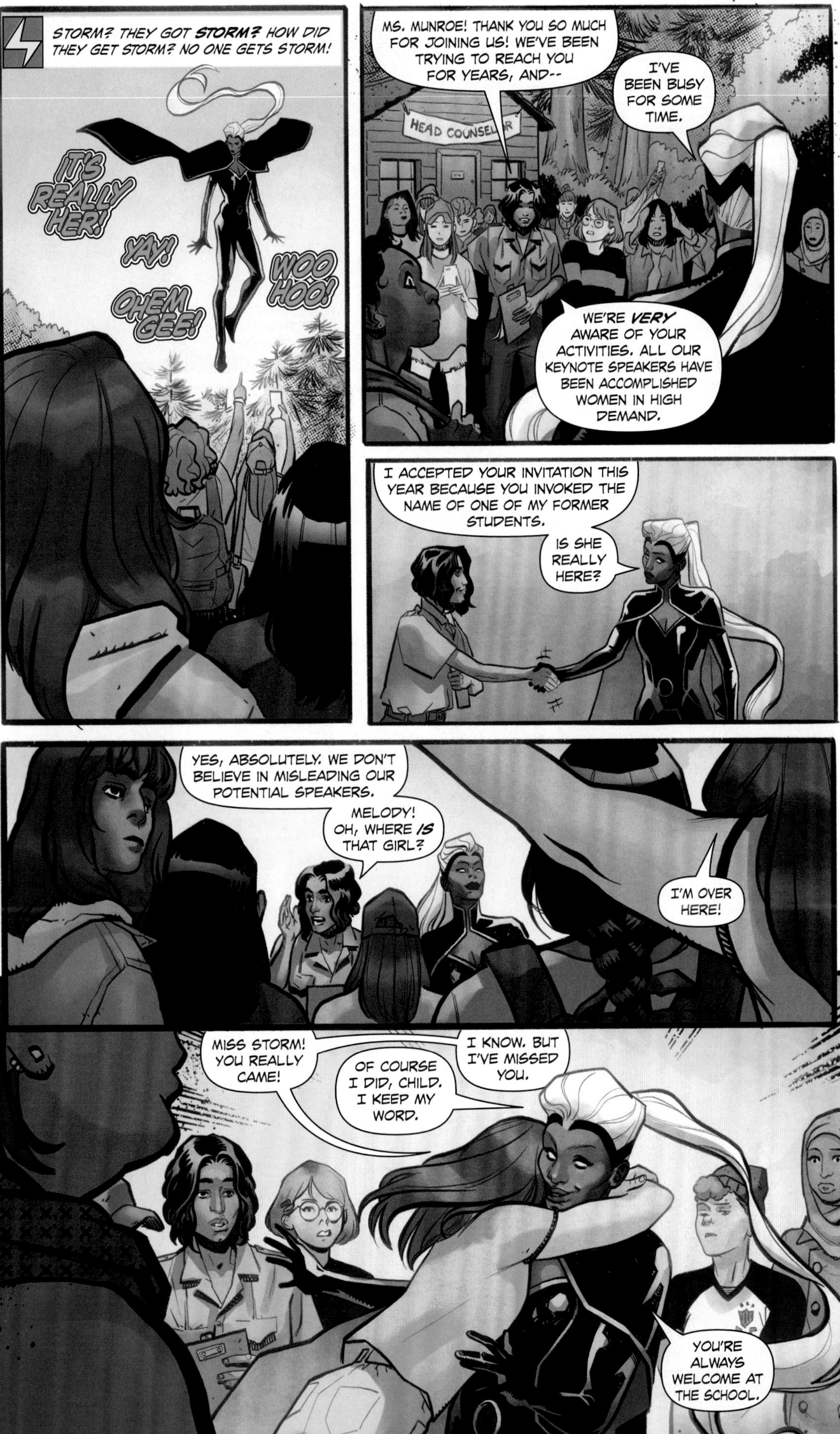
STORM? THEY GOT STORM? HOW DID THEY GET STORM? NO ONE GETS STORM!
IT'S REALLY HER!
YAY!
OHEM GEE!
WOO HOO!
MS. MUNROE! THANK YOU SO MUCH FOR JOINING US! WE'VE BEEN TRYING TO REACH YOU FOR YEARS, AND--
HEAD COUNSELOR
I'VE BEEN BUSY FOR SOME TIME.
WE'RE VERY AWARE OF YOUR ACTIVITIES. ALL OUR KEYNOTE SPEAKERS HAVE BEEN ACCOMPLISHED WOMEN IN HIGH DEMAND.
I ACCEPTED YOUR INVITATION THIS YEAR BECAUSE YOU INVOKED THE NAME OF ONE OF MY FORMER STUDENTS.
IS SHE REALLY HERE?
YES, ABSOLUTELY. WE DON'T BELIEVE IN MISLEADING OUR POTENTIAL SPEAKERS.
MELODY! OH, WHERE IS THAT GIRL?
I'M OVER HERE!
MISS STORM! YOU REALLY CAME!
OF COURSE I DID, CHILD. I KEEP MY WORD.
I KNOW. BUT I'VE MISSED YOU.
YOU'RE ALWAYS WELCOME AT THE SCHOOL.

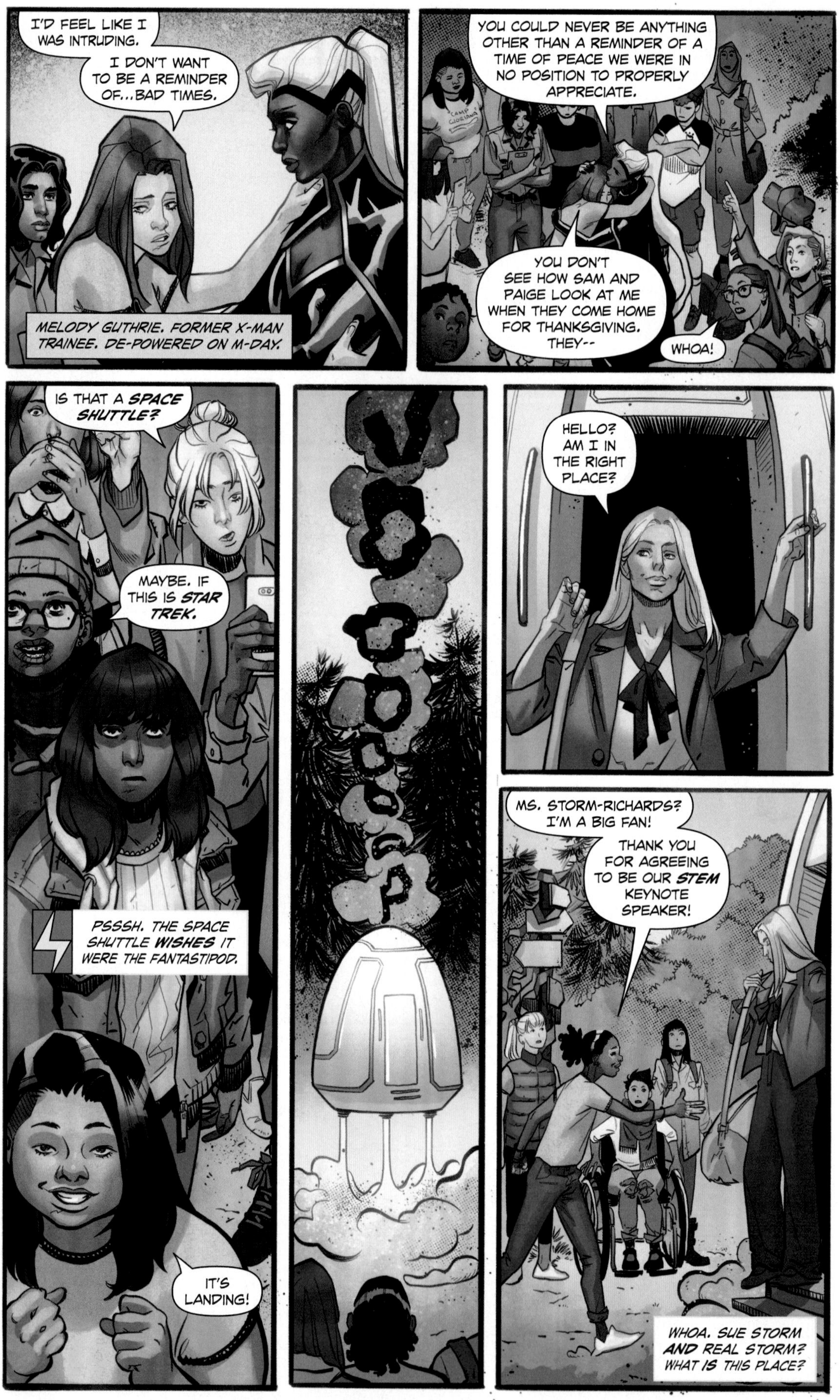
I'D FEEL LIKE I WAS INTRUDING.
I DON'T WANT TO BE A REMINDER OF... BAD TIMES.
MELODY GUTHRIE. FORMER X-MAN TRAINEE. DE-POWERED ON M-DAY.
YOU COULD NEVER BE ANYTHING OTHER THAN A REMINDER OF A TIME OF PEACE WE WERE IN NO POSITION TO PROPERLY APPRECIATE.
YOU DON'T SEE HOW SAM AND PAIGE LOOK AT ME WHEN THEY COME HOME FOR THANKSGIVING. THEY--
WHOA!
IS THAT A SPACE SHUTTLE?
MAYBE. IF THIS IS STAR TREK.
PSSSH. THE SPACE SHUTTLE WISHES IT WERE THE FANTASTIPOD.
IT'S LANDING!
HELLO? AM I IN THE RIGHT PLACE?
MS. STORM-RICHARDS? I'M A BIG FAN!
THANK YOU FOR AGREEING TO BE OUR STEM KEYNOTE SPEAKER!
WHOA. SUE STORM AND REAL STORM? WHAT IS THIS PLACE?

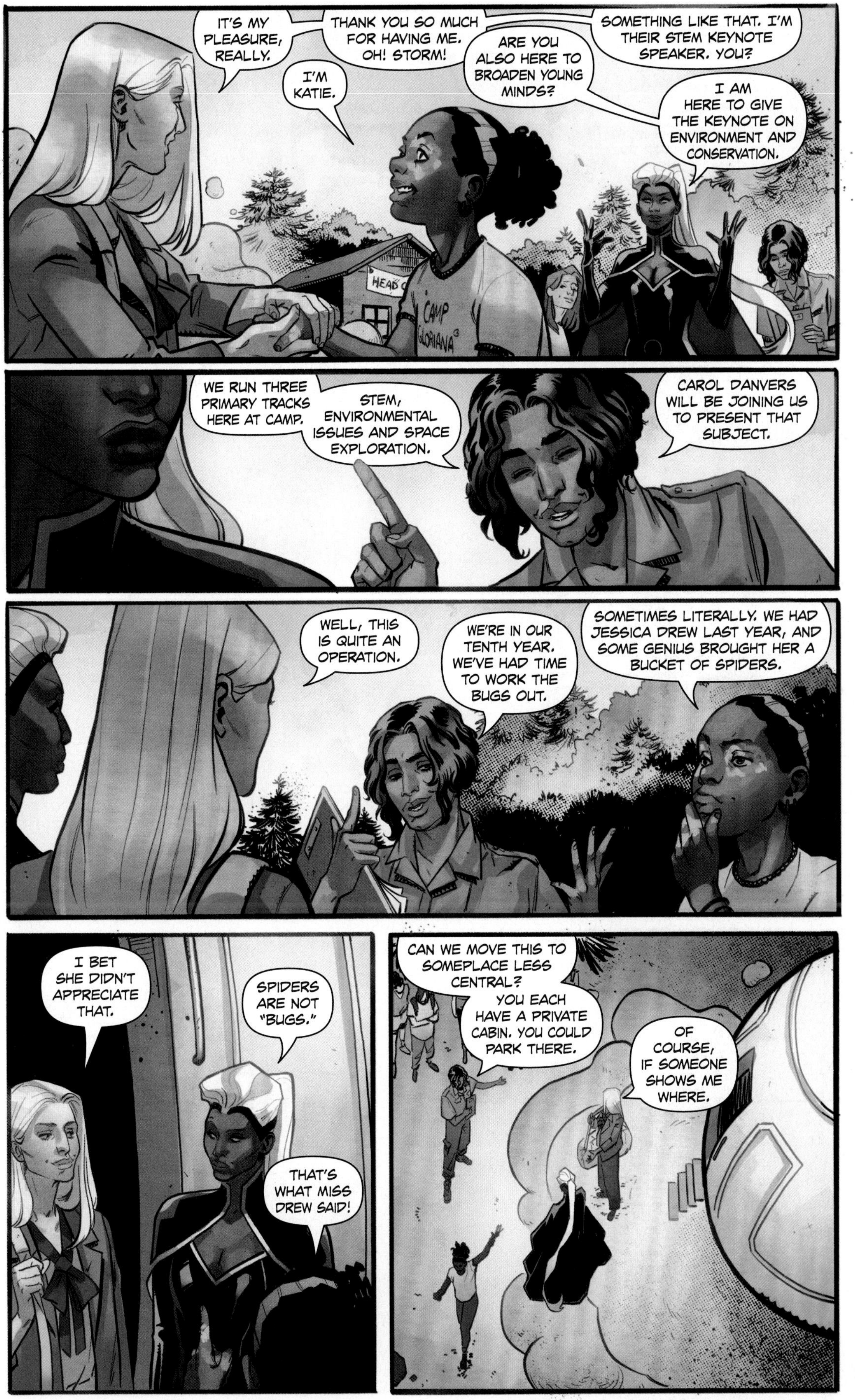
IT'S MY PLEASURE, REALLY.
THANK YOU SO MUCH FOR HAVING ME. OH! STORM!
I'M KATIE.
ARE YOU ALSO HERE TO BROADEN YOUNG MINDS?
SOMETHING LIKE THAT. I'M THEIR STEM KEYNOTE SPEAKER. YOU?
I AM HERE TO GIVE THE KEYNOTE ON ENVIRONMENT AND CONSERVATION.
HEAD
CAMP GLORIANA
WE RUN THREE PRIMARY TRACKS HERE AT CAMP.
STEM, ENVIRONMENTAL ISSUES AND SPACE EXPLORATION.
CAROL DANVERS WILL BE JOINING US TO PRESENT THAT SUBJECT.
WELL, THIS IS QUITE AN OPERATION.
WE'RE IN OUR TENTH YEAR. WE'VE HAD TIME TO WORK THE BUGS OUT.
SOMETIMES LITERALLY. WE HAD JESSICA DREW LAST YEAR, AND SOME GENIUS BROUGHT HER A BUCKET OF SPIDERS.
I BET SHE DIDN'T APPRECIATE THAT.
SPIDERS ARE NOT "BUGS."
THAT'S WHAT MISS DREW SAID!
CAN WE MOVE THIS TO SOMEPLACE LESS CENTRAL?
YOU EACH HAVE A PRIVATE CABIN. YOU COULD PARK THERE.
OF COURSE, IF SOMEONE SHOWS ME WHERE.

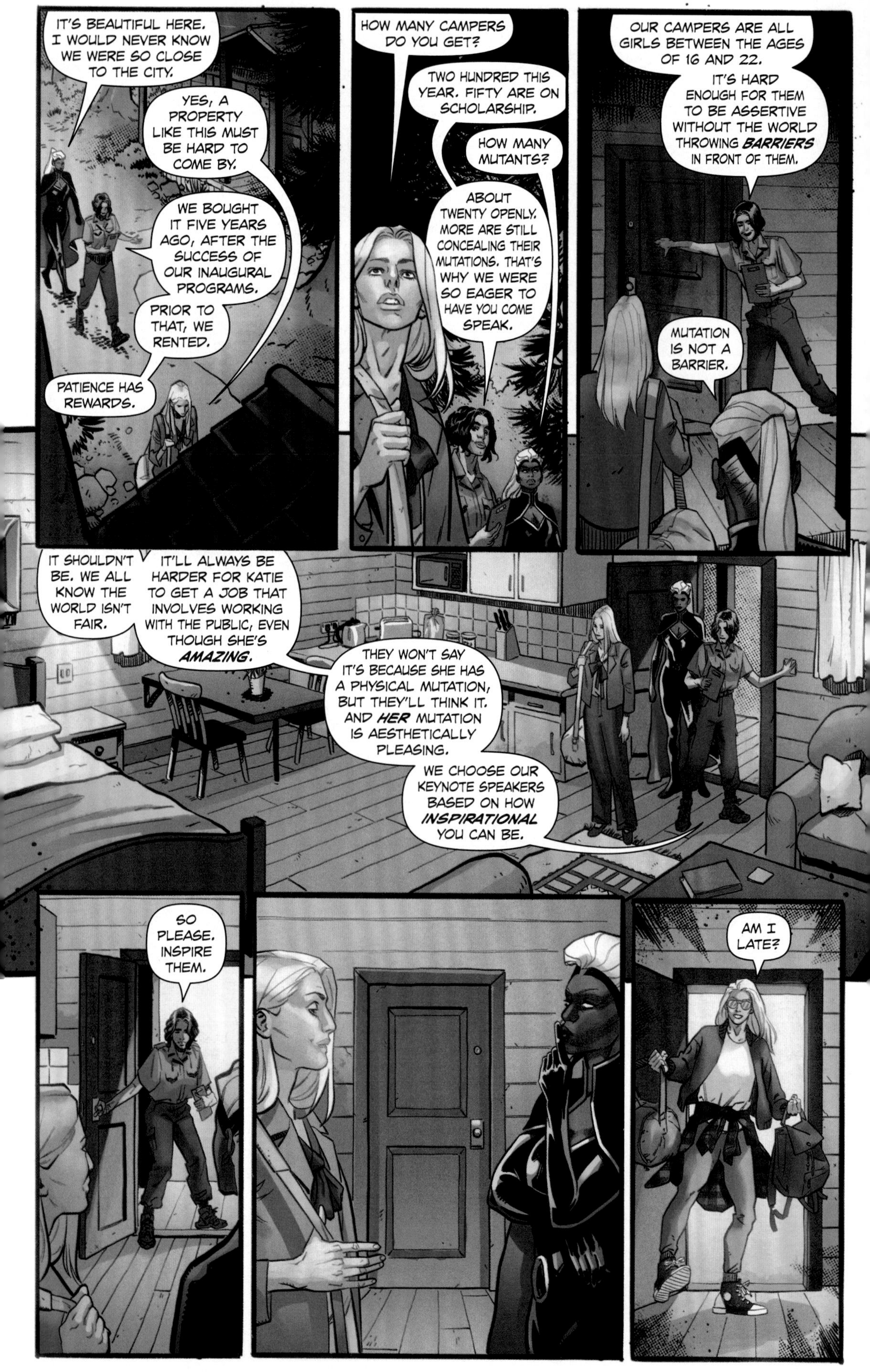

IT'S BEAUTIFUL HERE. I WOULD NEVER KNOW WE WERE SO CLOSE TO THE CITY.
YES, A PROPERTY LIKE THIS MUST BE HARD TO COME BY.
WE BOUGHT IT FIVE YEARS AGO, AFTER THE SUCCESS OF OUR INAUGURAL PROGRAMS.
PRIOR TO THAT, WE RENTED.
PATIENCE HAS REWARDS.
HOW MANY CAMPERS DO YOU GET?
TWO HUNDRED THIS YEAR. FIFTY ARE ON SCHOLARSHIP.
HOW MANY MUTANTS?
ABOUT TWENTY OPENLY. MORE ARE STILL CONCEALING THEIR MUTATIONS. THAT'S WHY WE WERE SO EAGER TO HAVE YOU COME SPEAK.
OUR CAMPERS ARE ALL GIRLS BETWEEN THE AGES OF 16 AND 22.
IT'S HARD ENOUGH FOR THEM TO BE ASSERTIVE WITHOUT THE WORLD THROWING BARRIERS IN FRONT OF THEM.
MUTATION IS NOT A BARRIER.
IT SHOULDN'T BE. WE ALL KNOW THE WORLD ISN'T FAIR.
IT'LL ALWAYS BE HARDER FOR KATIE TO GET A JOB THAT INVOLVES WORKING WITH THE PUBLIC, EVEN THOUGH SHE'S AMAZING.
THEY WON'T SAY IT'S BECAUSE SHE HAS A PHYSICAL MUTATION, BUT THEY'LL THINK IT. AND HER MUTATION IS AESTHETICALLY PLEASING.
WE CHOOSE OUR KEYNOTE SPEAKERS BASED ON HOW INSPIRATIONAL YOU CAN BE.
SO PLEASE. INSPIRE THEM.
AM I LATE?

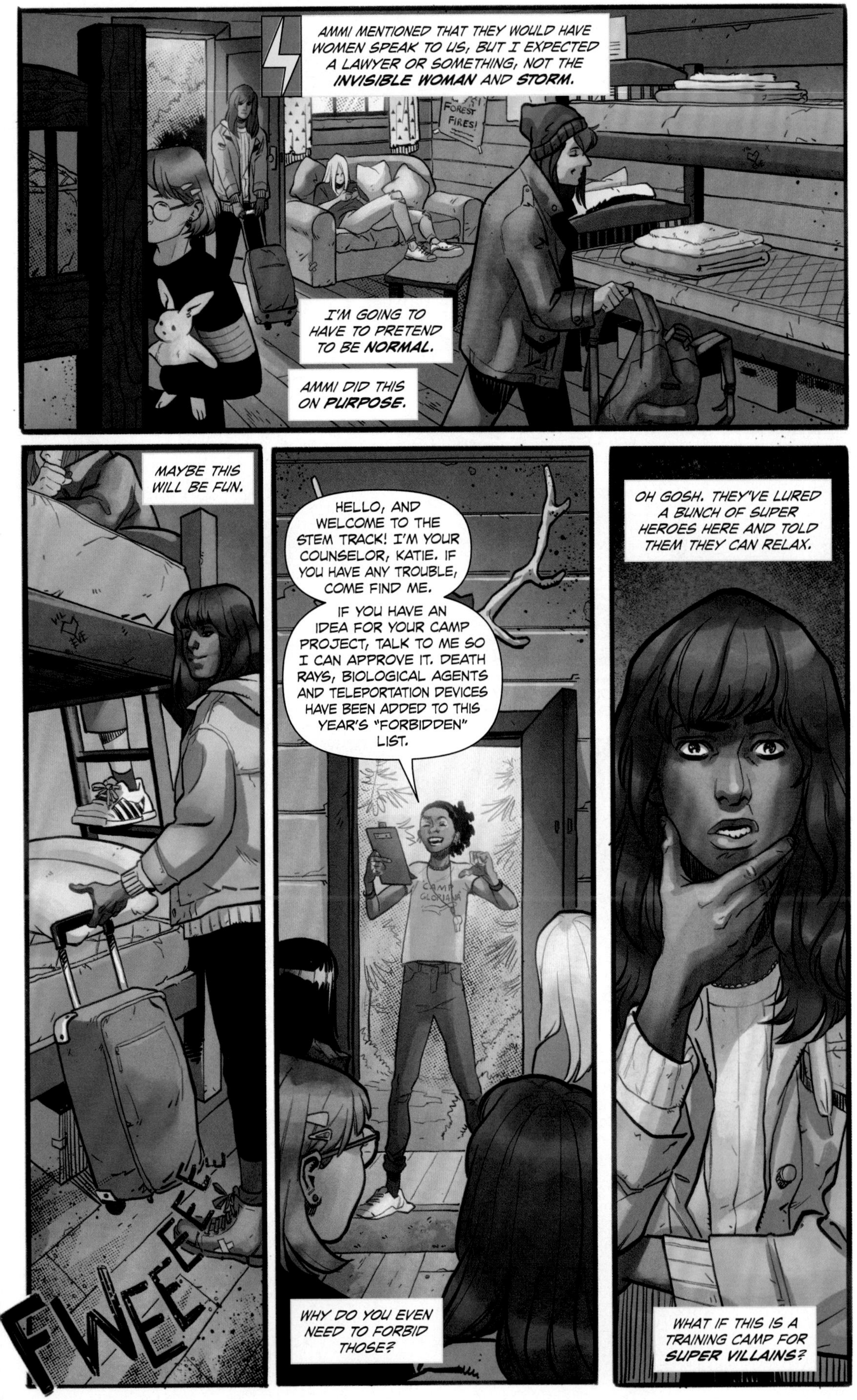
AMMI MENTIONED THAT THEY WOULD HAVE WOMEN SPEAK TO US, BUT I EXPECTED A LAWYER OR SOMETHING, NOT THE **INVISIBLE WOMAN** AND **STORM**.
FOREST FIRES!
I'M GOING TO HAVE TO PRETEND TO BE **NORMAL**.
AMMI DID THIS ON **PURPOSE**.
MAYBE THIS WILL BE FUN.
HELLO, AND WELCOME TO THE STEM TRACK! I'M YOUR COUNSELOR, KATIE. IF YOU HAVE ANY TROUBLE, COME FIND ME.
IF YOU HAVE AN IDEA FOR YOUR CAMP PROJECT, TALK TO ME SO I CAN APPROVE IT. DEATH RAYS, BIOLOGICAL AGENTS AND TELEPORTATION DEVICES HAVE BEEN ADDED TO THIS YEAR'S "FORBIDDEN" LIST.
CAMP GLORIANA
WHY DO YOU EVEN NEED TO FORBID THOSE?
FWEEEEEE
OH GOSH. THEY'VE LURED A BUNCH OF SUPER HEROES HERE AND TOLD THEM THEY CAN RELAX.
WHAT IF THIS IS A TRAINING CAMP FOR **SUPER VILLAINS**?

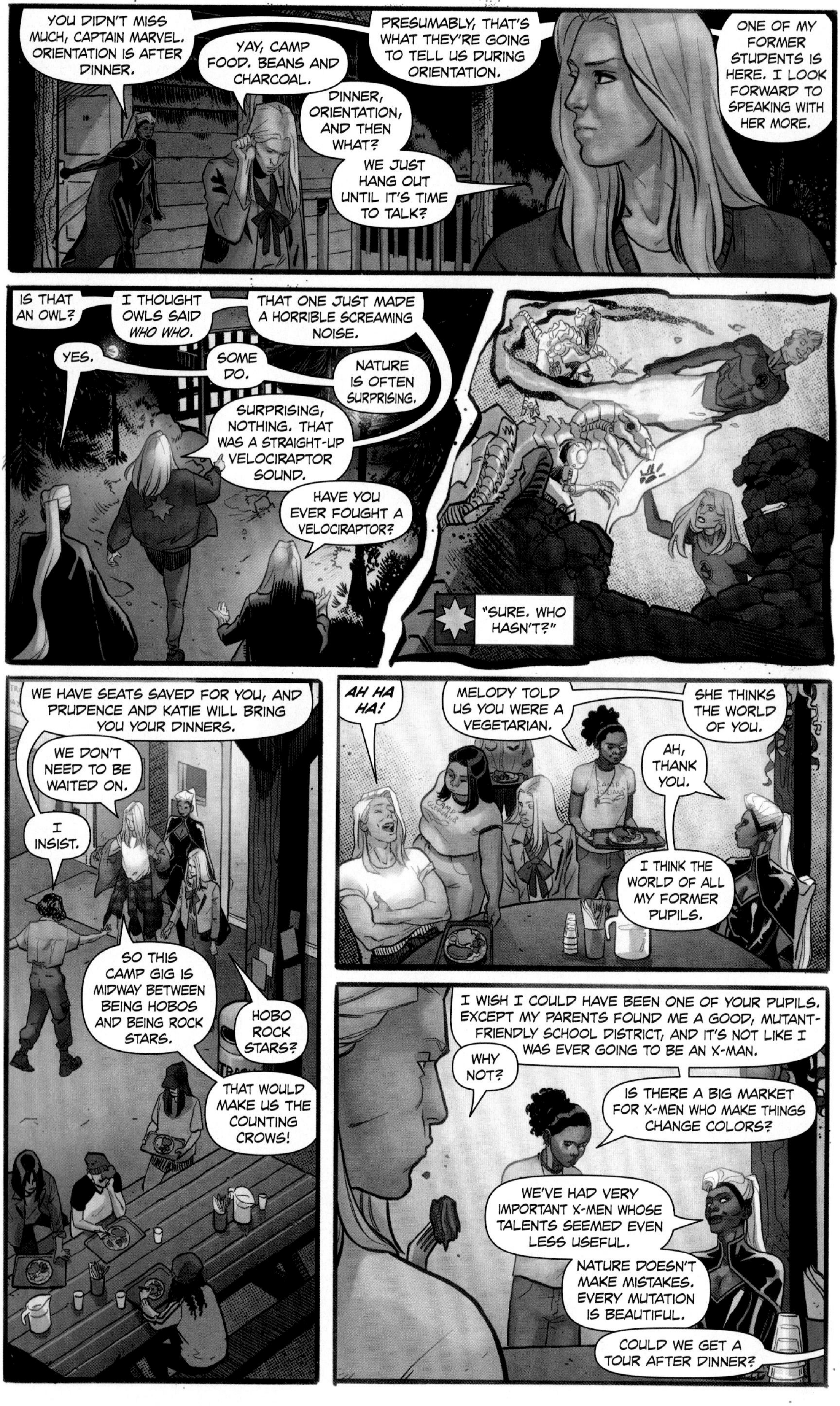

YOU DIDN'T MISS MUCH, CAPTAIN MARVEL. ORIENTATION IS AFTER DINNER.
YAY, CAMP FOOD. BEANS AND CHARCOAL.
PRESUMABLY, THAT'S WHAT THEY'RE GOING TO TELL US DURING ORIENTATION.
DINNER, ORIENTATION, AND THEN WHAT?
WE JUST HANG OUT UNTIL IT'S TIME TO TALK?
ONE OF MY FORMER STUDENTS IS HERE. I LOOK FORWARD TO SPEAKING WITH HER MORE.
IS THAT AN OWL?
I THOUGHT OWLS SAID *WHO WHO.*
THAT ONE JUST MADE A HORRIBLE SCREAMING NOISE.
YES.
SOME DO.
NATURE IS OFTEN SURPRISING.
SURPRISING, NOTHING. THAT WAS A STRAIGHT-UP VELOCIRAPTOR SOUND.
HAVE YOU EVER FOUGHT A VELOCIRAPTOR?
"SURE. WHO HASN'T?"
WE HAVE SEATS SAVED FOR YOU, AND PRUDENCE AND KATIE WILL BRING YOU YOUR DINNERS.
WE DON'T NEED TO BE WAITED ON.
I INSIST.
SO THIS CAMP GIG IS MIDWAY BETWEEN BEING HOBOS AND BEING ROCK STARS.
HOBO ROCK STARS?
THAT WOULD MAKE US THE COUNTING CROWS!
AH HA HA!
MELODY TOLD US YOU WERE A VEGETARIAN.
SHE THINKS THE WORLD OF YOU.
AH, THANK YOU.
I THINK THE WORLD OF ALL MY FORMER PUPILS.
I WISH I COULD HAVE BEEN ONE OF YOUR PUPILS. EXCEPT MY PARENTS FOUND ME A GOOD, MUTANT-FRIENDLY SCHOOL DISTRICT, AND IT'S NOT LIKE I WAS EVER GOING TO BE AN X-MAN.
WHY NOT?
IS THERE A BIG MARKET FOR X-MEN WHO MAKE THINGS CHANGE COLORS?
WE'VE HAD VERY IMPORTANT X-MEN WHOSE TALENTS SEEMED EVEN LESS USEFUL.
NATURE DOESN'T MAKE MISTAKES. EVERY MUTATION IS BEAUTIFUL.
COULD WE GET A TOUR AFTER DINNER?

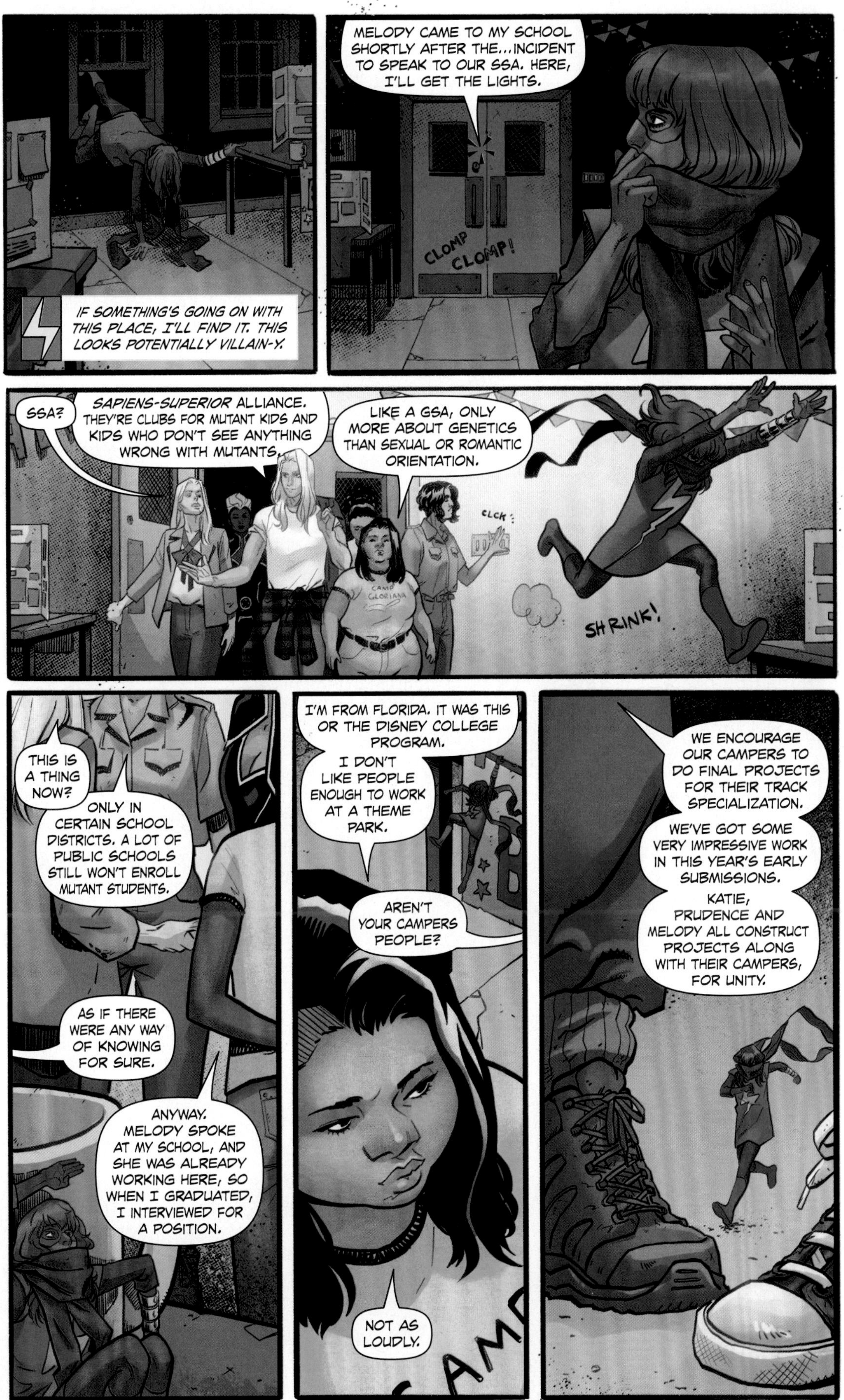

IF SOMETHING'S GOING ON WITH THIS PLACE, I'LL FIND IT. THIS LOOKS POTENTIALLY VILLAIN-Y.
MELODY CAME TO MY SCHOOL SHORTLY AFTER THE... INCIDENT TO SPEAK TO OUR SSA. HERE, I'LL GET THE LIGHTS.
CLOMP CLOMP!
SSA?
SAPIENS-SUPERIOR ALLIANCE. THEY'RE CLUBS FOR MUTANT KIDS AND KIDS WHO DON'T SEE ANYTHING WRONG WITH MUTANTS.
LIKE A GSA, ONLY MORE ABOUT GENETICS THAN SEXUAL OR ROMANTIC ORIENTATION.
CLCK
CAMP GLORIANA
SHRINK!
THIS IS A THING NOW?
ONLY IN CERTAIN SCHOOL DISTRICTS. A LOT OF PUBLIC SCHOOLS STILL WON'T ENROLL MUTANT STUDENTS.
AS IF THERE WERE ANY WAY OF KNOWING FOR SURE.
ANYWAY. MELODY SPOKE AT MY SCHOOL, AND SHE WAS ALREADY WORKING HERE, SO WHEN I GRADUATED, I INTERVIEWED FOR A POSITION.
I'M FROM FLORIDA. IT WAS THIS OR THE DISNEY COLLEGE PROGRAM.
I DON'T LIKE PEOPLE ENOUGH TO WORK AT A THEME PARK.
AREN'T YOUR CAMPERS PEOPLE?
NOT AS LOUDLY.
WE ENCOURAGE OUR CAMPERS TO DO FINAL PROJECTS FOR THEIR TRACK SPECIALIZATION.
WE'VE GOT SOME VERY IMPRESSIVE WORK IN THIS YEAR'S EARLY SUBMISSIONS.
KATIE, PRUDENCE AND MELODY ALL CONSTRUCT PROJECTS ALONG WITH THEIR CAMPERS, FOR UNITY.

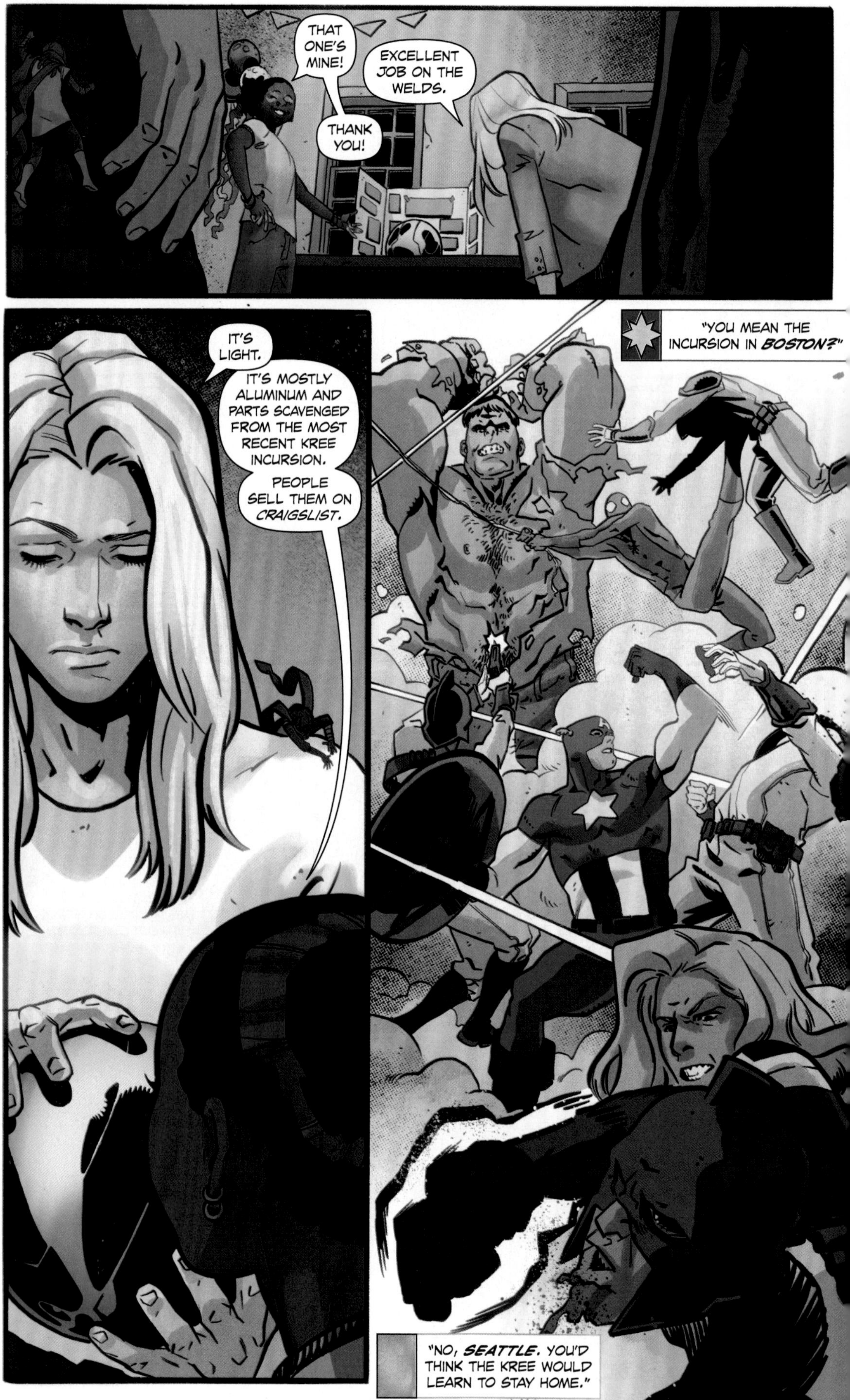
THAT ONE'S MINE!
THANK YOU!
EXCELLENT JOB ON THE WELDS.
IT'S LIGHT.
IT'S MOSTLY ALUMINUM AND PARTS SCAVENGED FROM THE MOST RECENT KREE INCURSION.
PEOPLE SELL THEM ON *CRAIGSLIST*.
"YOU MEAN THE INCURSION IN *BOSTON?*"
"NO, *SEATTLE*. YOU'D THINK THE KREE WOULD LEARN TO STAY HOME."

YOU'D THINK.

ANYWAY, NICE WORK.

THANK YOU!

BLINK BLINK!

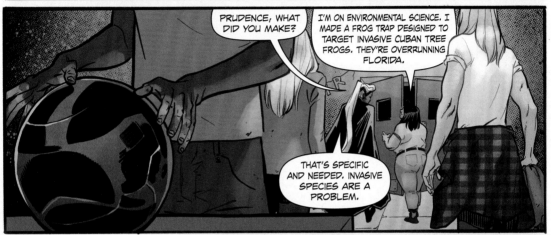

PRUDENCE, WHAT DID YOU MAKE?

I'M ON ENVIRONMENTAL SCIENCE. I MADE A FROG TRAP DESIGNED TO TARGET INVASIVE CUBAN TREE FROGS. THEY'RE OVERRUNNING FLORIDA.

THAT'S SPECIFIC AND NEEDED. INVASIVE SPECIES ARE A PROBLEM.

AND WE'RE BACK TO THE KREE!

INVASIVE SPECIES WITH *LASER GUNS.*

HEH.

I DON'T KNOW WHO THIS THING IS SIGNALING, BUT I KNOW IT'S PROBABLY *BAD NEWS BEARS.*

THIS CAMP IS A *TRAP* IN DISGUISE.

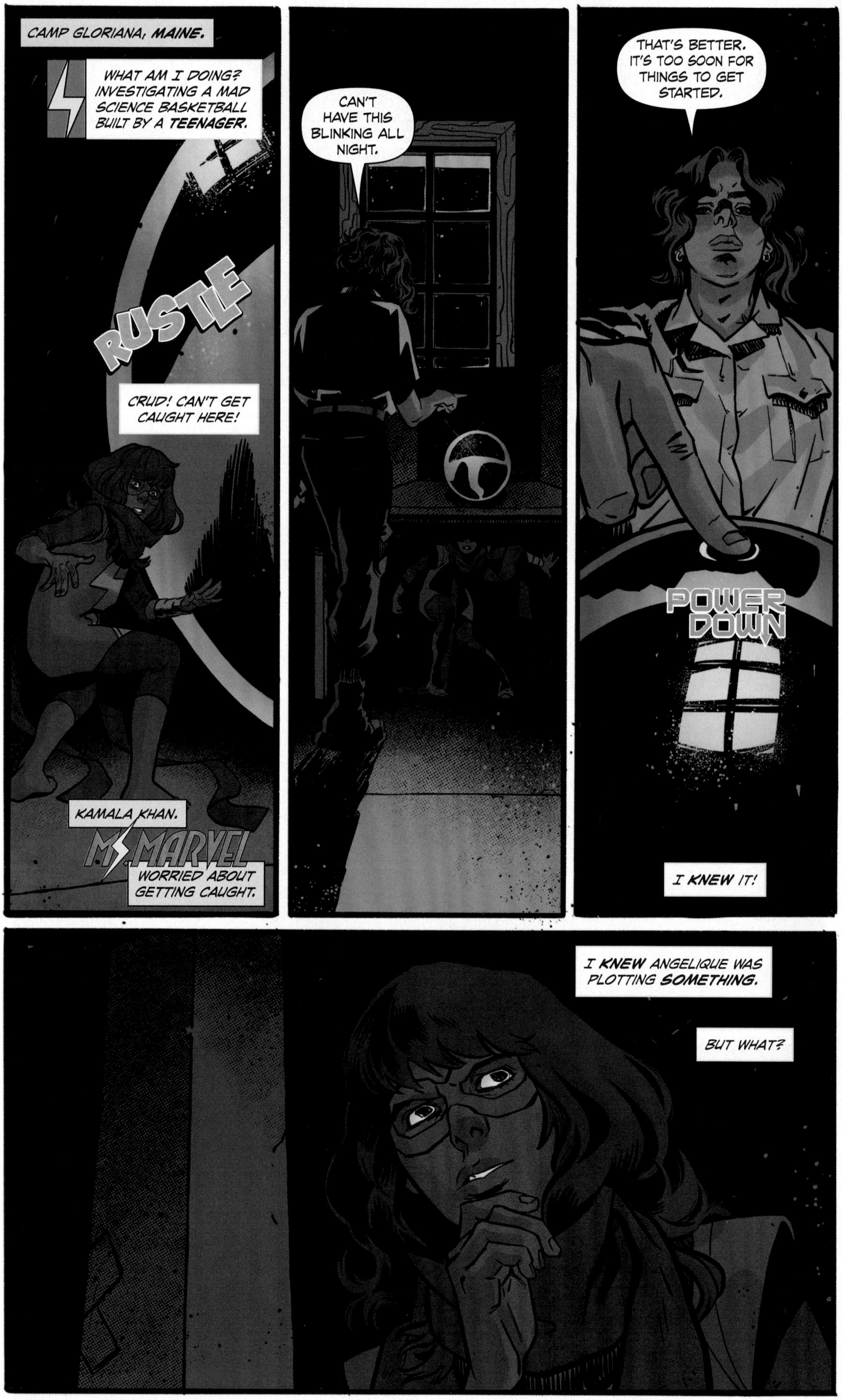

CAMP GLORIANA, MAINE.
WHAT AM I DOING? INVESTIGATING A MAD SCIENCE BASKETBALL BUILT BY A TEENAGER.
RUSTLE
CRUD! CAN'T GET CAUGHT HERE!
KAMALA KHAN.
MS. MARVEL
WORRIED ABOUT GETTING CAUGHT.
CAN'T HAVE THIS BLINKING ALL NIGHT.
THAT'S BETTER. IT'S TOO SOON FOR THINGS TO GET STARTED.
POWER DOWN
I KNEW IT!
I KNEW ANGELIQUE WAS PLOTTING SOMETHING.
BUT WHAT?

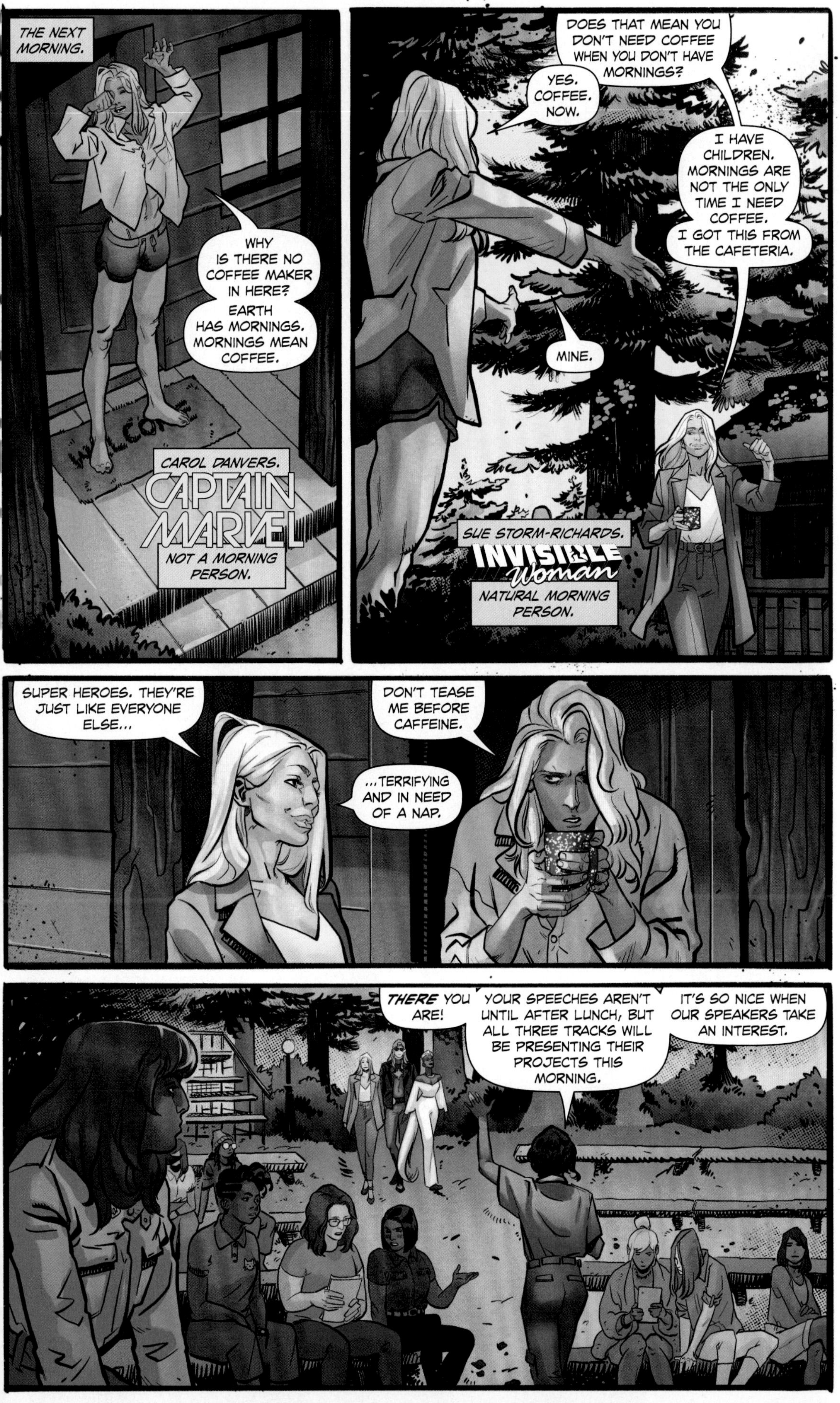
THE NEXT MORNING.
WHY IS THERE NO COFFEE MAKER IN HERE? EARTH HAS MORNINGS. MORNINGS MEAN COFFEE.
CAROL DANVERS.
CAPTAIN MARVEL
NOT A MORNING PERSON.
YES. COFFEE. NOW.
DOES THAT MEAN YOU DON'T NEED COFFEE WHEN YOU DON'T HAVE MORNINGS?
I HAVE CHILDREN. MORNINGS ARE NOT THE ONLY TIME I NEED COFFEE. I GOT THIS FROM THE CAFETERIA.
MINE.
SUE STORM-RICHARDS.
INVISIBLE Woman
NATURAL MORNING PERSON.
SUPER HEROES. THEY'RE JUST LIKE EVERYONE ELSE...
...TERRIFYING AND IN NEED OF A NAP.
DON'T TEASE ME BEFORE CAFFEINE.
THERE YOU ARE!
YOUR SPEECHES AREN'T UNTIL AFTER LUNCH, BUT ALL THREE TRACKS WILL BE PRESENTING THEIR PROJECTS THIS MORNING.
IT'S SO NICE WHEN OUR SPEAKERS TAKE AN INTEREST.

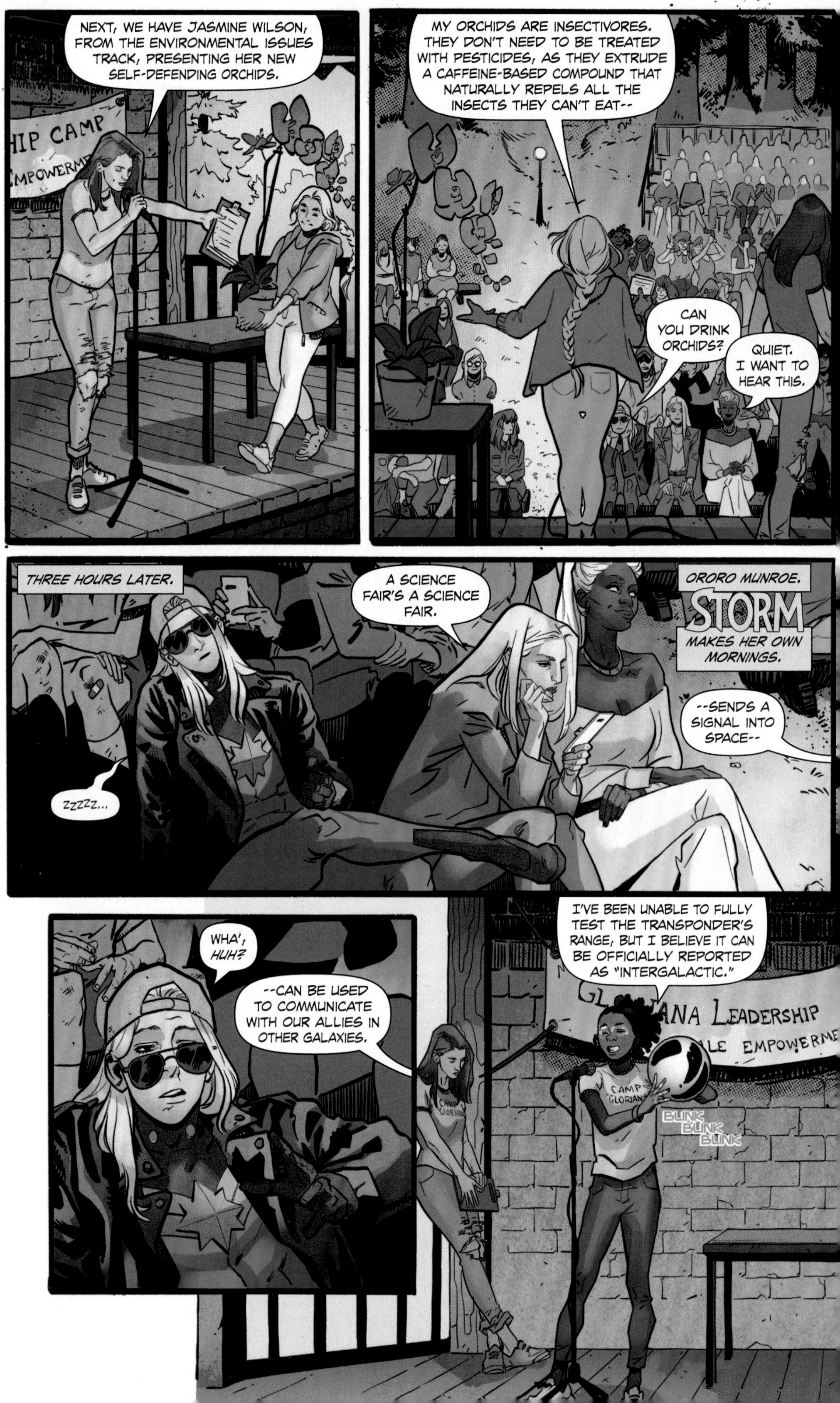

NEXT, WE HAVE JASMINE WILSON, FROM THE ENVIRONMENTAL ISSUES TRACK, PRESENTING HER NEW SELF-DEFENDING ORCHIDS.
HIP CAMP
EMPOWERM
MY ORCHIDS ARE INSECTIVORES. THEY DON'T NEED TO BE TREATED WITH PESTICIDES, AS THEY EXTRUDE A CAFFEINE-BASED COMPOUND THAT NATURALLY REPELS ALL THE INSECTS THEY CAN'T EAT--
CAN YOU DRINK ORCHIDS?
QUIET. I WANT TO HEAR THIS.
THREE HOURS LATER.
A SCIENCE FAIR'S A SCIENCE FAIR.
ORORO MUNROE.
STORM
MAKES HER OWN MORNINGS.
--SENDS A SIGNAL INTO SPACE--
ZZZZZ...
WHA', HUH?
--CAN BE USED TO COMMUNICATE WITH OUR ALLIES IN OTHER GALAXIES.
I'VE BEEN UNABLE TO FULLY TEST THE TRANSPONDER'S RANGE, BUT I BELIEVE IT CAN BE OFFICIALLY REPORTED AS "INTERGALACTIC."
ANA LEADERSHIP
LE EMPOWERME
CAMP GLORIANA
BLINK
BLINK
BLINK

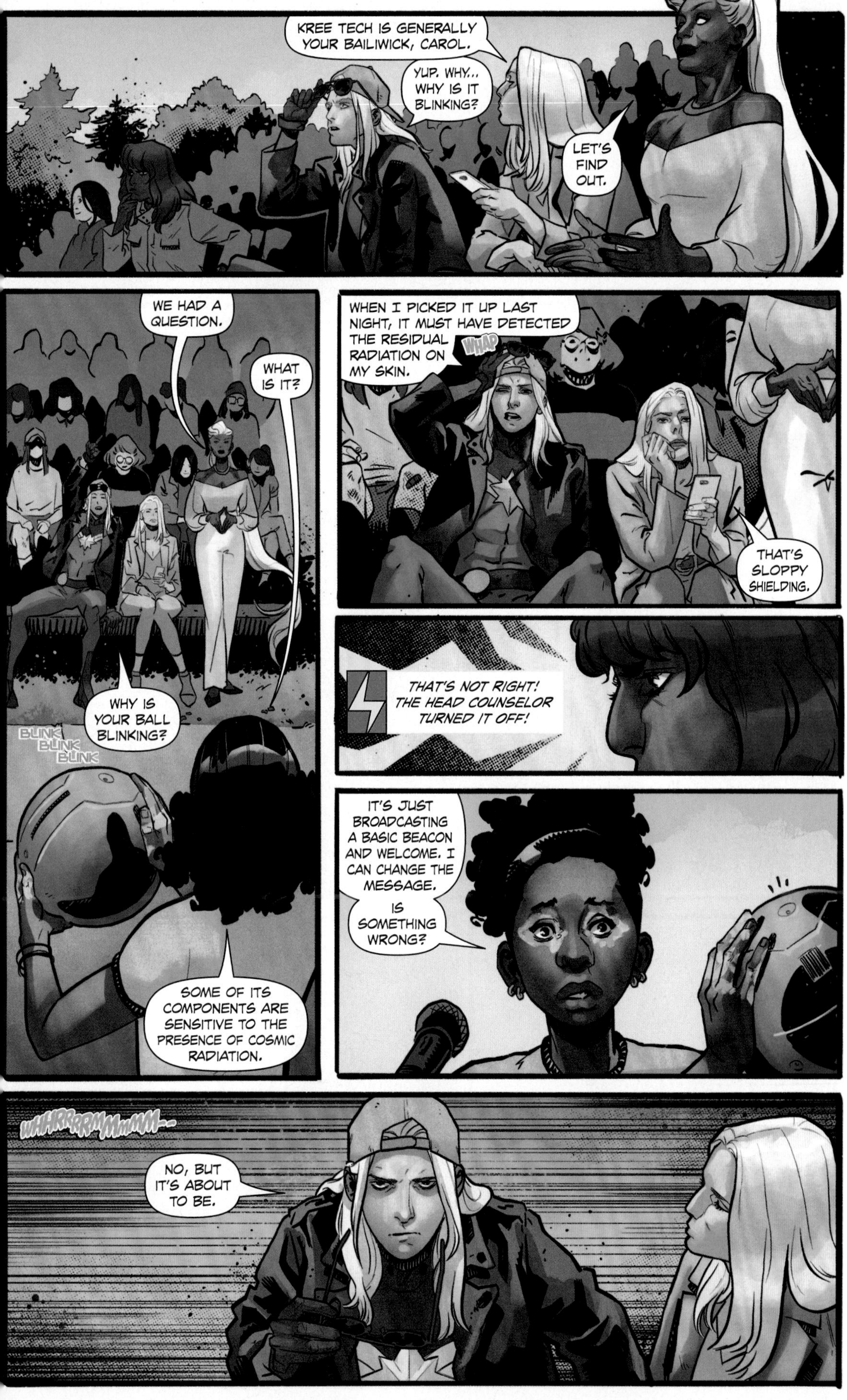
KREE TECH IS GENERALLY YOUR BAILIWICK, CAROL.
YUP. WHY... WHY IS IT BLINKING?
LET'S FIND OUT.
WE HAD A QUESTION.
WHAT IS IT?
WHY IS YOUR BALL BLINKING?
BLINK BLINK BLINK
SOME OF ITS COMPONENTS ARE SENSITIVE TO THE PRESENCE OF COSMIC RADIATION.
WHEN I PICKED IT UP LAST NIGHT, IT MUST HAVE DETECTED THE RESIDUAL RADIATION ON MY SKIN.
WHAP
THAT'S SLOPPY SHIELDING.
THAT'S NOT RIGHT! THE HEAD COUNSELOR TURNED IT OFF!
IT'S JUST BROADCASTING A BASIC BEACON AND WELCOME. I CAN CHANGE THE MESSAGE.
IS SOMETHING WRONG?
WHHRRRRMMmmM--
NO, BUT IT'S ABOUT TO BE.

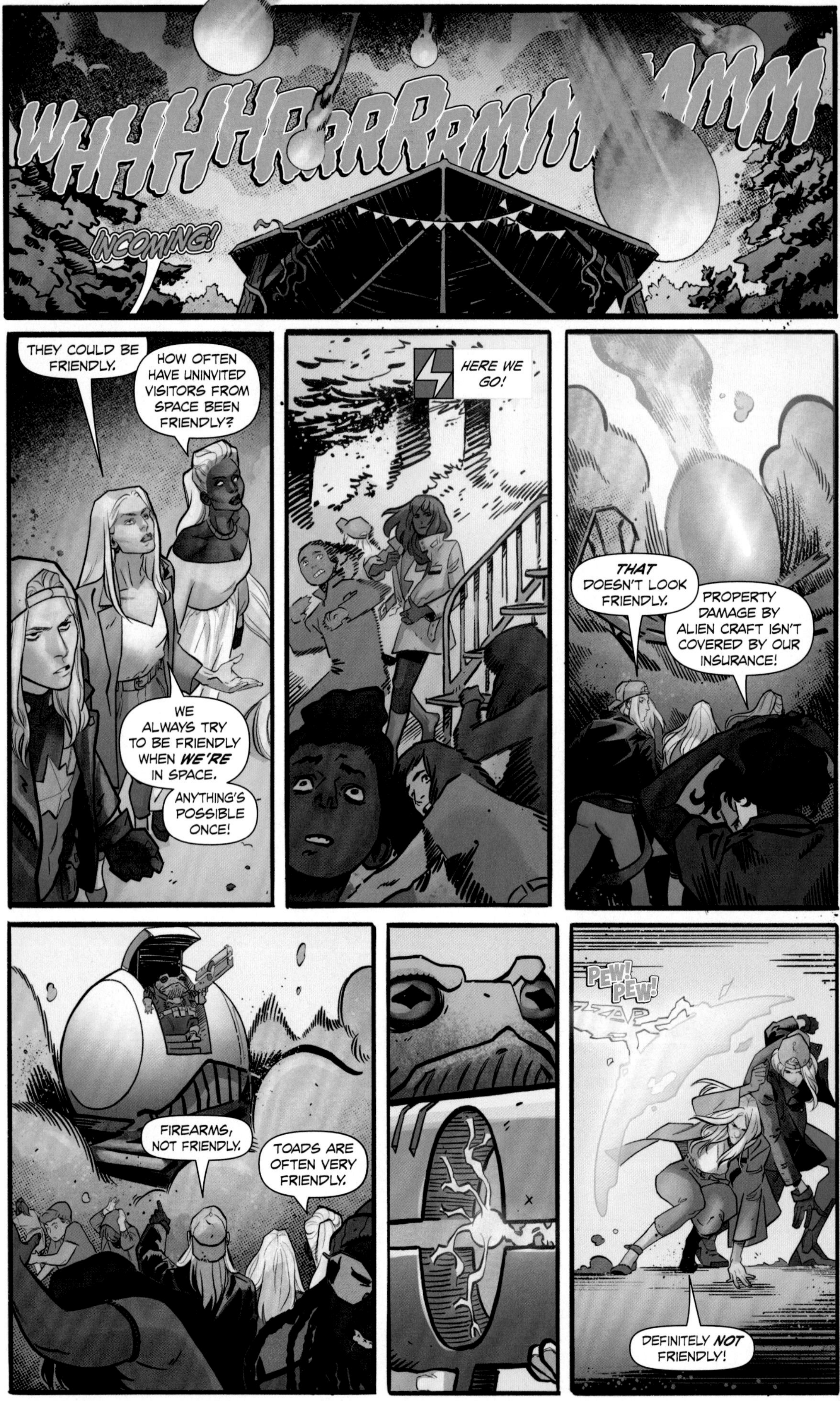
WHHHHRRRRRRMMMMMMM
INCOMING!
THEY COULD BE FRIENDLY.
HOW OFTEN HAVE UNINVITED VISITORS FROM SPACE BEEN FRIENDLY?
WE ALWAYS TRY TO BE FRIENDLY WHEN WE'RE IN SPACE.
ANYTHING'S POSSIBLE ONCE!
HERE WE GO!
THAT DOESN'T LOOK FRIENDLY.
PROPERTY DAMAGE BY ALIEN CRAFT ISN'T COVERED BY OUR INSURANCE!
FIREARMS, NOT FRIENDLY.
TOADS ARE OFTEN VERY FRIENDLY.
PEW! PEW!
ZZAP
DEFINITELY NOT FRIENDLY!

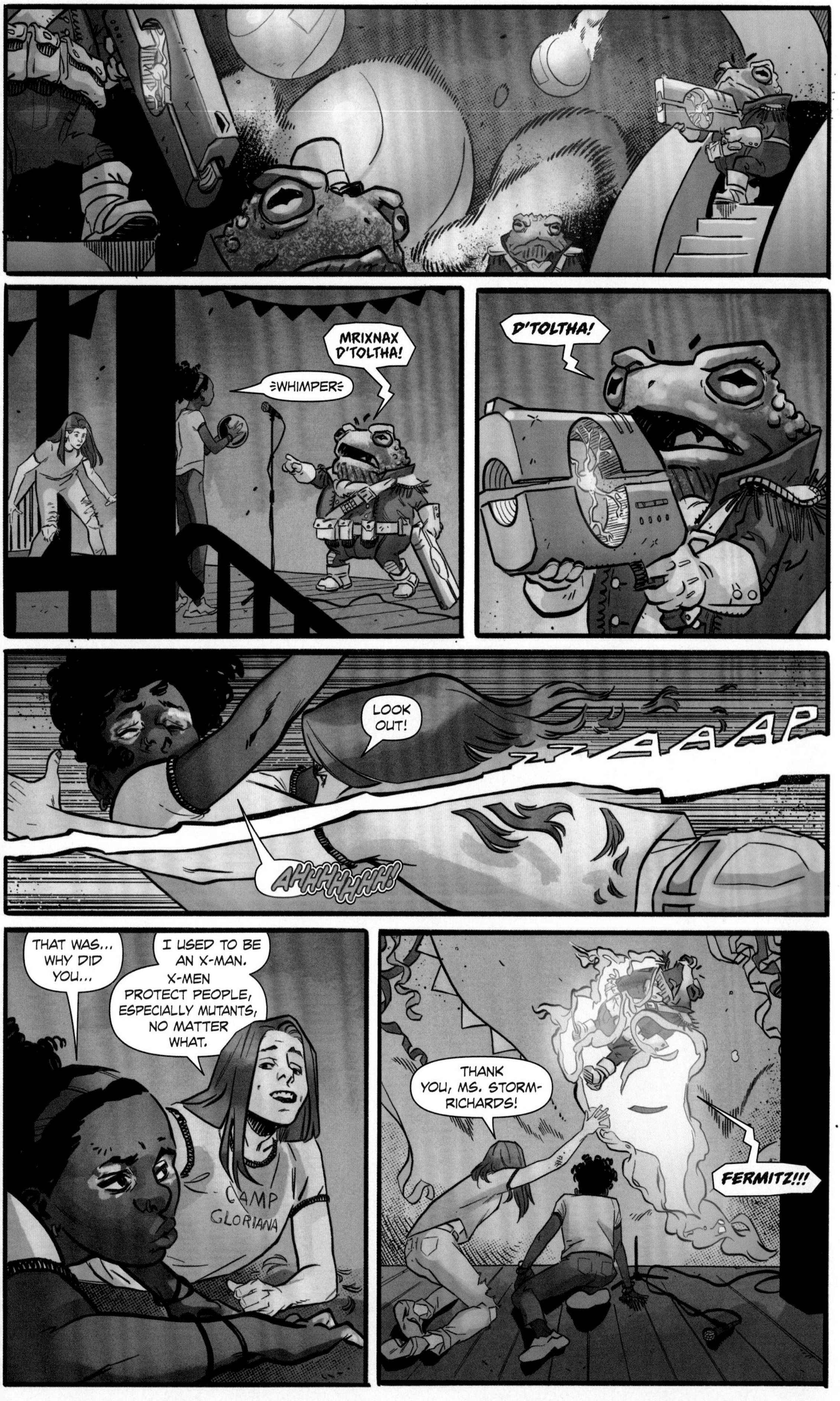
MRIXNAX D'TOLTHA!
WHIMPER
D'TOLTHA!
LOOK OUT!
ZWAAAAP
AHHHHHHH!
THAT WAS... WHY DID YOU...
I USED TO BE AN X-MAN.
X-MEN PROTECT PEOPLE, ESPECIALLY MUTANTS, NO MATTER WHAT.
CAMP GLORIANA
THANK YOU, MS. STORM-RICHARDS!
FERMITZ!!!

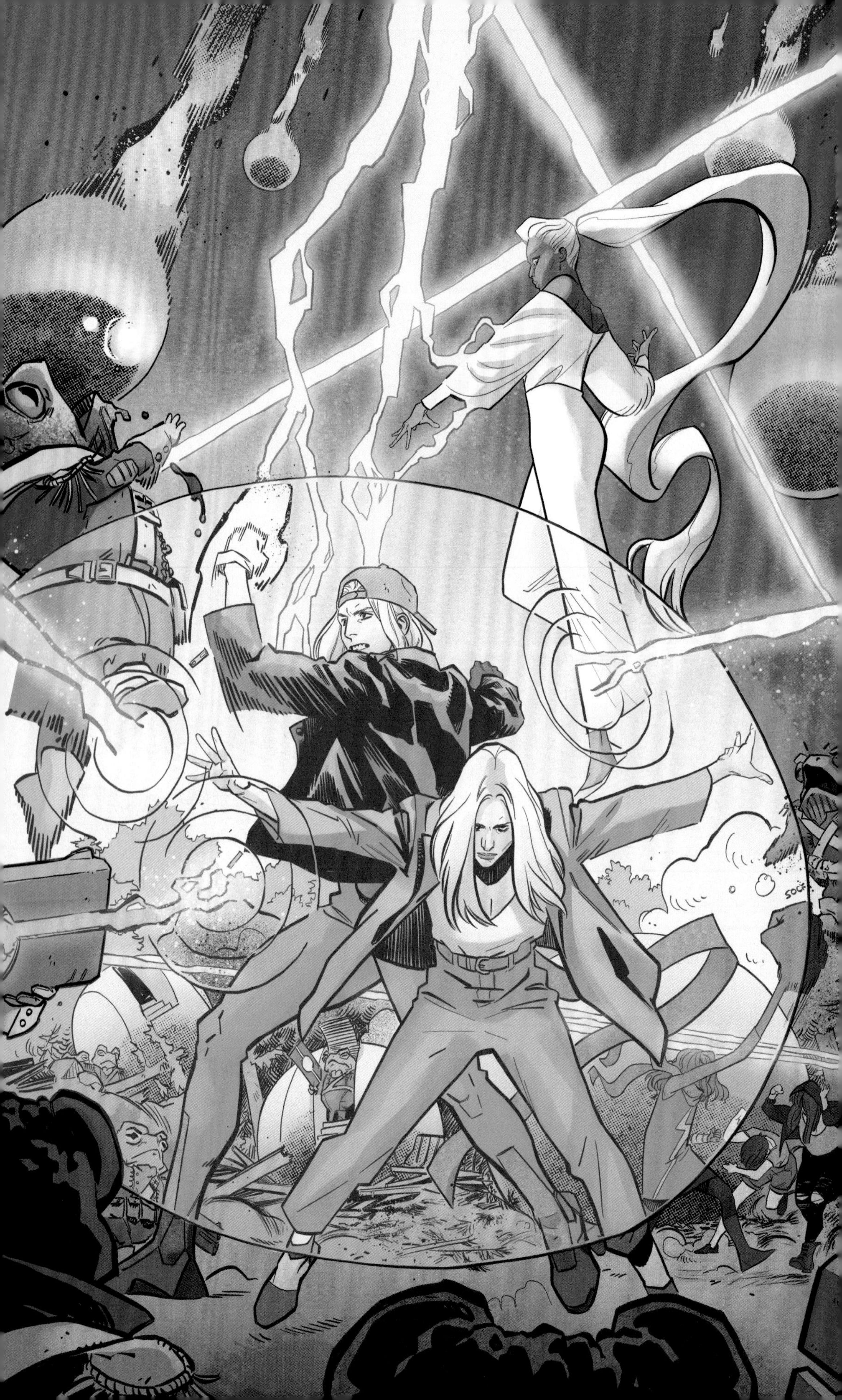
SOCK

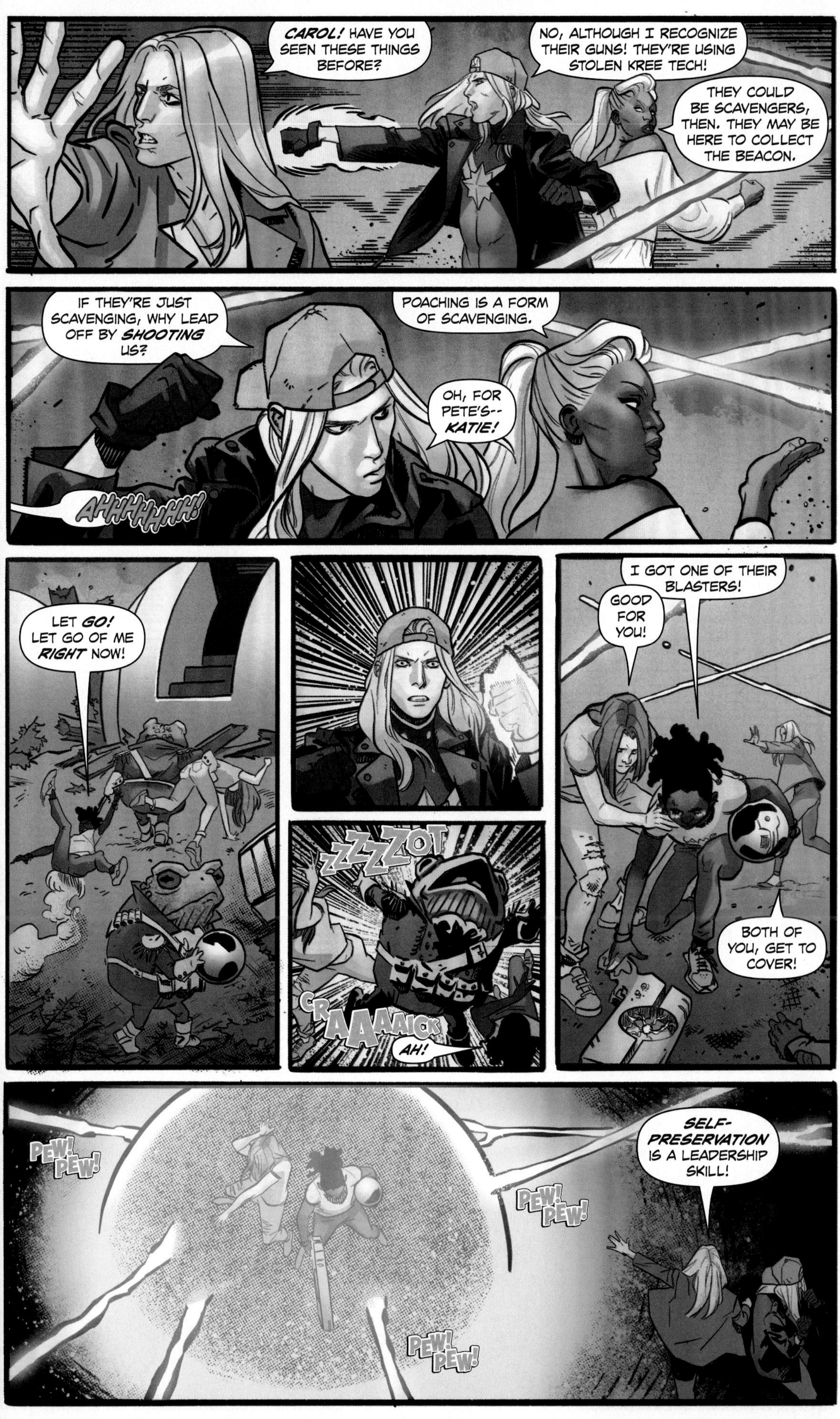
CAROL! HAVE YOU SEEN THESE THINGS BEFORE?
NO, ALTHOUGH I RECOGNIZE THEIR GUNS! THEY'RE USING STOLEN KREE TECH!
THEY COULD BE SCAVENGERS, THEN. THEY MAY BE HERE TO COLLECT THE BEACON.
IF THEY'RE JUST SCAVENGING, WHY LEAD OFF BY SHOOTING US?
POACHING IS A FORM OF SCAVENGING.
OH, FOR PETE'S-- KATIE!
AHHHHHHH!
LET GO! LET GO OF ME RIGHT NOW!
ZZZZZOT
CRAAAAAICK
AH!
I GOT ONE OF THEIR BLASTERS!
GOOD FOR YOU!
BOTH OF YOU, GET TO COVER!
PEW! PEW!
PEW! PEW!
PEW! PEW!
SELF-PRESERVATION IS A LEADERSHIP SKILL!

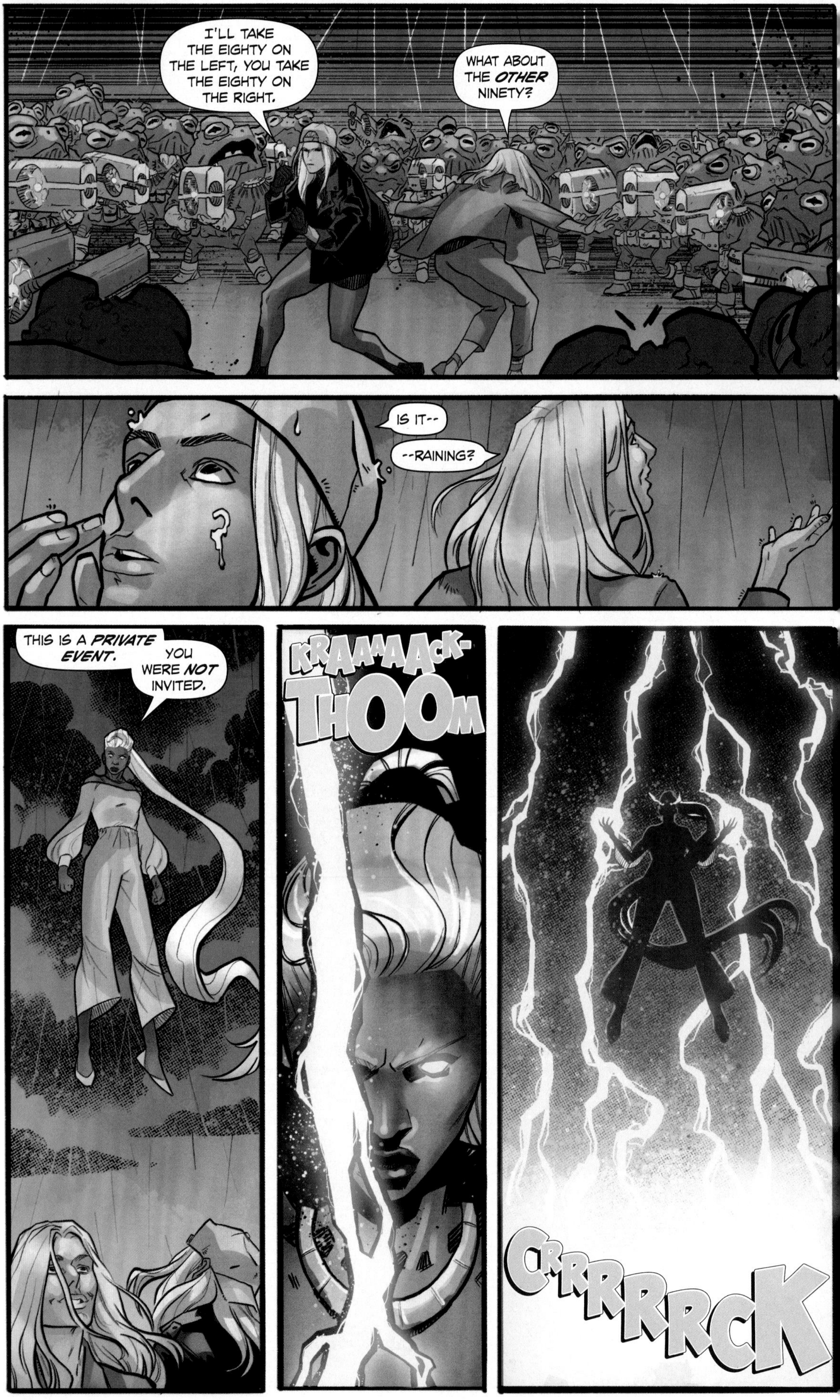
I'LL TAKE THE EIGHTY ON THE LEFT, YOU TAKE THE EIGHTY ON THE RIGHT.
WHAT ABOUT THE OTHER NINETY?
IS IT--
--RAINING?
THIS IS A PRIVATE EVENT.
YOU WERE NOT INVITED.
KRAAAAACK-THOOM
CRRRRRCK

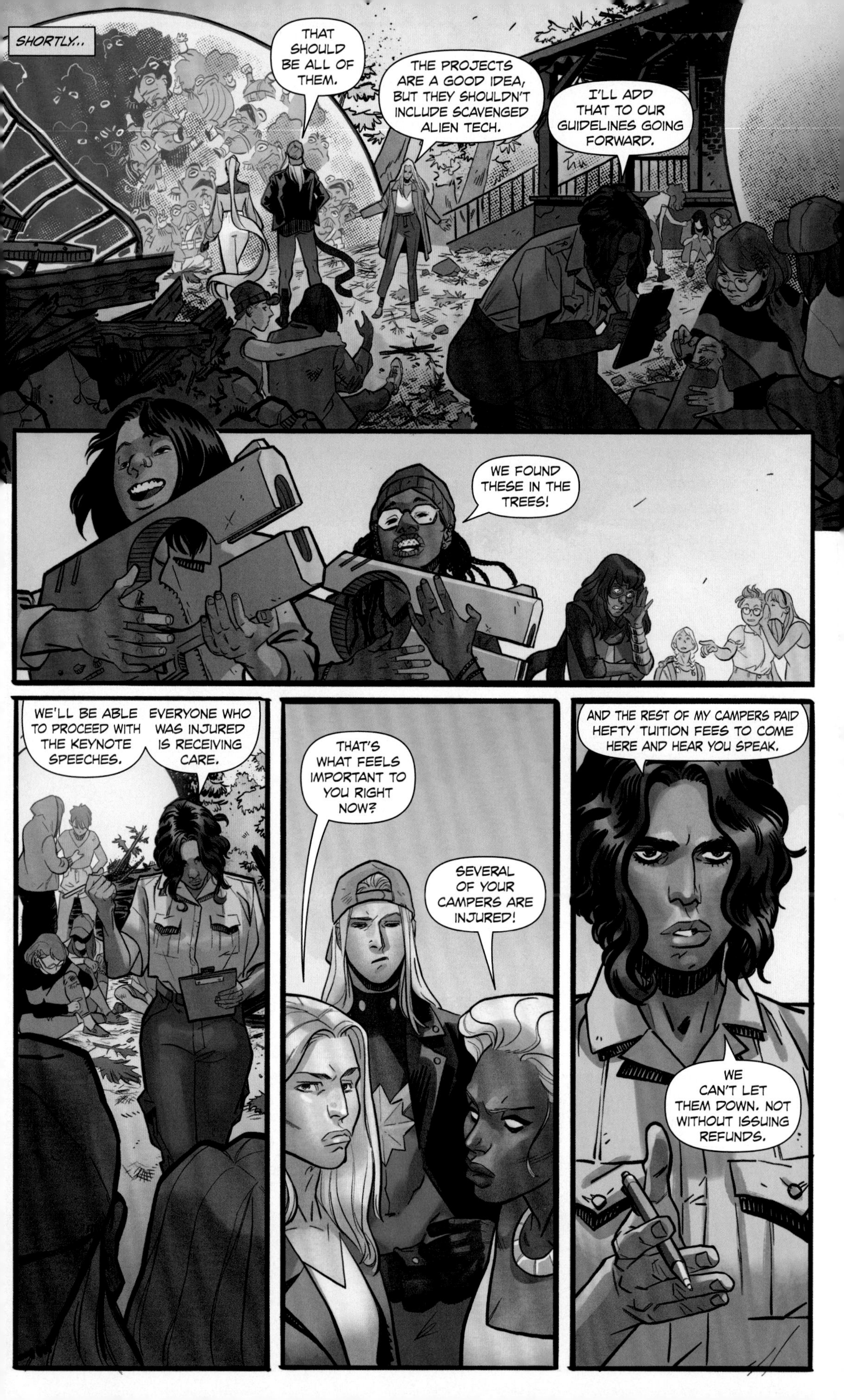
SHORTLY...
THAT SHOULD BE ALL OF THEM.
THE PROJECTS ARE A GOOD IDEA, BUT THEY SHOULDN'T INCLUDE SCAVENGED ALIEN TECH.
I'LL ADD THAT TO OUR GUIDELINES GOING FORWARD.
WE FOUND THESE IN THE TREES!
WE'LL BE ABLE TO PROCEED WITH THE KEYNOTE SPEECHES.
EVERYONE WHO WAS INJURED IS RECEIVING CARE.
THAT'S WHAT FEELS IMPORTANT TO YOU RIGHT NOW?
SEVERAL OF YOUR CAMPERS ARE INJURED!
AND THE REST OF MY CAMPERS PAID HEFTY TUITION FEES TO COME HERE AND HEAR YOU SPEAK.
WE CAN'T LET THEM DOWN. NOT WITHOUT ISSUING REFUNDS.

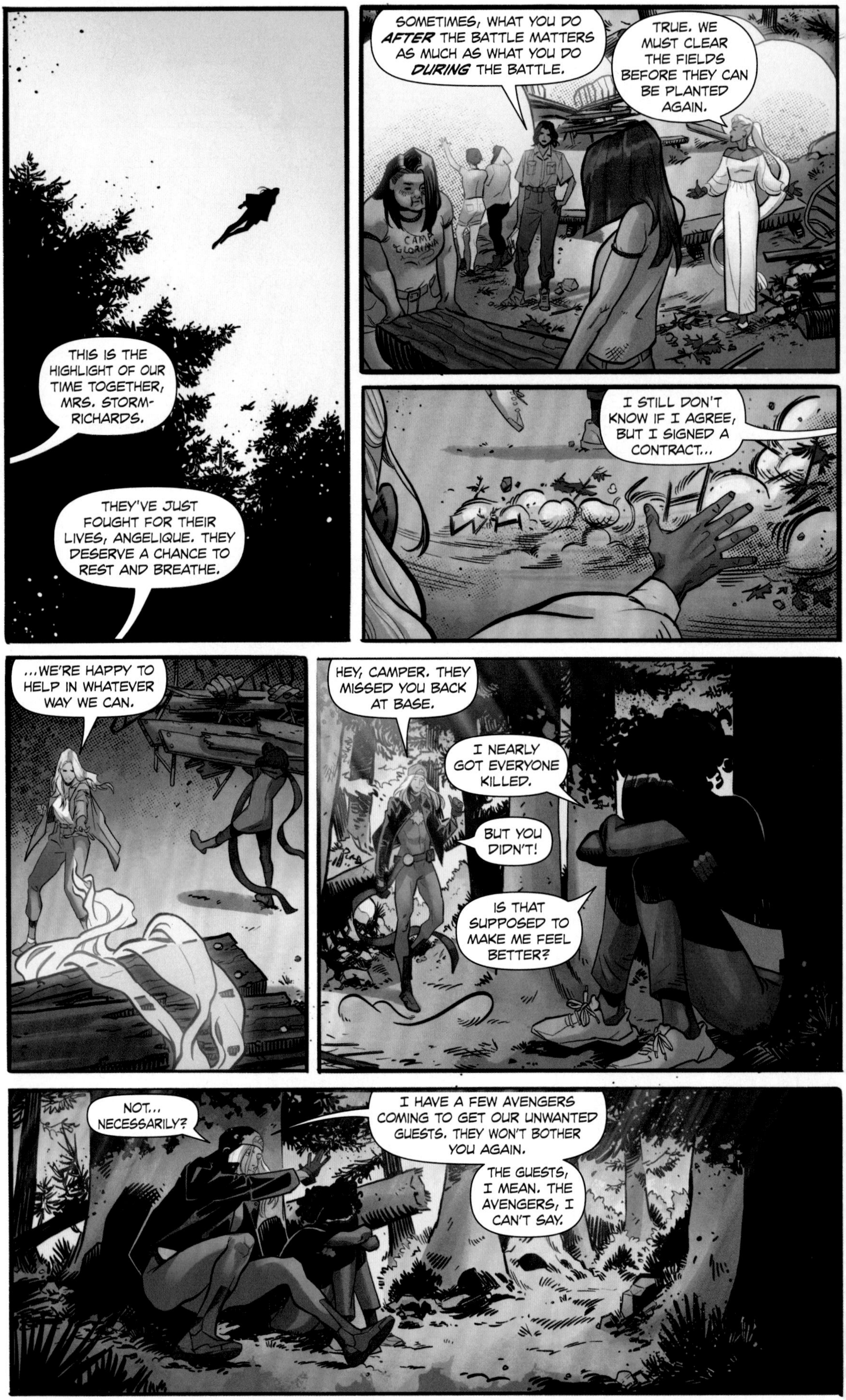
THIS IS THE HIGHLIGHT OF OUR TIME TOGETHER, MRS. STORM-RICHARDS.
THEY'VE JUST FOUGHT FOR THEIR LIVES, ANGELIQUE. THEY DESERVE A CHANCE TO REST AND BREATHE.
SOMETIMES, WHAT YOU DO AFTER THE BATTLE MATTERS AS MUCH AS WHAT YOU DO DURING THE BATTLE.
TRUE. WE MUST CLEAR THE FIELDS BEFORE THEY CAN BE PLANTED AGAIN.
CAMP GLORIANA
I STILL DON'T KNOW IF I AGREE, BUT I SIGNED A CONTRACT...
WHOOOSH
...WE'RE HAPPY TO HELP IN WHATEVER WAY WE CAN.
HEY, CAMPER. THEY MISSED YOU BACK AT BASE.
I NEARLY GOT EVERYONE KILLED.
BUT YOU DIDN'T!
IS THAT SUPPOSED TO MAKE ME FEEL BETTER?
NOT... NECESSARILY?
I HAVE A FEW AVENGERS COMING TO GET OUR UNWANTED GUESTS. THEY WON'T BOTHER YOU AGAIN.
THE GUESTS, I MEAN. THE AVENGERS, I CAN'T SAY.

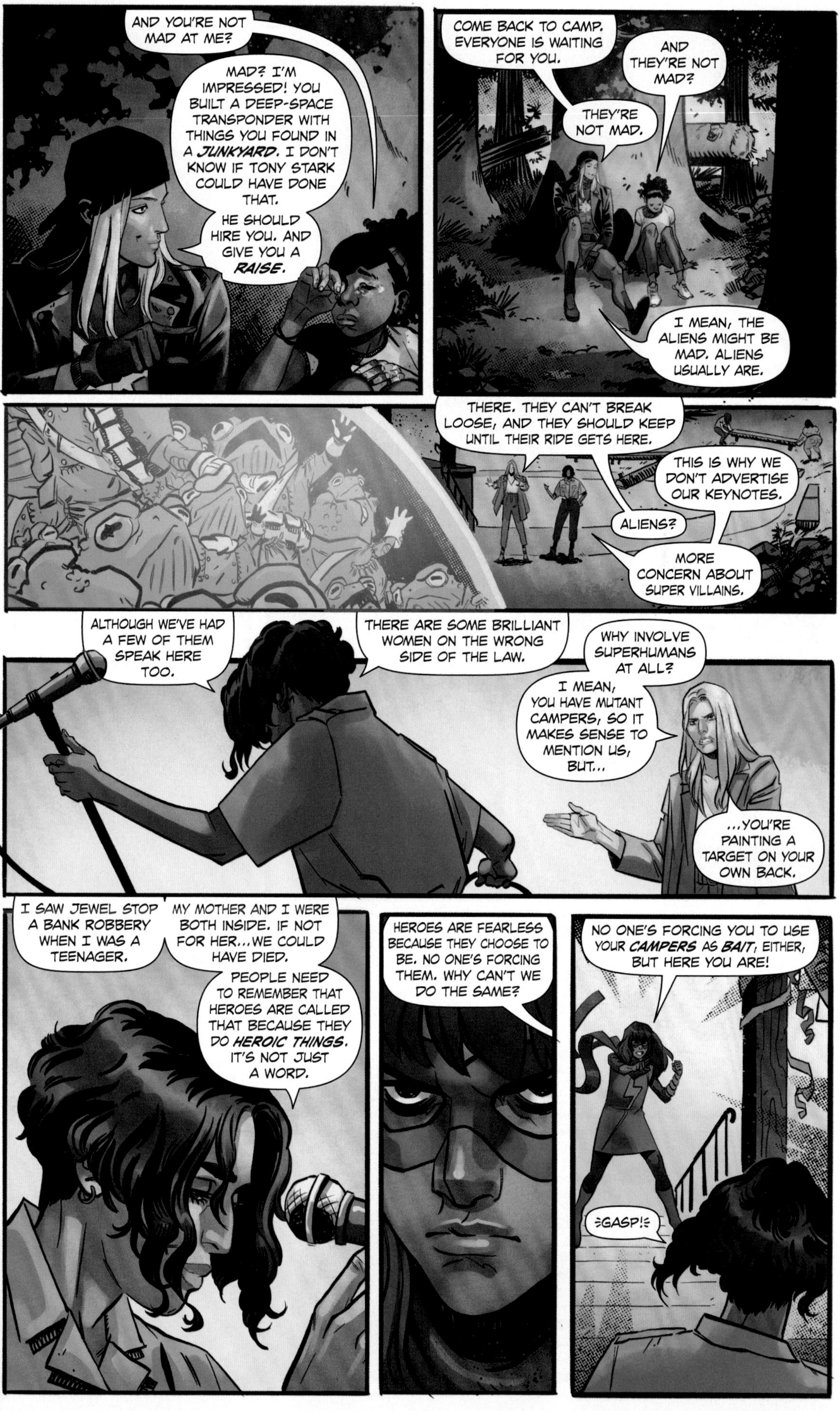
AND YOU'RE NOT MAD AT ME?
MAD? I'M IMPRESSED! YOU BUILT A DEEP-SPACE TRANSPONDER WITH THINGS YOU FOUND IN A JUNKYARD. I DON'T KNOW IF TONY STARK COULD HAVE DONE THAT.
HE SHOULD HIRE YOU. AND GIVE YOU A RAISE.
COME BACK TO CAMP. EVERYONE IS WAITING FOR YOU.
AND THEY'RE NOT MAD?
THEY'RE NOT MAD.
I MEAN, THE ALIENS MIGHT BE MAD. ALIENS USUALLY ARE.
THERE. THEY CAN'T BREAK LOOSE, AND THEY SHOULD KEEP UNTIL THEIR RIDE GETS HERE.
THIS IS WHY WE DON'T ADVERTISE OUR KEYNOTES.
ALIENS?
MORE CONCERN ABOUT SUPER VILLAINS.
ALTHOUGH WE'VE HAD A FEW OF THEM SPEAK HERE TOO.
THERE ARE SOME BRILLIANT WOMEN ON THE WRONG SIDE OF THE LAW.
WHY INVOLVE SUPERHUMANS AT ALL?
I MEAN, YOU HAVE MUTANT CAMPERS, SO IT MAKES SENSE TO MENTION US, BUT...
...YOU'RE PAINTING A TARGET ON YOUR OWN BACK.
I SAW JEWEL STOP A BANK ROBBERY WHEN I WAS A TEENAGER.
MY MOTHER AND I WERE BOTH INSIDE. IF NOT FOR HER...WE COULD HAVE DIED.
PEOPLE NEED TO REMEMBER THAT HEROES ARE CALLED THAT BECAUSE THEY DO HEROIC THINGS. IT'S NOT JUST A WORD.
HEROES ARE FEARLESS BECAUSE THEY CHOOSE TO BE. NO ONE'S FORCING THEM. WHY CAN'T WE DO THE SAME?
NO ONE'S FORCING YOU TO USE YOUR CAMPERS AS BAIT, EITHER, BUT HERE YOU ARE!
GASP!

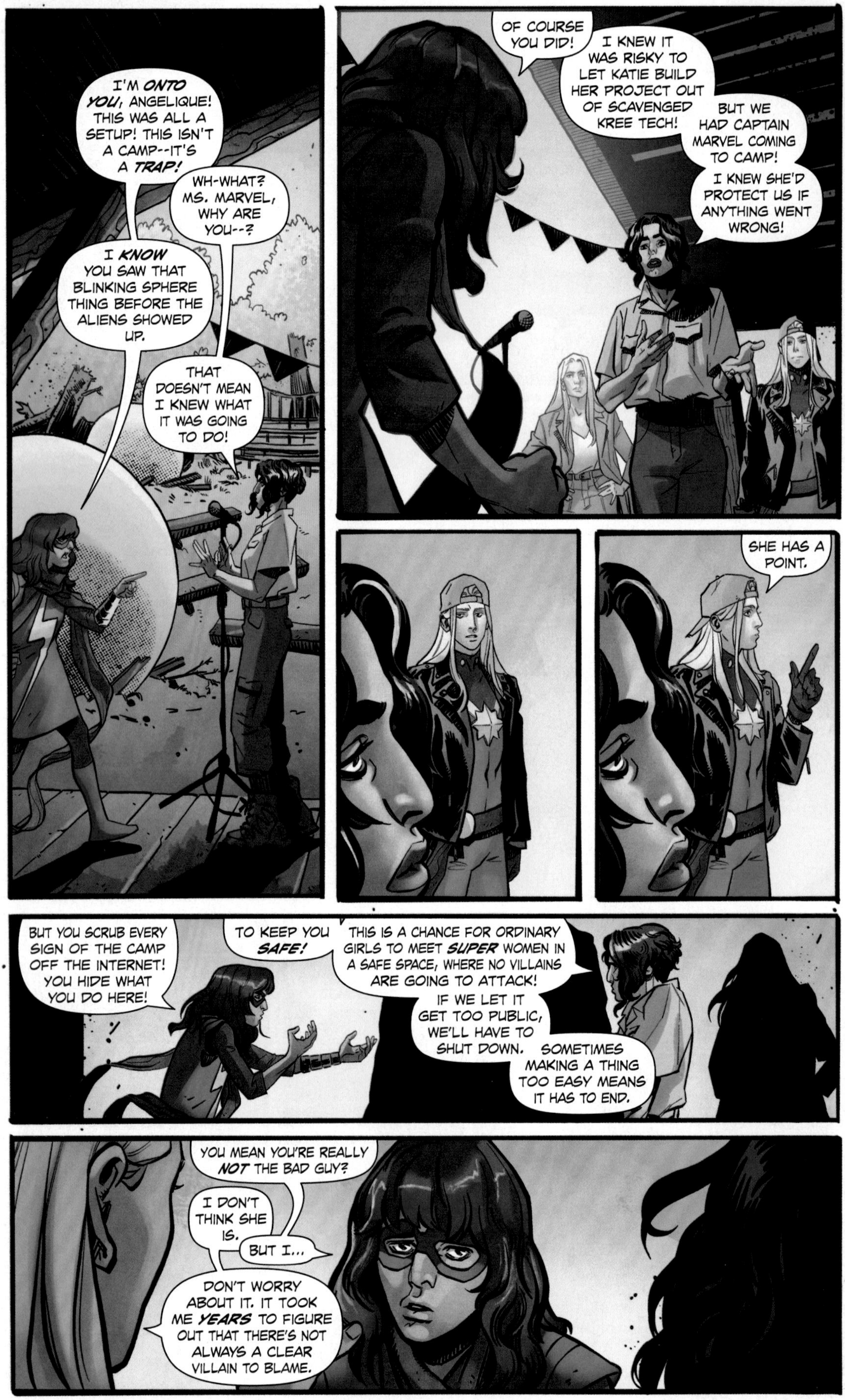
I'M ONTO YOU, ANGELIQUE! THIS WAS ALL A SETUP! THIS ISN'T A CAMP--IT'S A TRAP!
WH-WHAT? MS. MARVEL, WHY ARE YOU--?
I KNOW YOU SAW THAT BLINKING SPHERE THING BEFORE THE ALIENS SHOWED UP.
THAT DOESN'T MEAN I KNEW WHAT IT WAS GOING TO DO!
OF COURSE YOU DID!
I KNEW IT WAS RISKY TO LET KATIE BUILD HER PROJECT OUT OF SCAVENGED KREE TECH!
BUT WE HAD CAPTAIN MARVEL COMING TO CAMP!
I KNEW SHE'D PROTECT US IF ANYTHING WENT WRONG!
SHE HAS A POINT.
BUT YOU SCRUB EVERY SIGN OF THE CAMP OFF THE INTERNET! YOU HIDE WHAT YOU DO HERE!
TO KEEP YOU SAFE!
THIS IS A CHANCE FOR ORDINARY GIRLS TO MEET SUPER WOMEN IN A SAFE SPACE, WHERE NO VILLAINS ARE GOING TO ATTACK!
IF WE LET IT GET TOO PUBLIC, WE'LL HAVE TO SHUT DOWN.
SOMETIMES MAKING A THING TOO EASY MEANS IT HAS TO END.
YOU MEAN YOU'RE REALLY NOT THE BAD GUY?
I DON'T THINK SHE IS.
BUT I...
DON'T WORRY ABOUT IT. IT TOOK ME YEARS TO FIGURE OUT THAT THERE'S NOT ALWAYS A CLEAR VILLAIN TO BLAME.

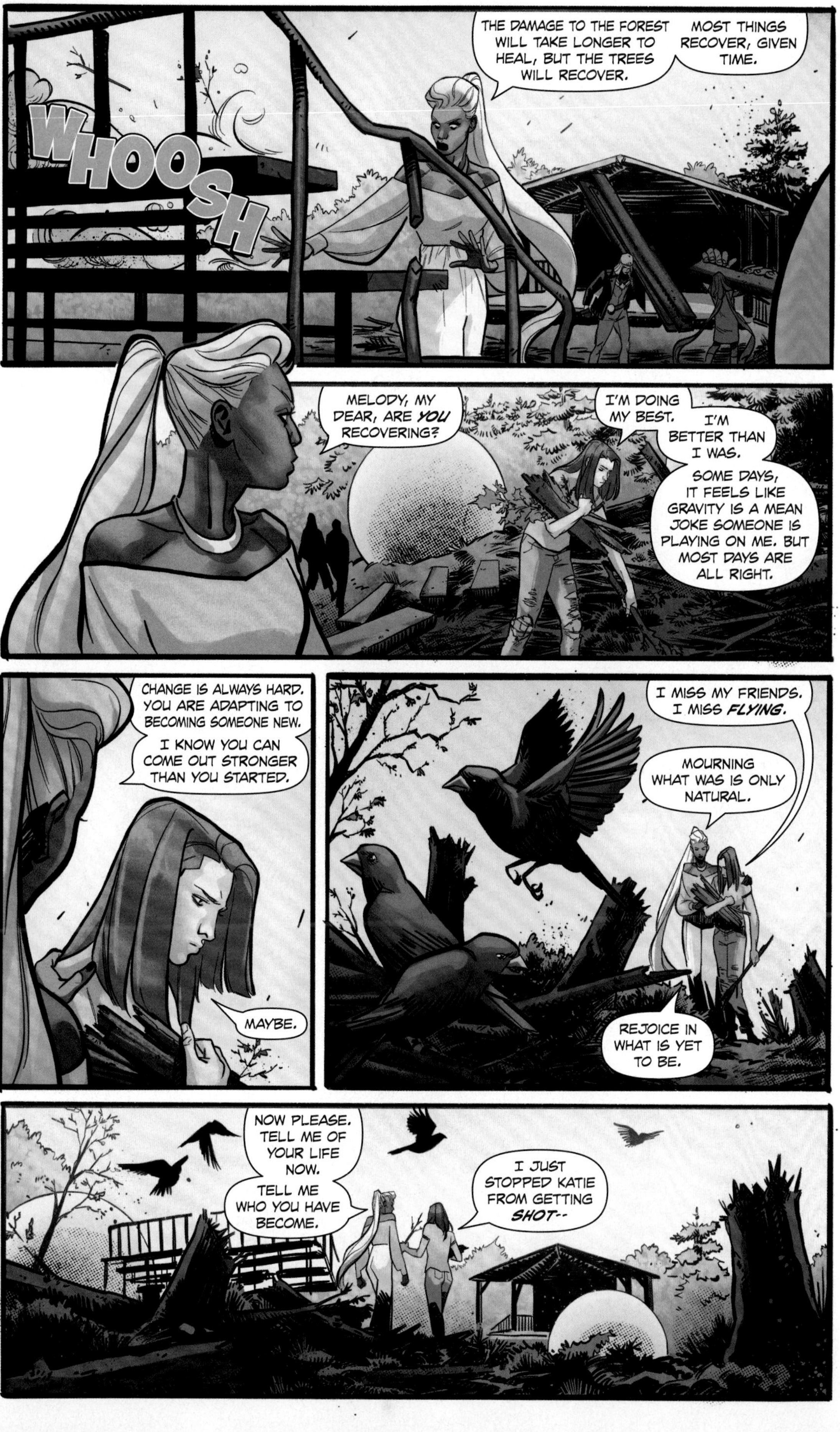
WHOOSH
THE DAMAGE TO THE FOREST WILL TAKE LONGER TO HEAL, BUT THE TREES WILL RECOVER.
MOST THINGS RECOVER, GIVEN TIME.
MELODY, MY DEAR, ARE *YOU* RECOVERING?
I'M DOING MY BEST.
I'M BETTER THAN I WAS.
SOME DAYS, IT FEELS LIKE GRAVITY IS A MEAN JOKE SOMEONE IS PLAYING ON ME. BUT MOST DAYS ARE ALL RIGHT.
CHANGE IS ALWAYS HARD. YOU ARE ADAPTING TO BECOMING SOMEONE NEW.
I KNOW YOU CAN COME OUT STRONGER THAN YOU STARTED.
MAYBE.
I MISS MY FRIENDS. I MISS *FLYING*.
MOURNING WHAT WAS IS ONLY NATURAL.
REJOICE IN WHAT IS YET TO BE.
NOW PLEASE. TELL ME OF YOUR LIFE NOW.
TELL ME WHO YOU HAVE BECOME.
I JUST STOPPED KATIE FROM GETTING *SHOT*--

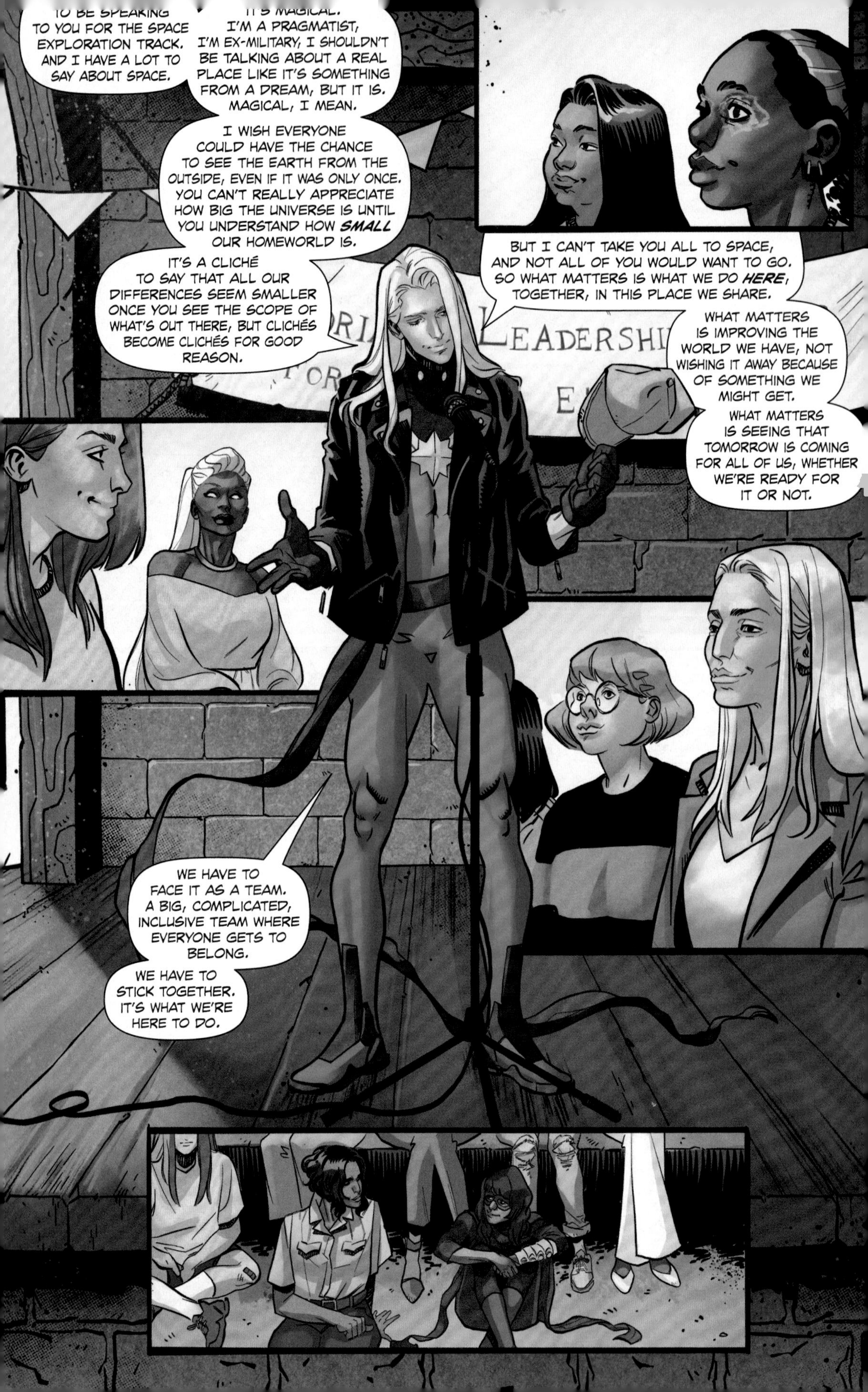

TO BE SPEAKING TO YOU FOR THE SPACE EXPLORATION TRACK. AND I HAVE A LOT TO SAY ABOUT SPACE.
IT'S MAGICAL. I'M A PRAGMATIST, I'M EX-MILITARY, I SHOULDN'T BE TALKING ABOUT A REAL PLACE LIKE IT'S SOMETHING FROM A DREAM, BUT IT IS. MAGICAL, I MEAN.
I WISH EVERYONE COULD HAVE THE CHANCE TO SEE THE EARTH FROM THE OUTSIDE, EVEN IF IT WAS ONLY ONCE. YOU CAN'T REALLY APPRECIATE HOW BIG THE UNIVERSE IS UNTIL YOU UNDERSTAND HOW ***SMALL*** OUR HOMEWORLD IS.
IT'S A CLICHÉ TO SAY THAT ALL OUR DIFFERENCES SEEM SMALLER ONCE YOU SEE THE SCOPE OF WHAT'S OUT THERE, BUT CLICHÉS BECOME CLICHÉS FOR GOOD REASON.
BUT I CAN'T TAKE YOU ALL TO SPACE, AND NOT ALL OF YOU WOULD WANT TO GO. SO WHAT MATTERS IS WHAT WE DO ***HERE***, TOGETHER, IN THIS PLACE WE SHARE.
WHAT MATTERS IS IMPROVING THE WORLD WE HAVE, NOT WISHING IT AWAY BECAUSE OF SOMETHING WE MIGHT GET.
WHAT MATTERS IS SEEING THAT TOMORROW IS COMING FOR ALL OF US, WHETHER WE'RE READY FOR IT OR NOT.
WE HAVE TO FACE IT AS A TEAM. A BIG, COMPLICATED, INCLUSIVE TEAM WHERE EVERYONE GETS TO BELONG.
WE HAVE TO STICK TOGETHER. IT'S WHAT WE'RE HERE TO DO.

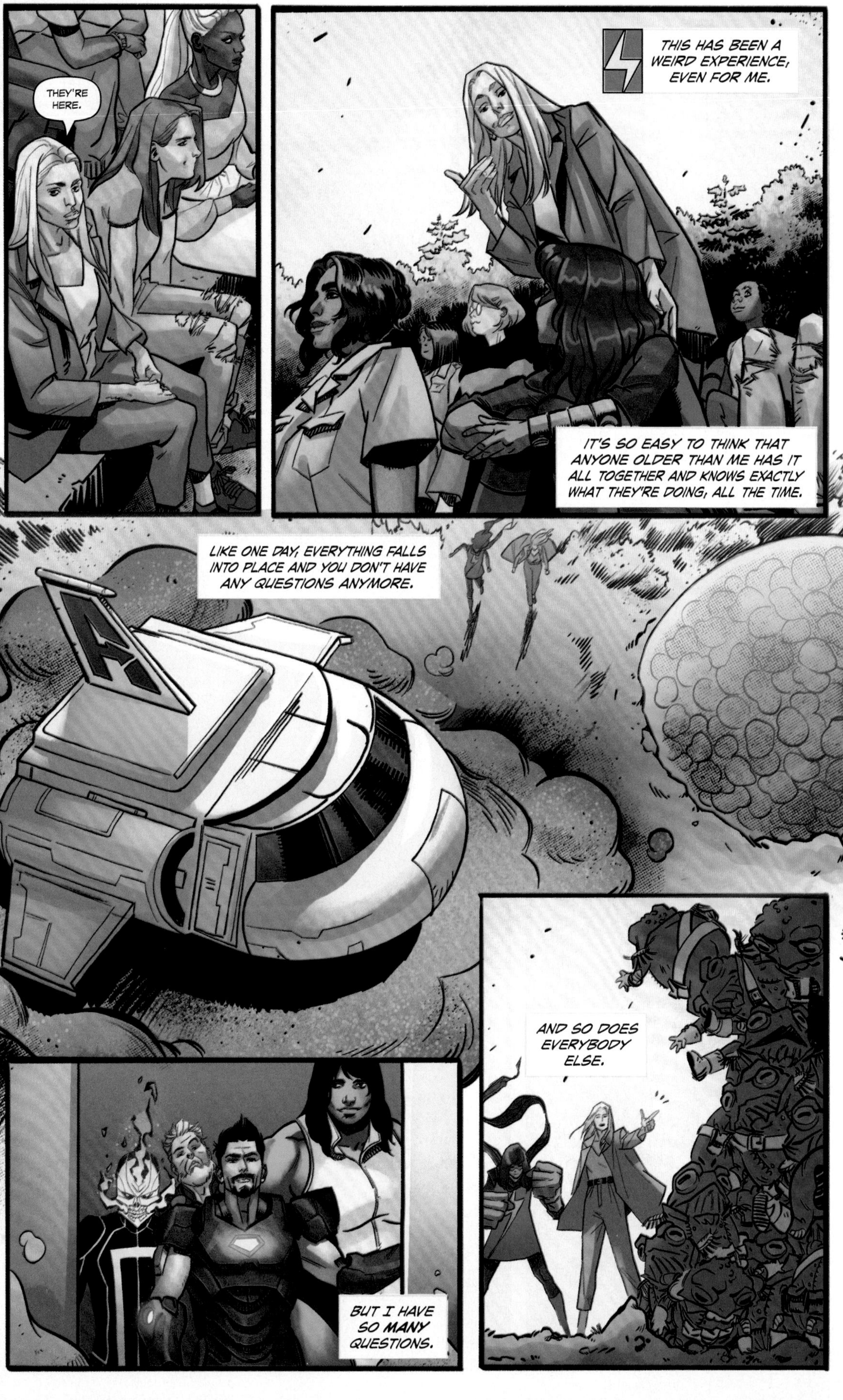
THEY'RE HERE.
THIS HAS BEEN A WEIRD EXPERIENCE, EVEN FOR ME.
IT'S SO EASY TO THINK THAT ANYONE OLDER THAN ME HAS IT ALL TOGETHER AND KNOWS EXACTLY WHAT THEY'RE DOING, ALL THE TIME.
LIKE ONE DAY, EVERYTHING FALLS INTO PLACE AND YOU DON'T HAVE ANY QUESTIONS ANYMORE.
AND SO DOES EVERYBODY ELSE.
BUT I HAVE SO MANY QUESTIONS.

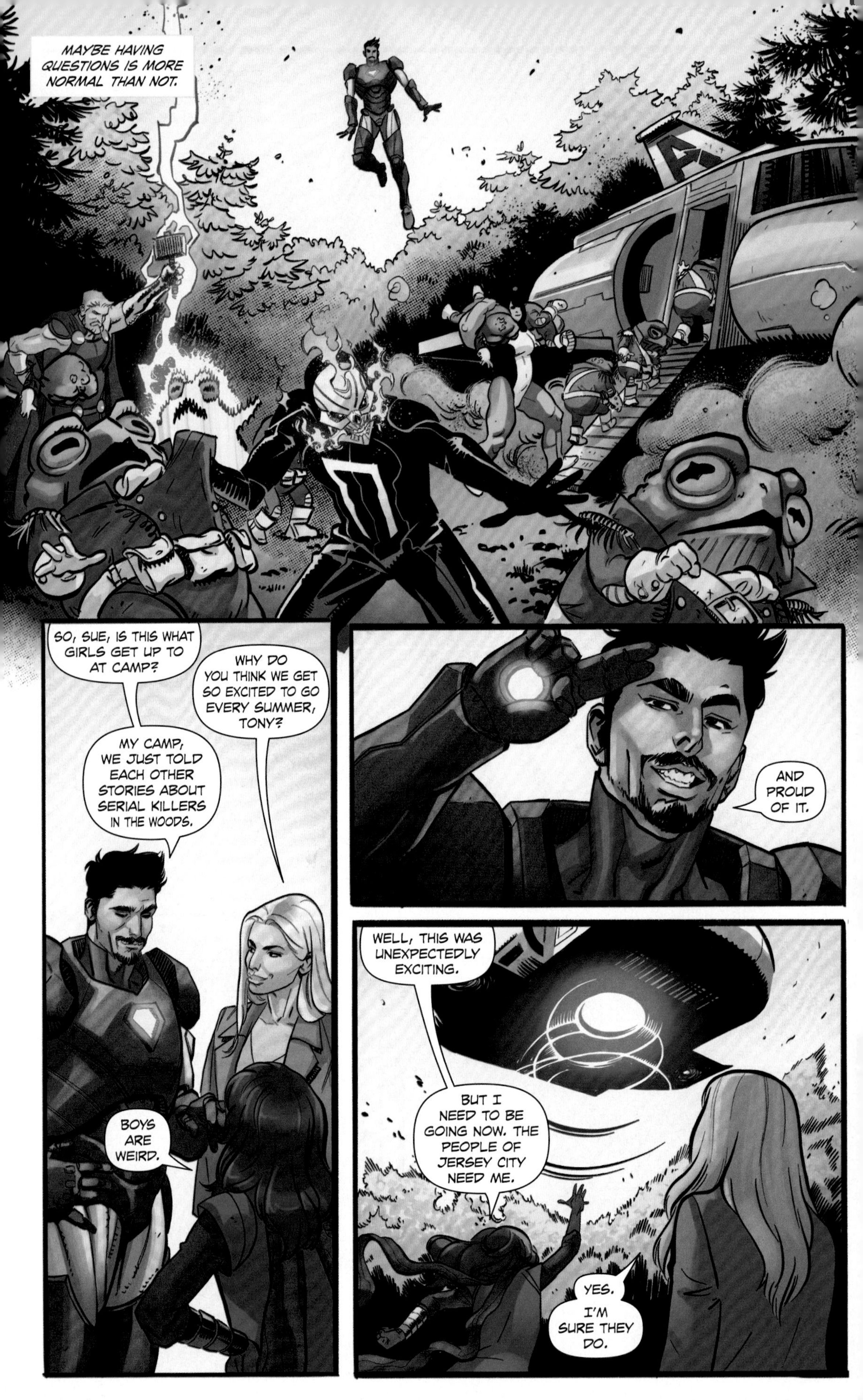
MAYBE HAVING QUESTIONS IS MORE NORMAL THAN NOT.
SO, SUE, IS THIS WHAT GIRLS GET UP TO AT CAMP?
MY CAMP, WE JUST TOLD EACH OTHER STORIES ABOUT SERIAL KILLERS IN THE WOODS.
WHY DO YOU THINK WE GET SO EXCITED TO GO EVERY SUMMER, TONY?
BOYS ARE WEIRD.
AND PROUD OF IT.
WELL, THIS WAS UNEXPECTEDLY EXCITING.
BUT I NEED TO BE GOING NOW. THE PEOPLE OF JERSEY CITY NEED ME.
YES. I'M SURE THEY DO.

IS EVERYTHING WELL?

YUP. JUST SUPERVISING THE CLEANUP.

WE ARE CAPABLE OF SO MUCH MORE THAN WE THINK WE ARE. ALL WE HAVE TO DO IS REACH FOR IT. ALL WE HAVE TO BE IS FEARLESS.

GO CAPTAIN MARVEL!

YEAH!

WOO!

THANK YOU, COLONEL DANVERS, FOR THAT INSPIRING SPEECH.

GLORIANA LEADERSHIP CAMP FOR FEMALE EMPOWER

WE WILL BE MOVING OUR TWO REMAINING KEYNOTES TO TOMORROW TO GIVE US TIME TO CLEAN UP THE DAMAGE FROM TODAY'S "EXCITEMENT."

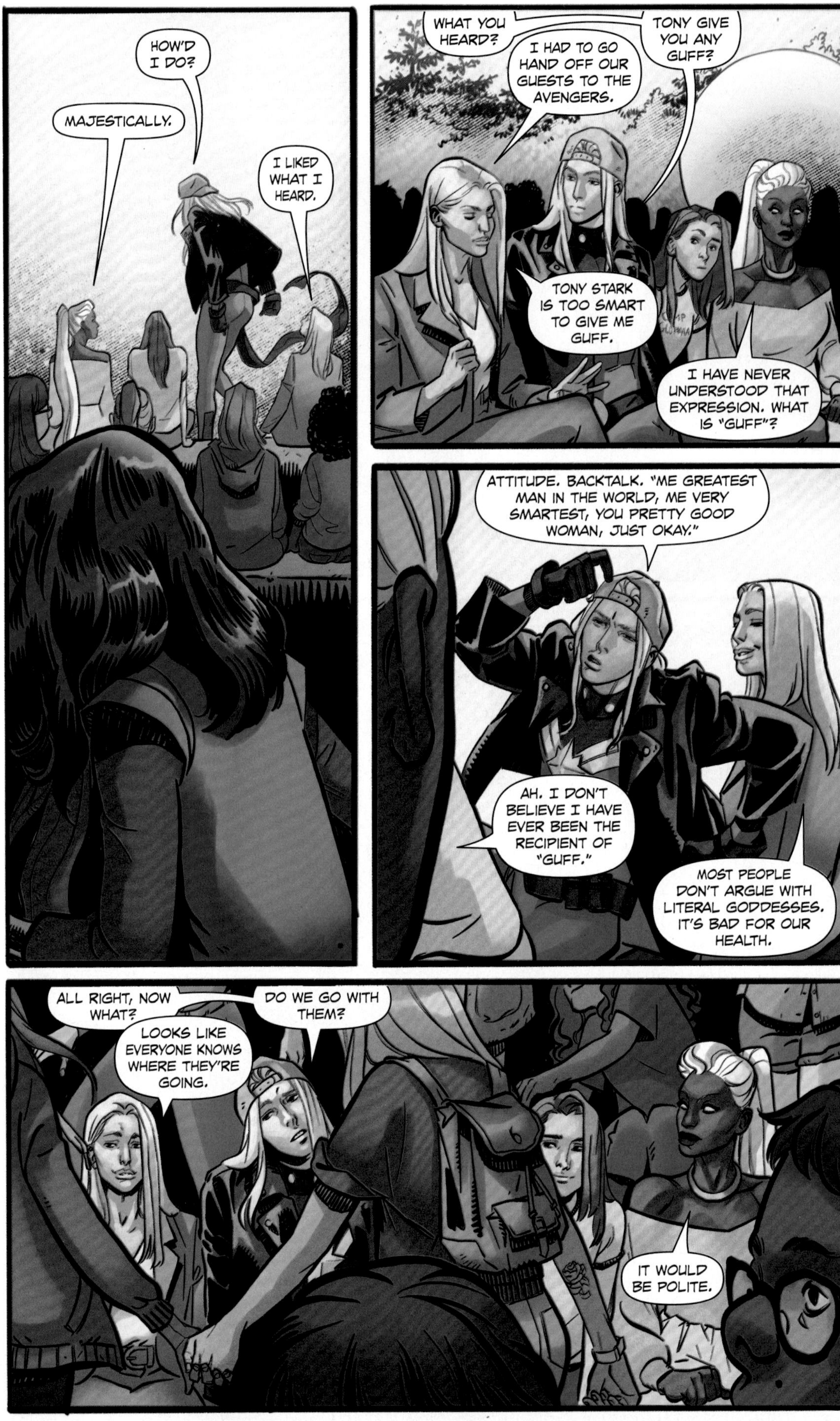
HOW'D I DO?
MAJESTICALLY.
I LIKED WHAT I HEARD.
WHAT YOU HEARD?
I HAD TO GO HAND OFF OUR GUESTS TO THE AVENGERS.
TONY GIVE YOU ANY GUFF?
TONY STARK IS TOO SMART TO GIVE ME GUFF.
I HAVE NEVER UNDERSTOOD THAT EXPRESSION. WHAT IS "GUFF"?
ATTITUDE. BACKTALK. "ME GREATEST MAN IN THE WORLD, ME VERY SMARTEST, YOU PRETTY GOOD WOMAN, JUST OKAY."
AH. I DON'T BELIEVE I HAVE EVER BEEN THE RECIPIENT OF "GUFF."
MOST PEOPLE DON'T ARGUE WITH LITERAL GODDESSES. IT'S BAD FOR OUR HEALTH.
ALL RIGHT, NOW WHAT?
DO WE GO WITH THEM?
LOOKS LIKE EVERYONE KNOWS WHERE THEY'RE GOING.
IT WOULD BE POLITE.

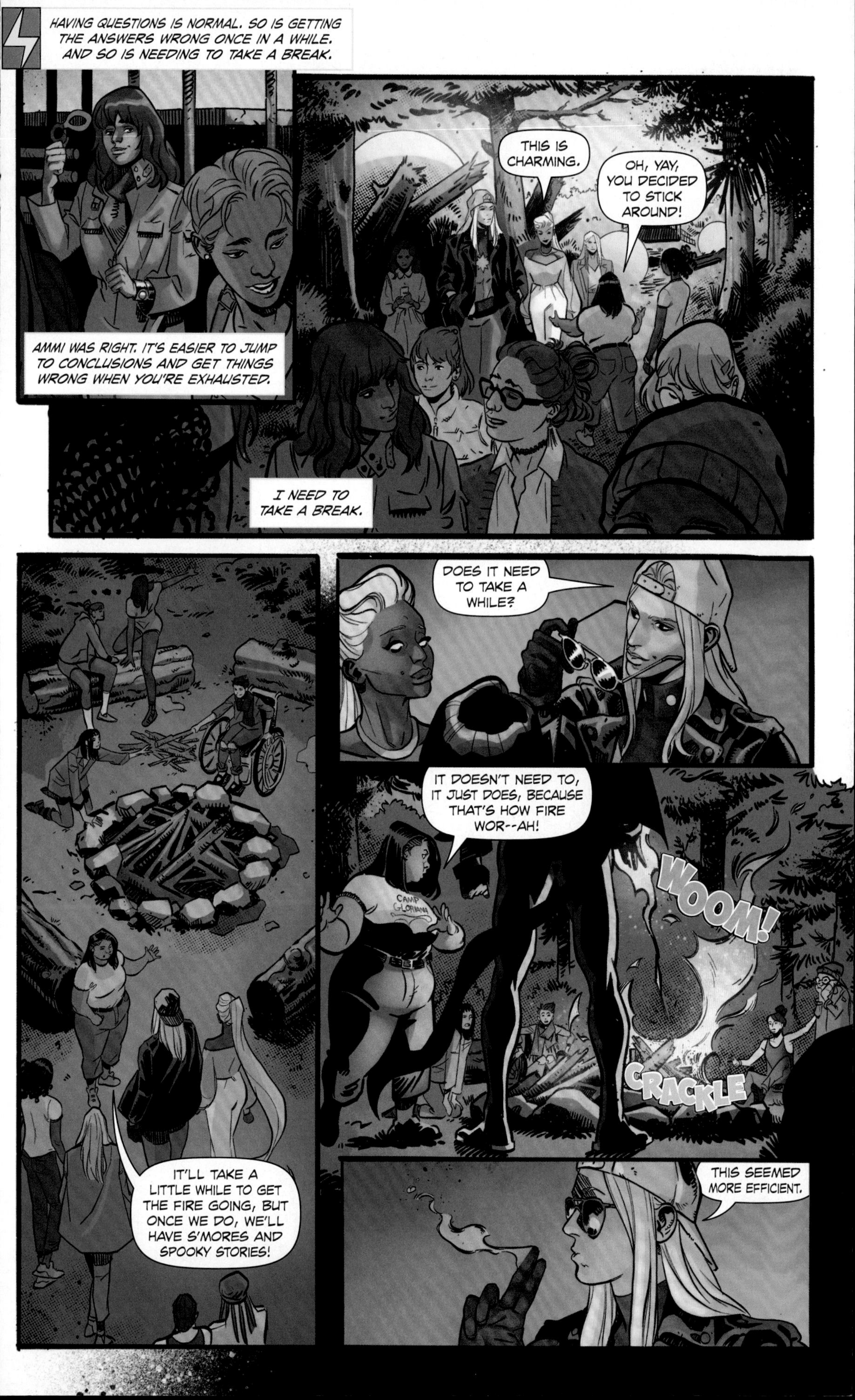
HAVING QUESTIONS IS NORMAL. SO IS GETTING THE ANSWERS WRONG ONCE IN A WHILE. AND SO IS NEEDING TO TAKE A BREAK.
AMMI WAS RIGHT. IT'S EASIER TO JUMP TO CONCLUSIONS AND GET THINGS WRONG WHEN YOU'RE EXHAUSTED.
THIS IS CHARMING.
OH, YAY, YOU DECIDED TO STICK AROUND!
I NEED TO TAKE A BREAK.
IT'LL TAKE A LITTLE WHILE TO GET THE FIRE GOING, BUT ONCE WE DO, WE'LL HAVE S'MORES AND SPOOKY STORIES!
DOES IT NEED TO TAKE A WHILE?
IT DOESN'T NEED TO, IT JUST DOES, BECAUSE THAT'S HOW FIRE WOR--AH!
CAMP GLORIANA
WOOM!
CRACKLE
THIS SEEMED MORE EFFICIENT.

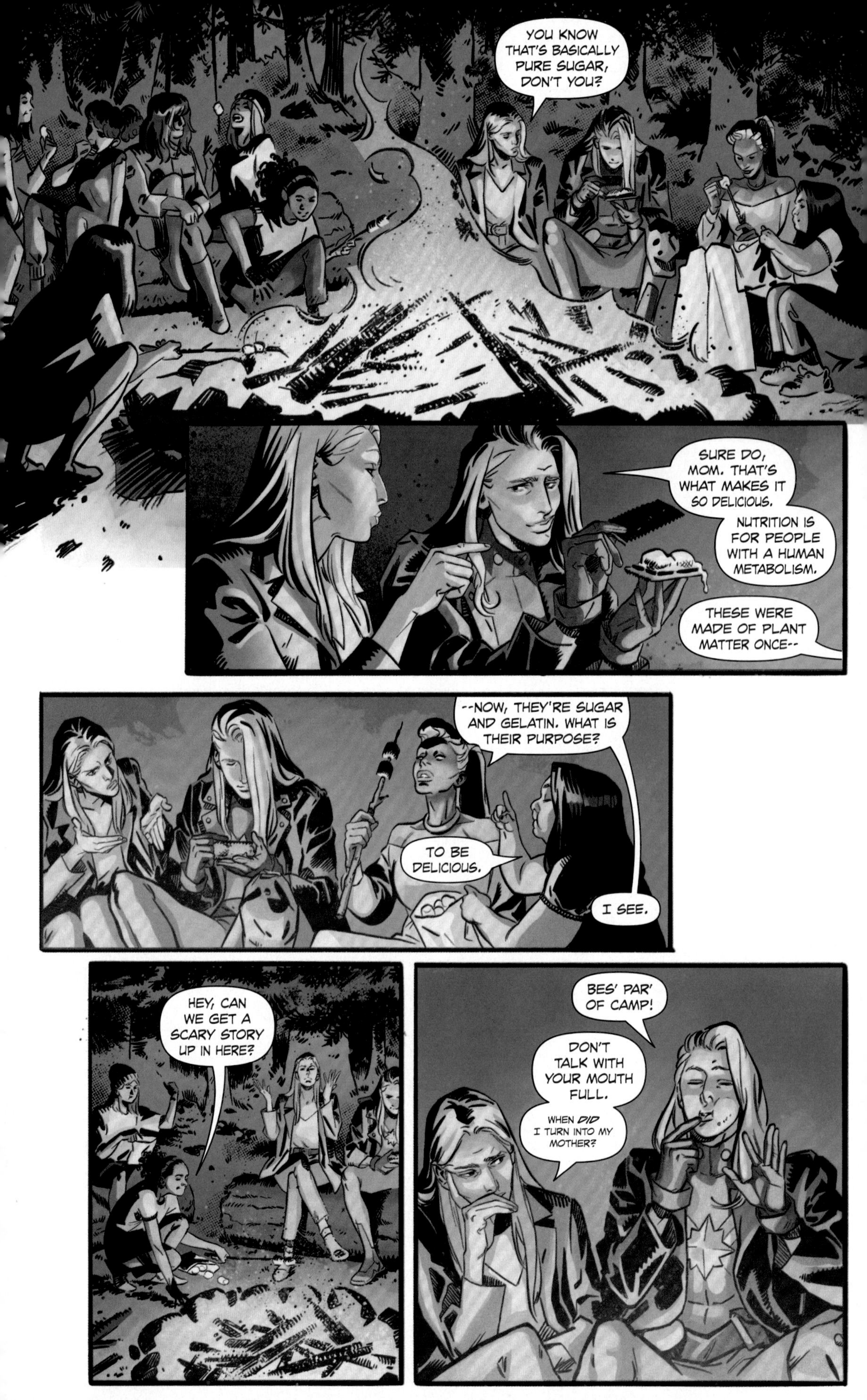
YOU KNOW THAT'S BASICALLY PURE SUGAR, DON'T YOU?
SURE DO, MOM. THAT'S WHAT MAKES IT SO DELICIOUS.
NUTRITION IS FOR PEOPLE WITH A HUMAN METABOLISM.
THESE WERE MADE OF PLANT MATTER ONCE--
--NOW, THEY'RE SUGAR AND GELATIN. WHAT IS THEIR PURPOSE?
TO BE DELICIOUS.
I SEE.
HEY, CAN WE GET A SCARY STORY UP IN HERE?
BES' PAR' OF CAMP!
DON'T TALK WITH YOUR MOUTH FULL.
WHEN DID I TURN INTO MY MOTHER?

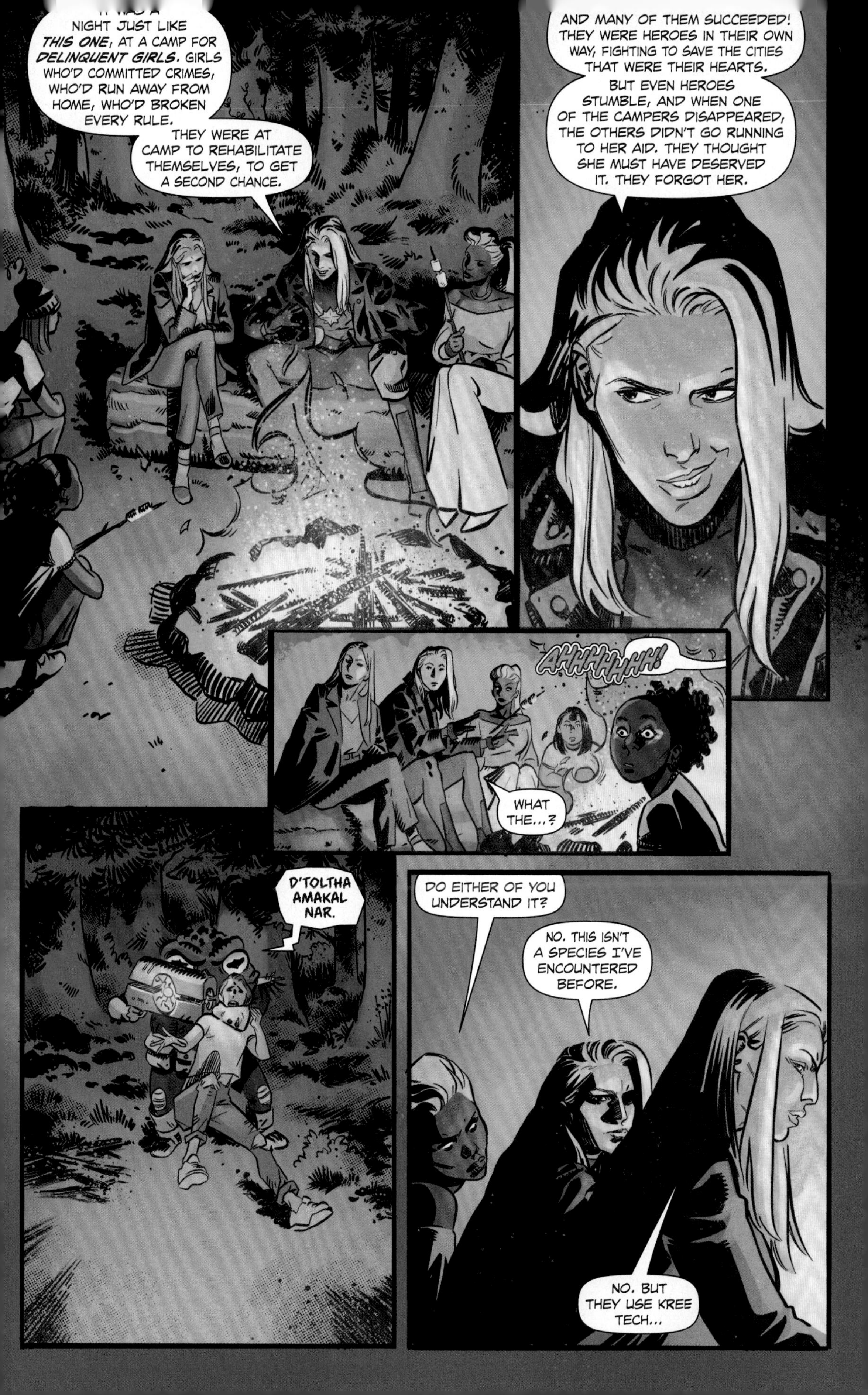
NIGHT JUST LIKE THIS ONE, AT A CAMP FOR DELINQUENT GIRLS. GIRLS WHO'D COMMITTED CRIMES, WHO'D RUN AWAY FROM HOME, WHO'D BROKEN EVERY RULE.
THEY WERE AT CAMP TO REHABILITATE THEMSELVES, TO GET A SECOND CHANCE.
AND MANY OF THEM SUCCEEDED! THEY WERE HEROES IN THEIR OWN WAY, FIGHTING TO SAVE THE CITIES THAT WERE THEIR HEARTS.
BUT EVEN HEROES STUMBLE, AND WHEN ONE OF THE CAMPERS DISAPPEARED, THE OTHERS DIDN'T GO RUNNING TO HER AID. THEY THOUGHT SHE MUST HAVE DESERVED IT. THEY FORGOT HER.
AHHHHHHH!
WHAT THE...?
D'TOLTHA AMAKAL NAR.
DO EITHER OF YOU UNDERSTAND IT?
NO. THIS ISN'T A SPECIES I'VE ENCOUNTERED BEFORE.
NO. BUT THEY USE KREE TECH...

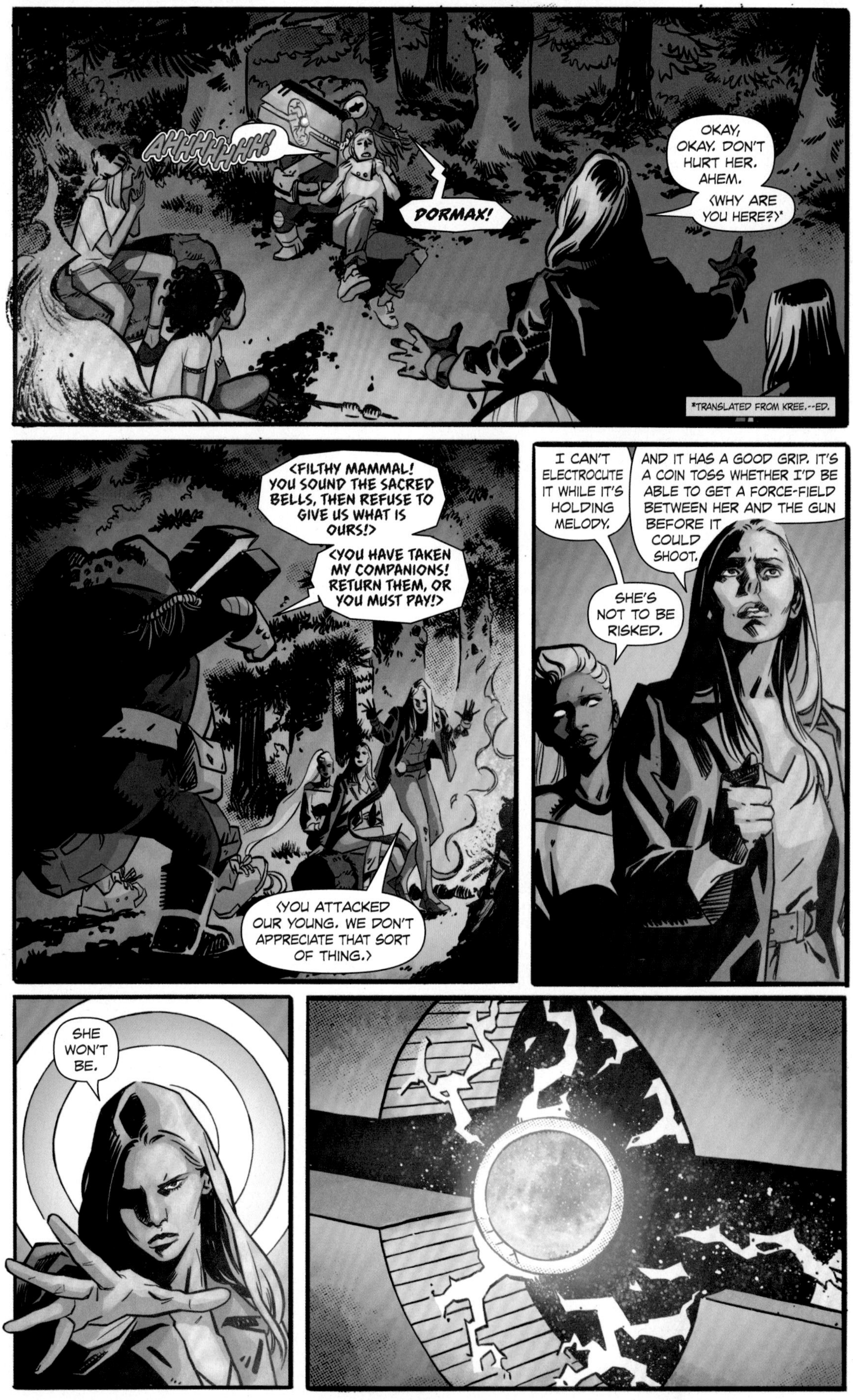
AHHHHHHH!
DORMAX!
OKAY, OKAY. DON'T HURT HER. AHEM.
‹WHY ARE YOU HERE?›*
*TRANSLATED FROM KREE.--ED.
‹FILTHY MAMMAL! YOU SOUND THE SACRED BELLS, THEN REFUSE TO GIVE US WHAT IS OURS!›
‹YOU HAVE TAKEN MY COMPANIONS! RETURN THEM, OR YOU MUST PAY!›
‹YOU ATTACKED OUR YOUNG. WE DON'T APPRECIATE THAT SORT OF THING.›
I CAN'T ELECTROCUTE IT WHILE IT'S HOLDING MELODY.
AND IT HAS A GOOD GRIP. IT'S A COIN TOSS WHETHER I'D BE ABLE TO GET A FORCE-FIELD BETWEEN HER AND THE GUN BEFORE IT COULD SHOOT.
SHE'S NOT TO BE RISKED.
SHE WON'T BE.

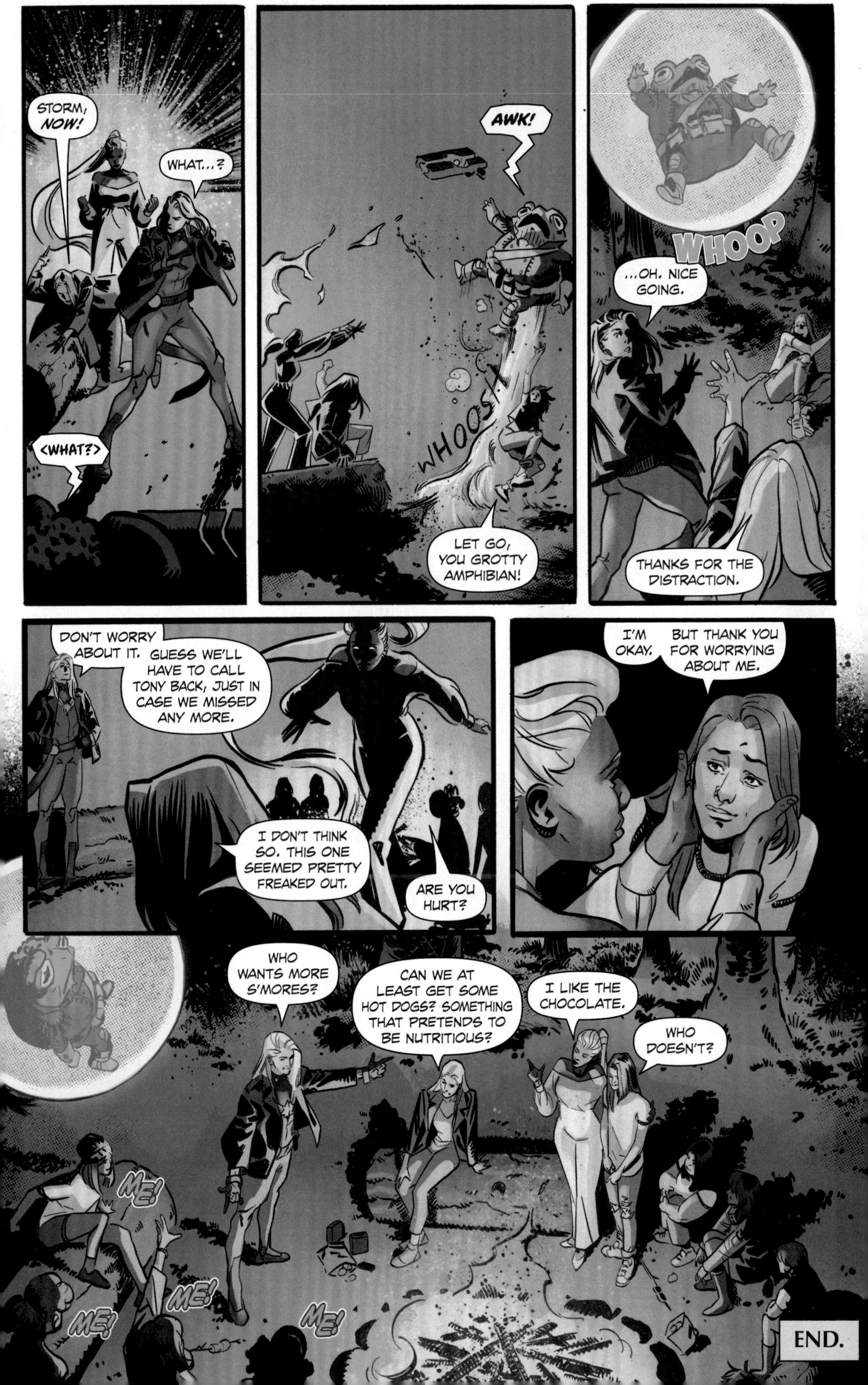
STORM, NOW!
WHAT...?
<WHAT?>
AWK!
WHOOSH
LET GO, YOU GROTTY AMPHIBIAN!
WHOOP
...OH. NICE GOING.
THANKS FOR THE DISTRACTION.
DON'T WORRY ABOUT IT.
GUESS WE'LL HAVE TO CALL TONY BACK, JUST IN CASE WE MISSED ANY MORE.
I DON'T THINK SO. THIS ONE SEEMED PRETTY FREAKED OUT.
ARE YOU HURT?
I'M OKAY.
BUT THANK YOU FOR WORRYING ABOUT ME.
WHO WANTS MORE S'MORES?
CAN WE AT LEAST GET SOME HOT DOGS? SOMETHING THAT PRETENDS TO BE NUTRITIOUS?
I LIKE THE CHOCOLATE.
WHO DOESN'T?
ME!
ME!
ME!
ME!
END.

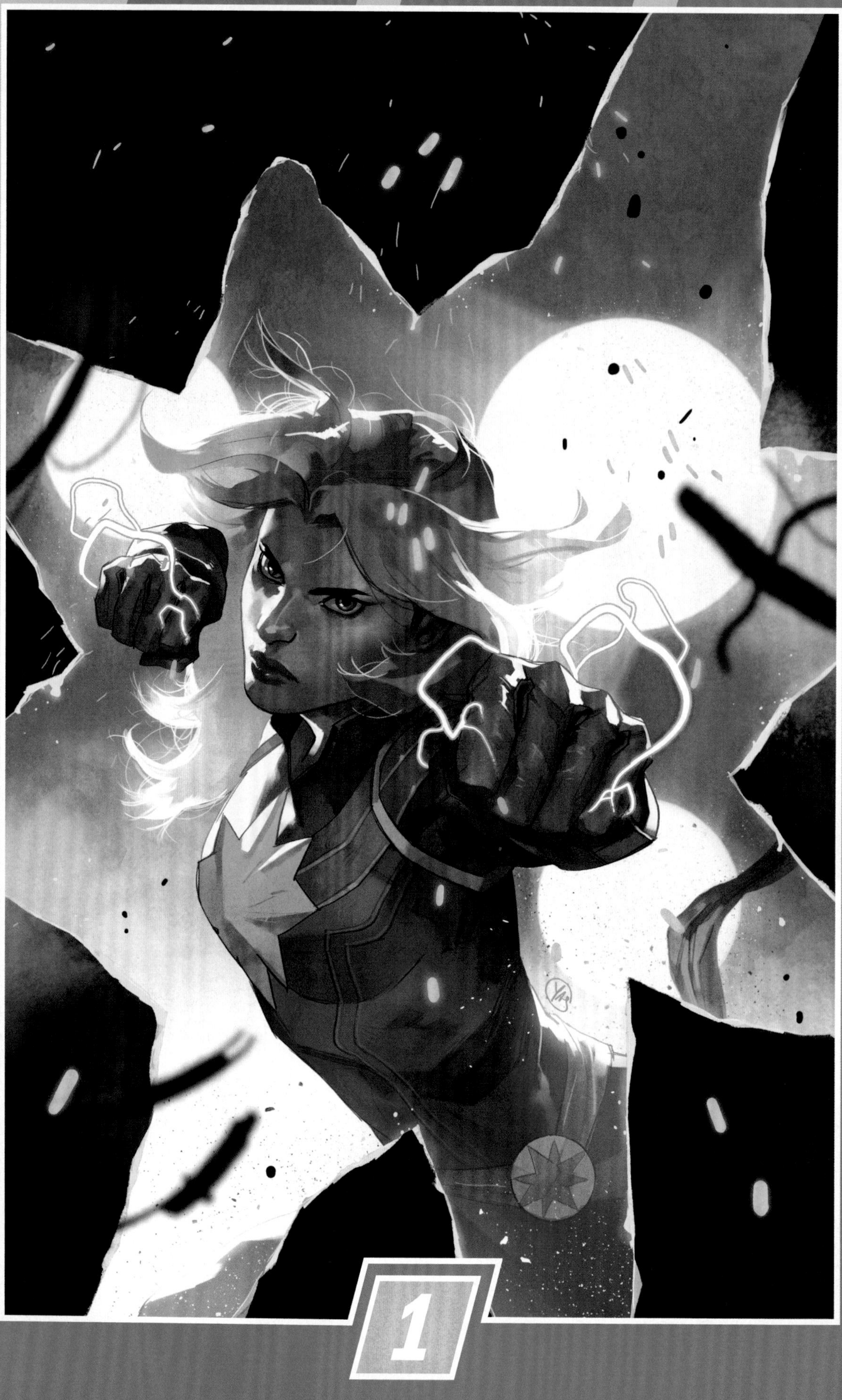
1

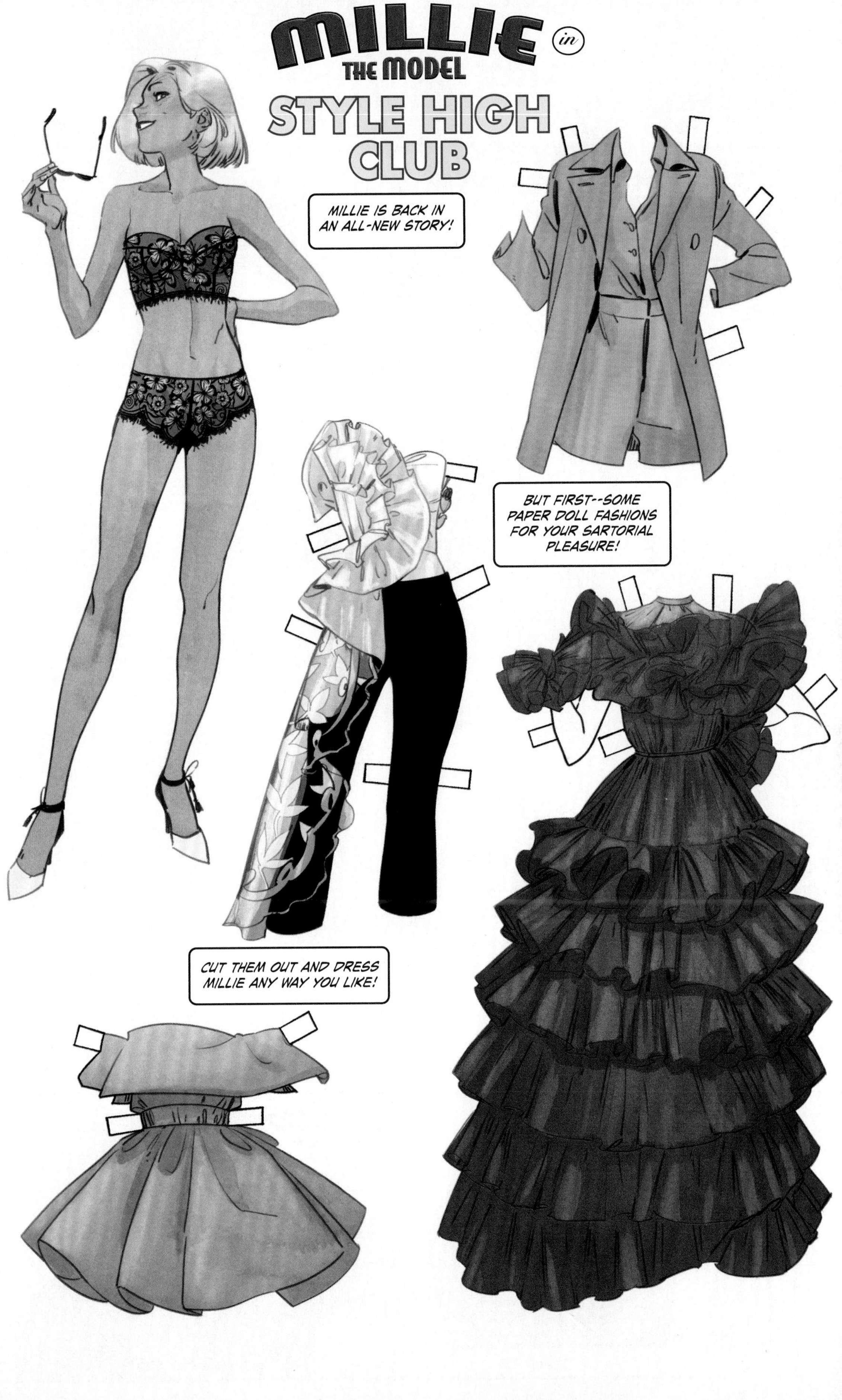
MILLIE in THE MODEL
STYLE HIGH CLUB
MILLIE IS BACK IN AN ALL-NEW STORY!
BUT FIRST--SOME PAPER DOLL FASHIONS FOR YOUR SARTORIAL PLEASURE!
CUT THEM OUT AND DRESS MILLIE ANY WAY YOU LIKE!

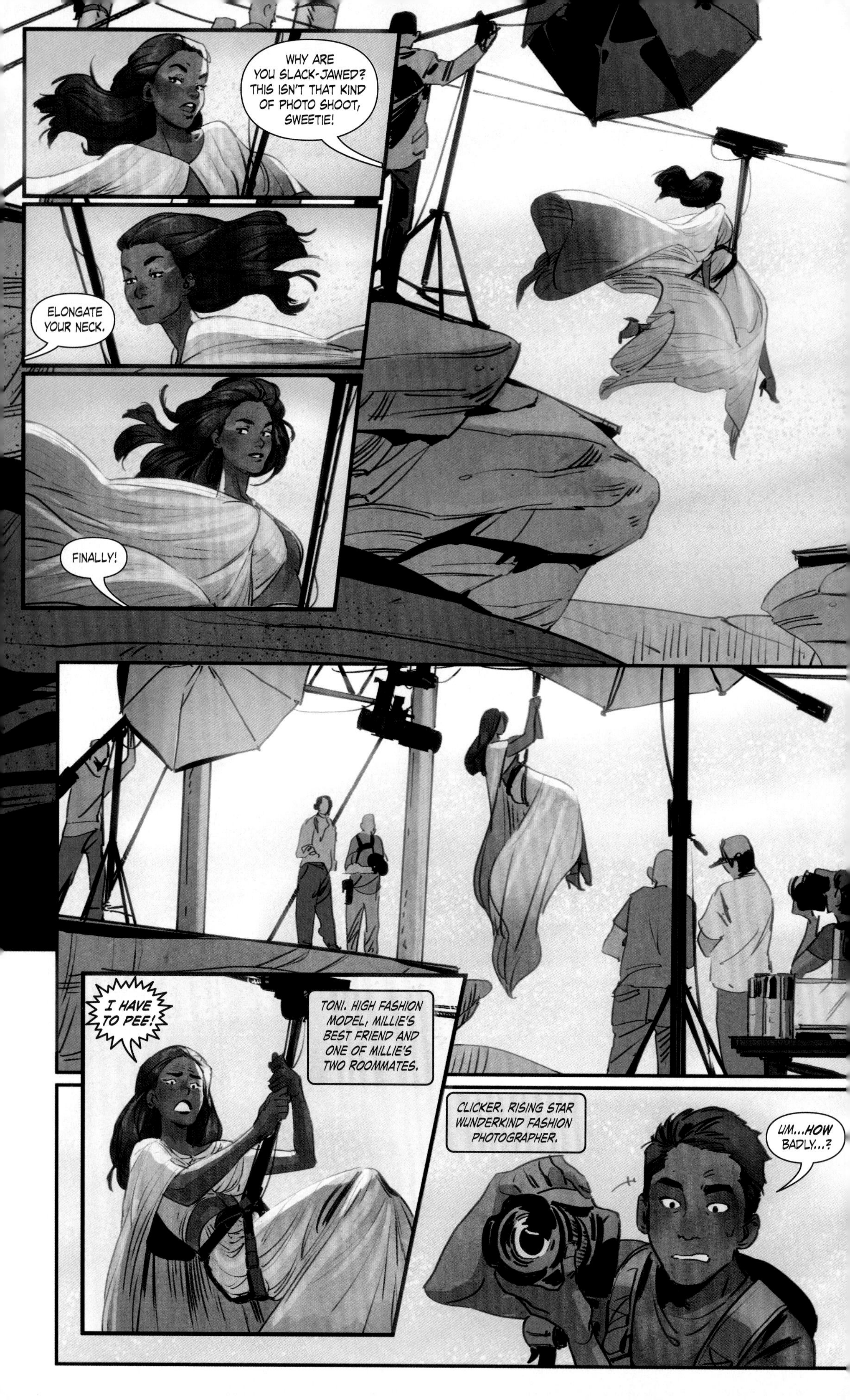
WHY ARE YOU SLACK-JAWED? THIS ISN'T THAT KIND OF PHOTO SHOOT, SWEETIE!
ELONGATE YOUR NECK.
FINALLY!
I HAVE TO PEE!
TONI. HIGH FASHION MODEL, MILLIE'S BEST FRIEND AND ONE OF MILLIE'S TWO ROOMMATES.
CLICKER. RISING STAR WUNDERKIND FASHION PHOTOGRAPHER.
UM...HOW BADLY...?

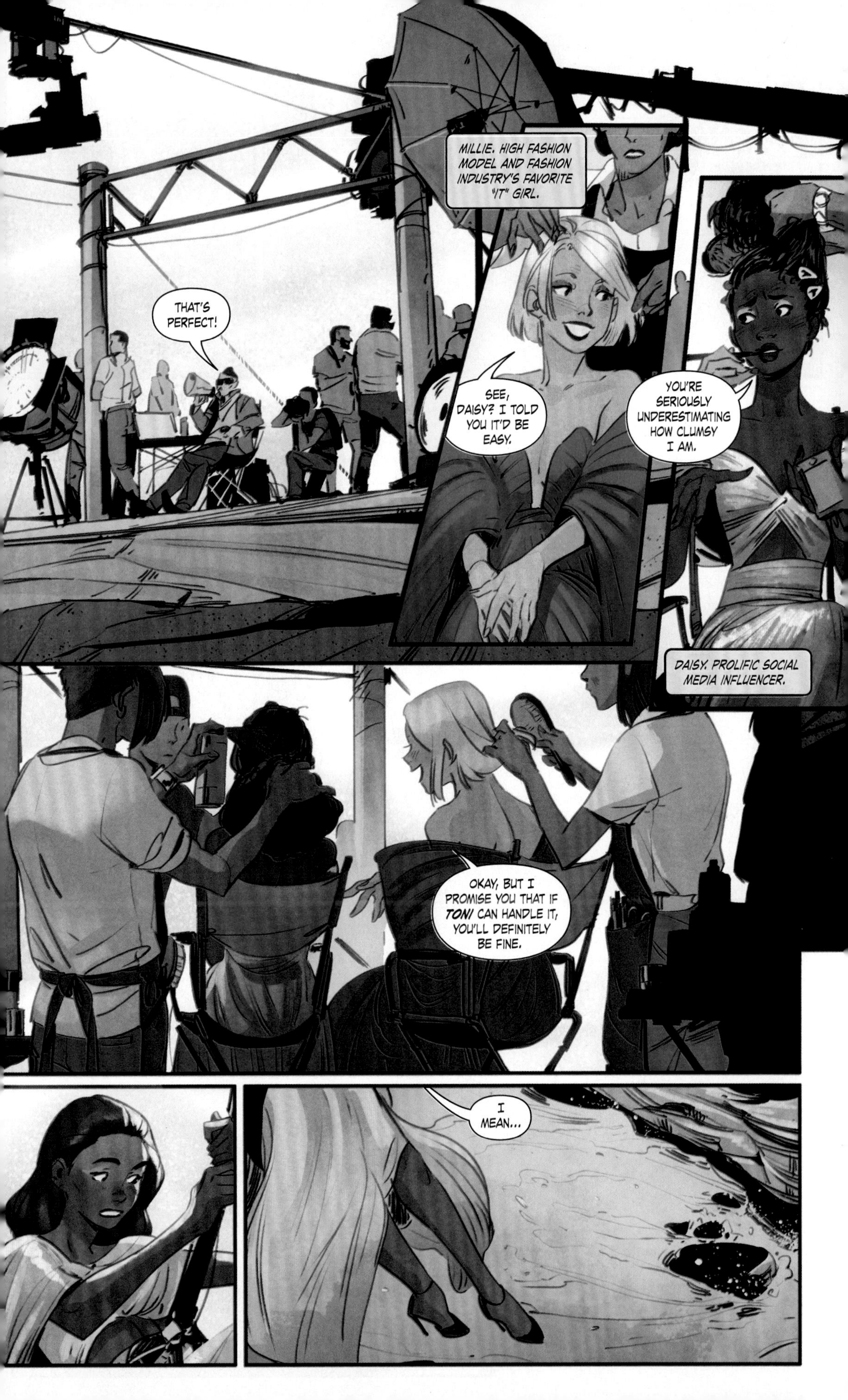
MILLIE. HIGH FASHION MODEL AND FASHION INDUSTRY'S FAVORITE "IT" GIRL.
THAT'S PERFECT!
SEE, DAISY? I TOLD YOU IT'D BE EASY.
YOU'RE SERIOUSLY UNDERESTIMATING HOW CLUMSY I AM.
DAISY. PROLIFIC SOCIAL MEDIA INFLUENCER.
OKAY, BUT I PROMISE YOU THAT IF TONI CAN HANDLE IT, YOU'LL DEFINITELY BE FINE.
I MEAN...

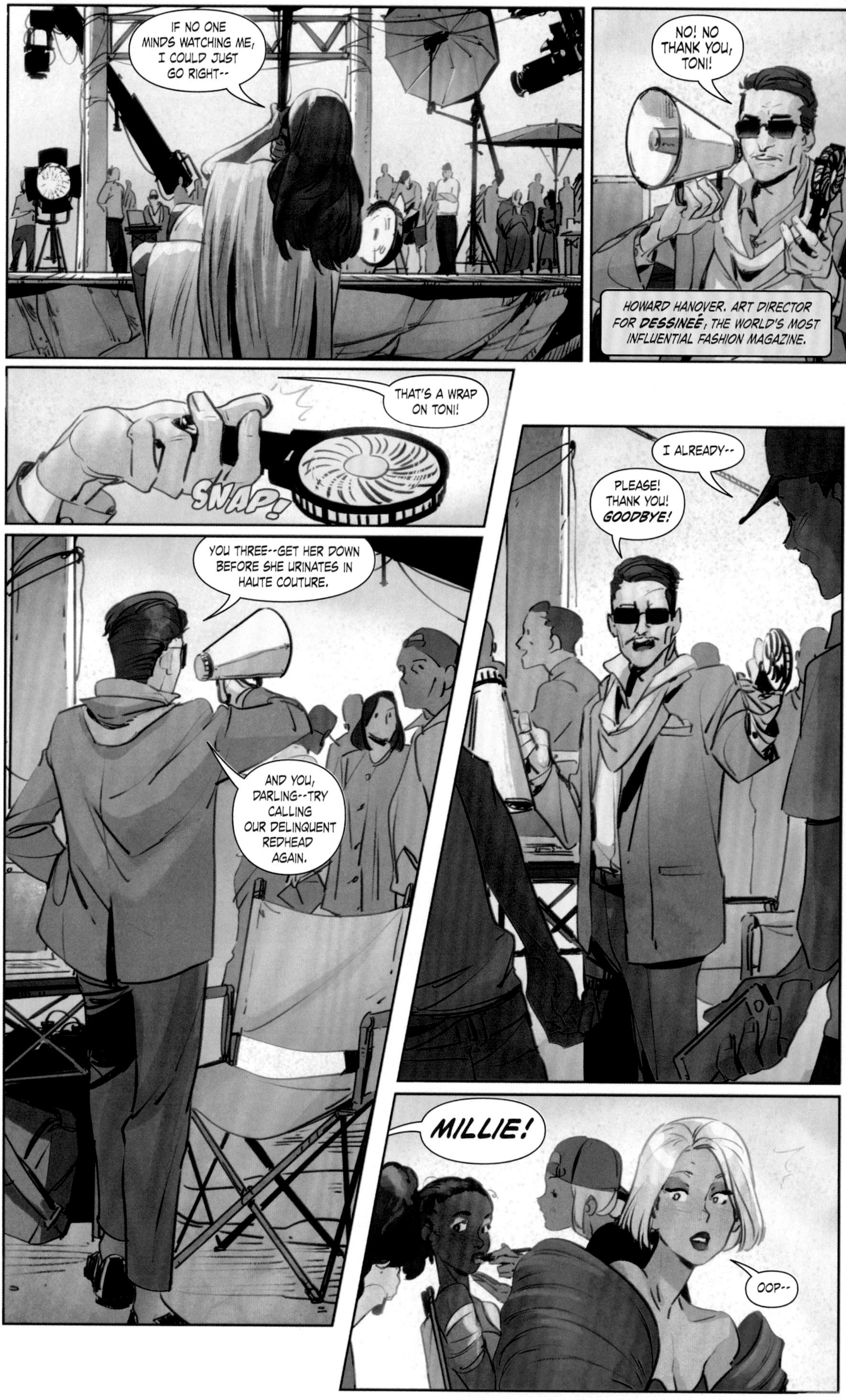
IF NO ONE MINDS WATCHING ME, I COULD JUST GO RIGHT--
NO! NO THANK YOU, TONI!
HOWARD HANOVER. ART DIRECTOR FOR DESSINEÉ; THE WORLD'S MOST INFLUENTIAL FASHION MAGAZINE.
THAT'S A WRAP ON TONI!
SNAP!
I ALREADY--
PLEASE! THANK YOU! GOODBYE!
YOU THREE--GET HER DOWN BEFORE SHE URINATES IN HAUTE COUTURE.
AND YOU, DARLING--TRY CALLING OUR DELINQUENT REDHEAD AGAIN.
MILLIE!
OOP--

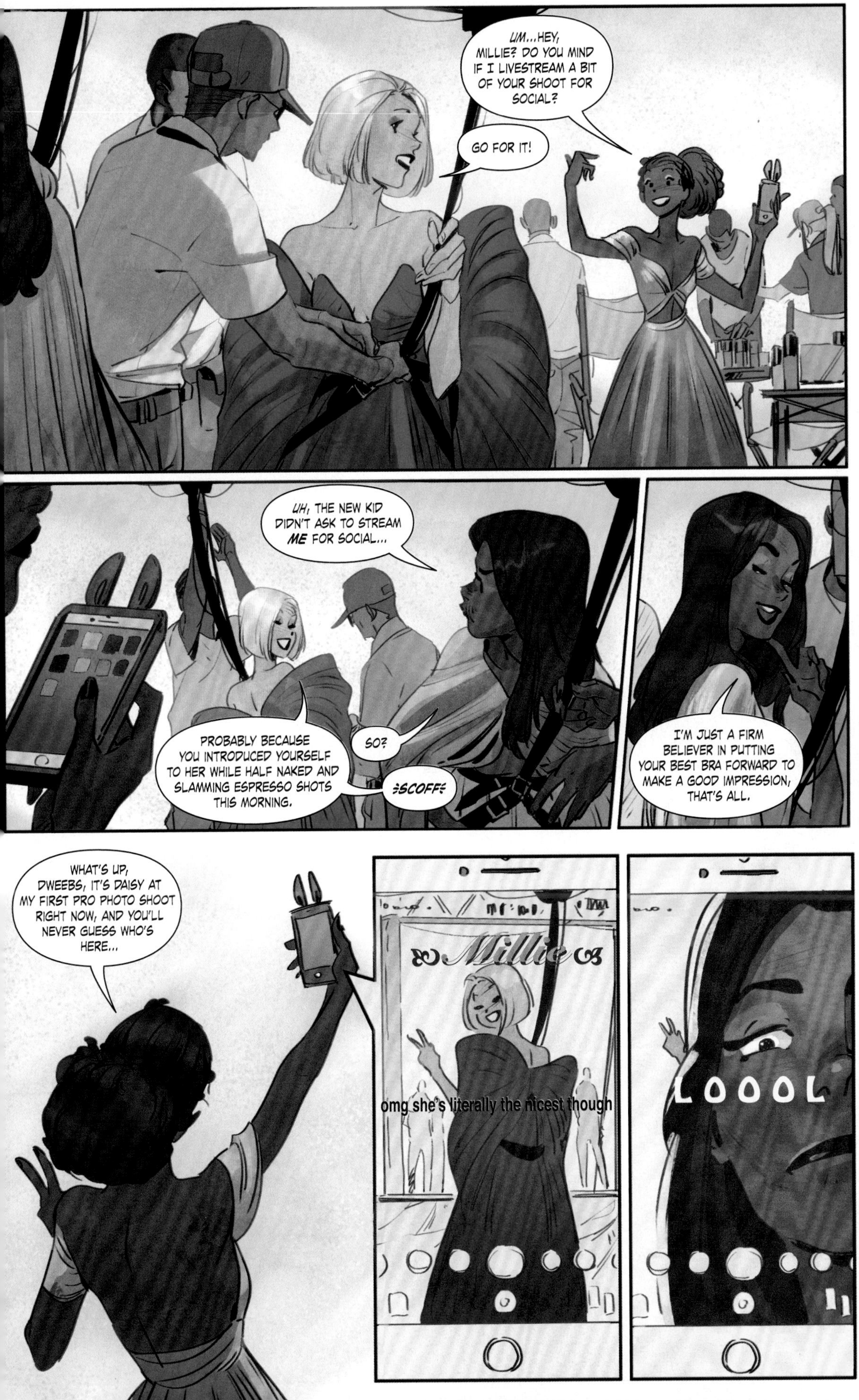
UM...HEY, MILLIE? DO YOU MIND IF I LIVESTREAM A BIT OF YOUR SHOOT FOR SOCIAL?
GO FOR IT!
UH, THE NEW KID DIDN'T ASK TO STREAM ME FOR SOCIAL...
PROBABLY BECAUSE YOU INTRODUCED YOURSELF TO HER WHILE HALF NAKED AND SLAMMING ESPRESSO SHOTS THIS MORNING.
SO?
SCOFF
I'M JUST A FIRM BELIEVER IN PUTTING YOUR BEST BRA FORWARD TO MAKE A GOOD IMPRESSION, THAT'S ALL.
WHAT'S UP, DWEEBS, IT'S DAISY AT MY FIRST PRO PHOTO SHOOT RIGHT NOW, AND YOU'LL NEVER GUESS WHO'S HERE...
Millie
omg she's literally the nicest though
LOOOL

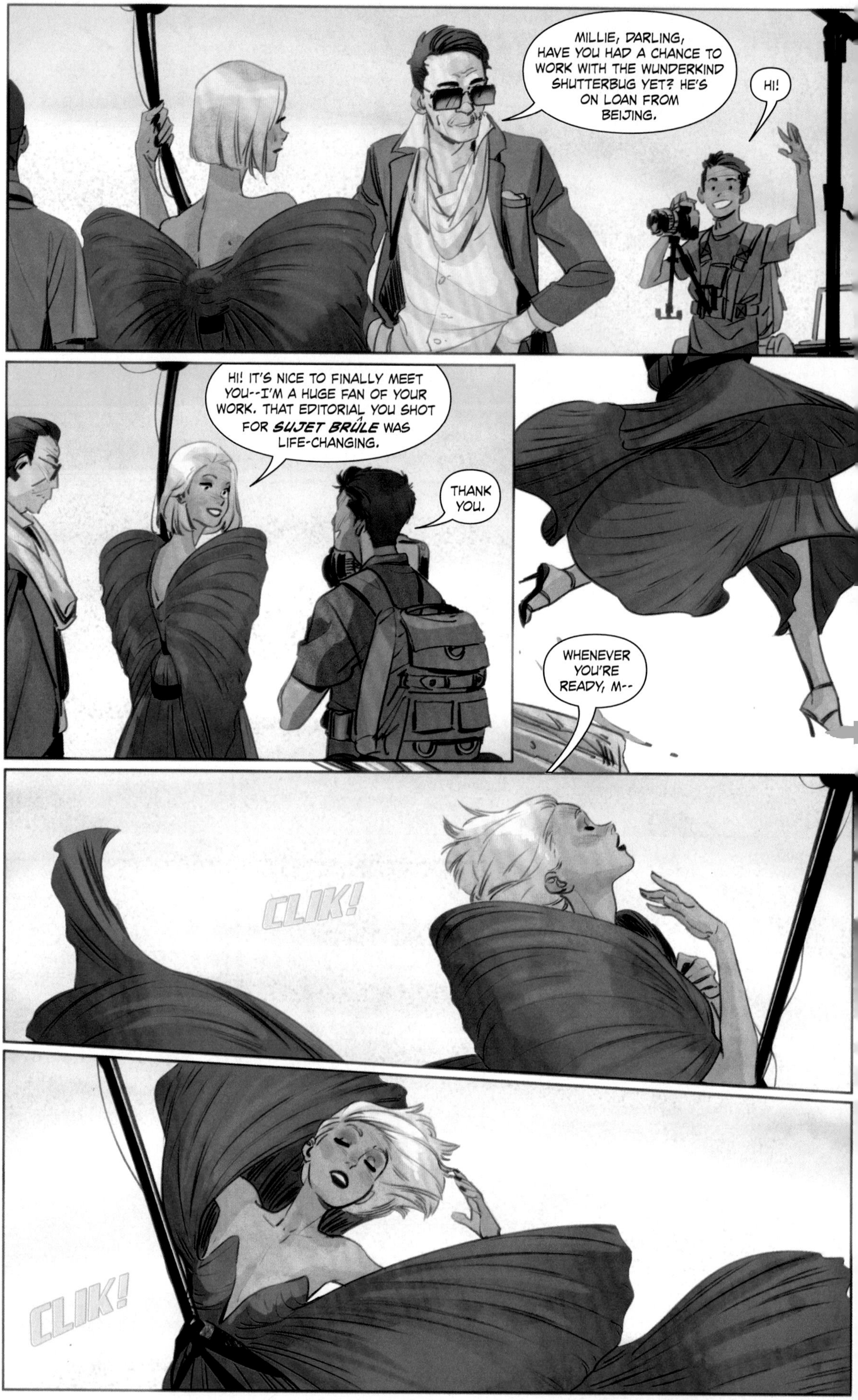
MILLIE, DARLING, HAVE YOU HAD A CHANCE TO WORK WITH THE WUNDERKIND SHUTTERBUG YET? HE'S ON LOAN FROM BEIJING.
HI!
HI! IT'S NICE TO FINALLY MEET YOU--I'M A HUGE FAN OF YOUR WORK. THAT EDITORIAL YOU SHOT FOR SUJET BRÛLE WAS LIFE-CHANGING.
THANK YOU.
WHENEVER YOU'RE READY, M--
CLIK!
CLIK!

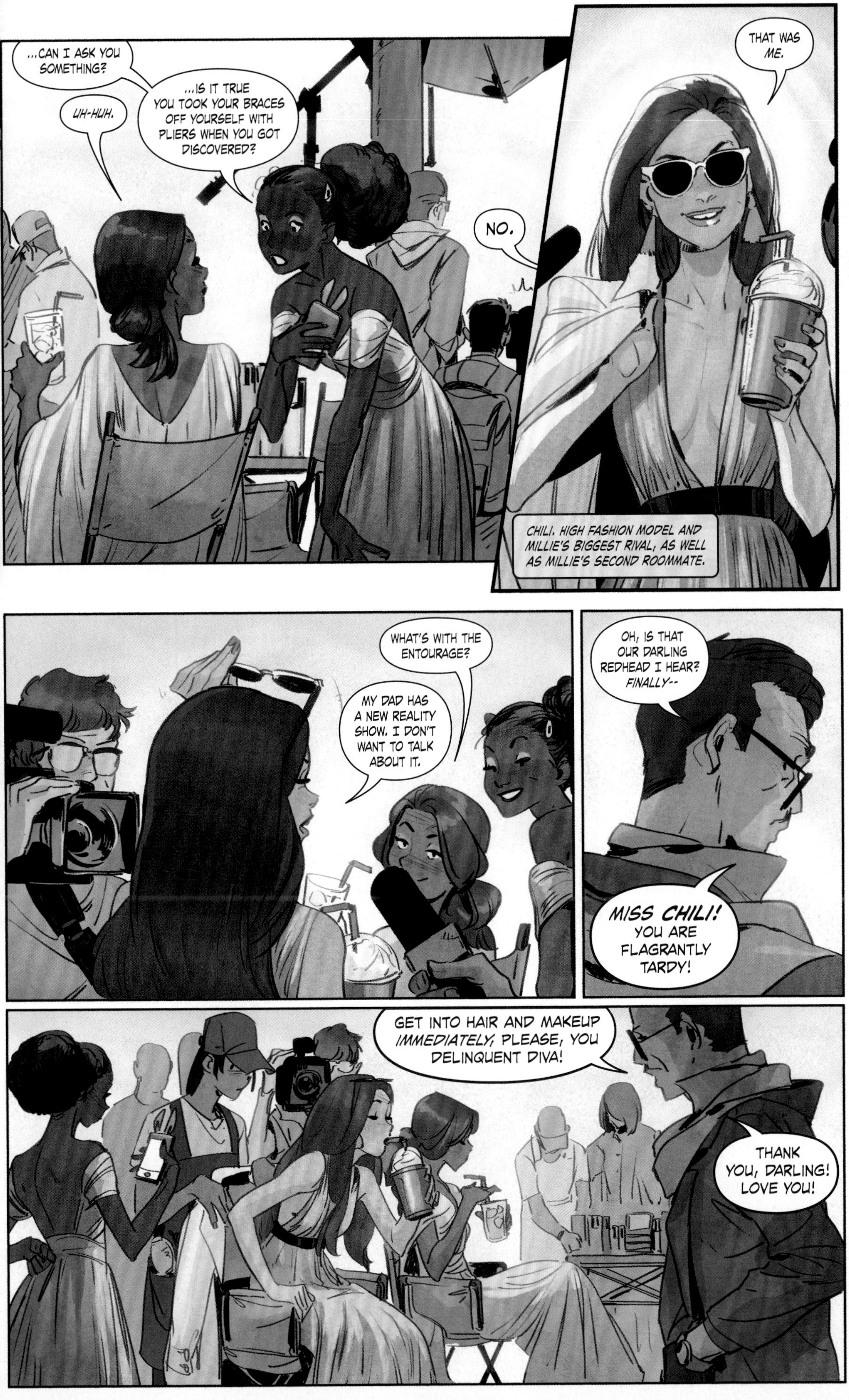
...CAN I ASK YOU SOMETHING?
UH-HUH.
...IS IT TRUE YOU TOOK YOUR BRACES OFF YOURSELF WITH PLIERS WHEN YOU GOT DISCOVERED?
NO.
THAT WAS *ME.*
CHILI. HIGH FASHION MODEL AND MILLIE'S BIGGEST RIVAL, AS WELL AS MILLIE'S SECOND ROOMMATE.
WHAT'S WITH THE ENTOURAGE?
MY DAD HAS A NEW REALITY SHOW. I DON'T WANT TO TALK ABOUT IT.
OH, IS THAT OUR DARLING REDHEAD I HEAR? *FINALLY--*
MISS CHILI! YOU ARE FLAGRANTLY TARDY!
GET INTO HAIR AND MAKEUP *IMMEDIATELY,* PLEASE, YOU DELINQUENT DIVA!
THANK YOU, DARLING! LOVE YOU!

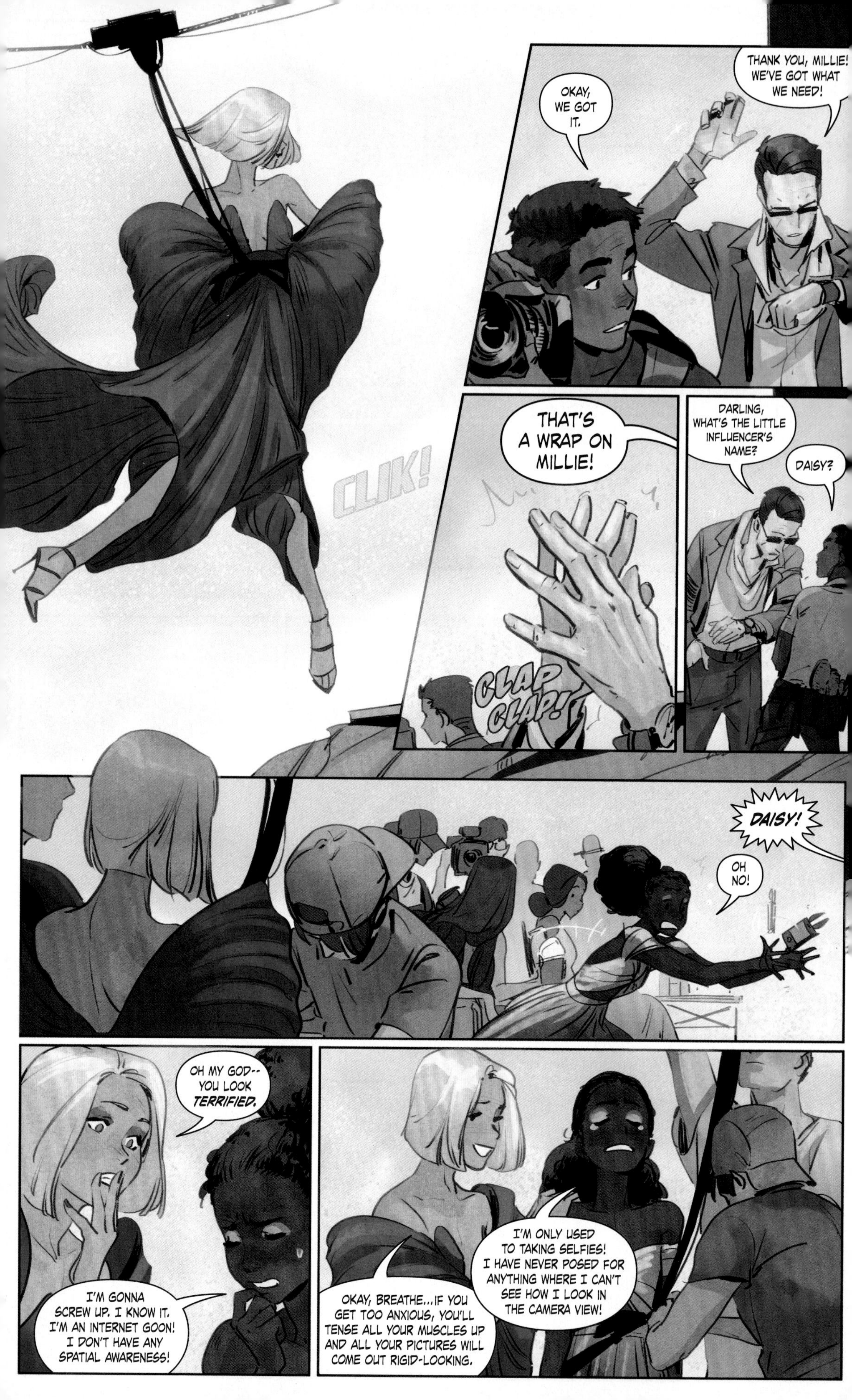
OKAY, WE GOT IT.
THANK YOU, MILLIE! WE'VE GOT WHAT WE NEED!
CLIK!
THAT'S A WRAP ON MILLIE!
CLAP CLAP!
DARLING, WHAT'S THE LITTLE INFLUENCER'S NAME?
DAISY?
DAISY!
OH NO!
OH MY GOD-- YOU LOOK TERRIFIED.
I'M GONNA SCREW UP. I KNOW IT. I'M AN INTERNET GOON! I DON'T HAVE ANY SPATIAL AWARENESS!
I'M ONLY USED TO TAKING SELFIES! I HAVE NEVER POSED FOR ANYTHING WHERE I CAN'T SEE HOW I LOOK IN THE CAMERA VIEW!
OKAY, BREATHE...IF YOU GET TOO ANXIOUS, YOU'LL TENSE ALL YOUR MUSCLES UP AND ALL YOUR PICTURES WILL COME OUT RIGID-LOOKING.

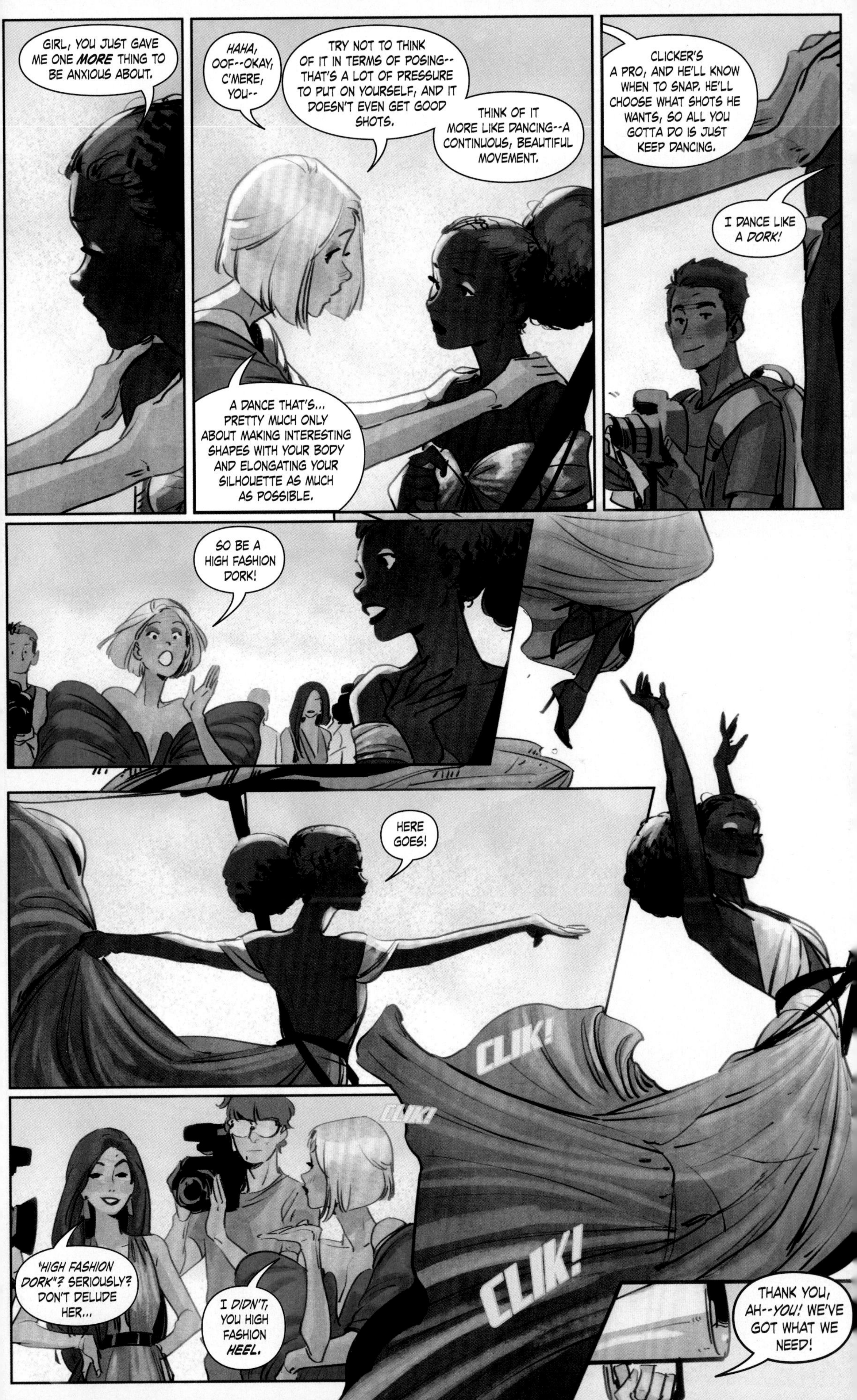
GIRL, YOU JUST GAVE ME ONE *MORE* THING TO BE ANXIOUS ABOUT.
HAHA, OOF--OKAY, C'MERE, YOU--
TRY NOT TO THINK OF IT IN TERMS OF POSING--THAT'S A LOT OF PRESSURE TO PUT ON YOURSELF, AND IT DOESN'T EVEN GET GOOD SHOTS.
THINK OF IT MORE LIKE DANCING--A CONTINUOUS, BEAUTIFUL MOVEMENT.
A DANCE THAT'S... PRETTY MUCH ONLY ABOUT MAKING INTERESTING SHAPES WITH YOUR BODY AND ELONGATING YOUR SILHOUETTE AS MUCH AS POSSIBLE.
CLICKER'S A PRO, AND HE'LL KNOW WHEN TO SNAP. HE'LL CHOOSE WHAT SHOTS HE WANTS, SO ALL YOU GOTTA DO IS JUST KEEP DANCING.
I DANCE LIKE A *DORK!*
SO BE A HIGH FASHION DORK!
HERE GOES!
CLIK!
CLIK!
CLIK!
"HIGH FASHION DORK"? SERIOUSLY? DON'T DELUDE HER...
I DIDN'T, YOU HIGH FASHION ***HEEL.***
THANK YOU, AH--*YOU!* WE'VE GOT WHAT WE NEED!

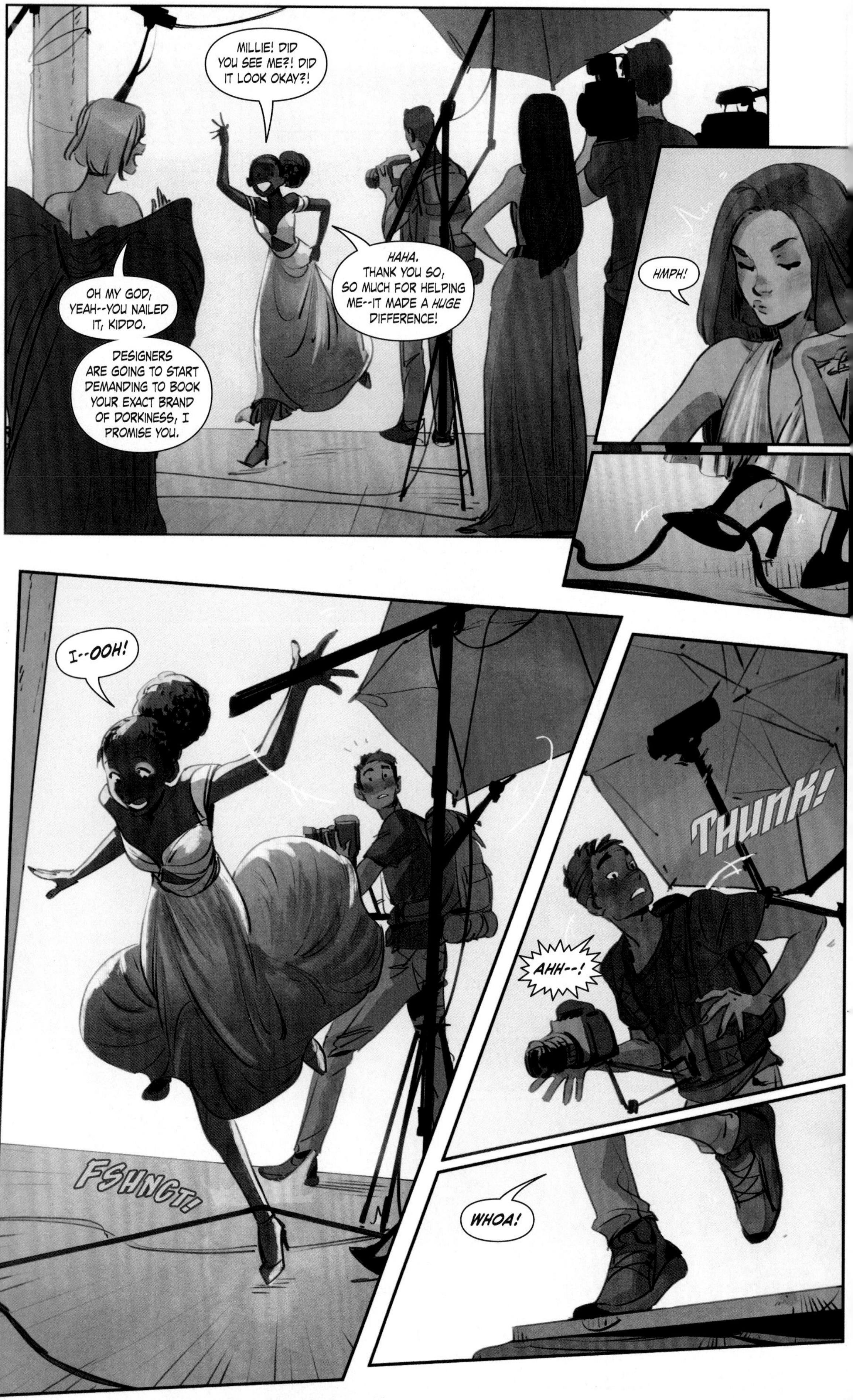
MILLIE! DID YOU SEE ME?! DID IT LOOK OKAY?!
OH MY GOD, YEAH--YOU NAILED IT, KIDDO.
DESIGNERS ARE GOING TO START DEMANDING TO BOOK YOUR EXACT BRAND OF DORKINESS, I PROMISE YOU.
HAHA. THANK YOU SO, SO MUCH FOR HELPING ME--IT MADE A HUGE DIFFERENCE!
HMPH!
I--OOH!
FSHNGT!
THUNK!
AHH--!
WHOA!

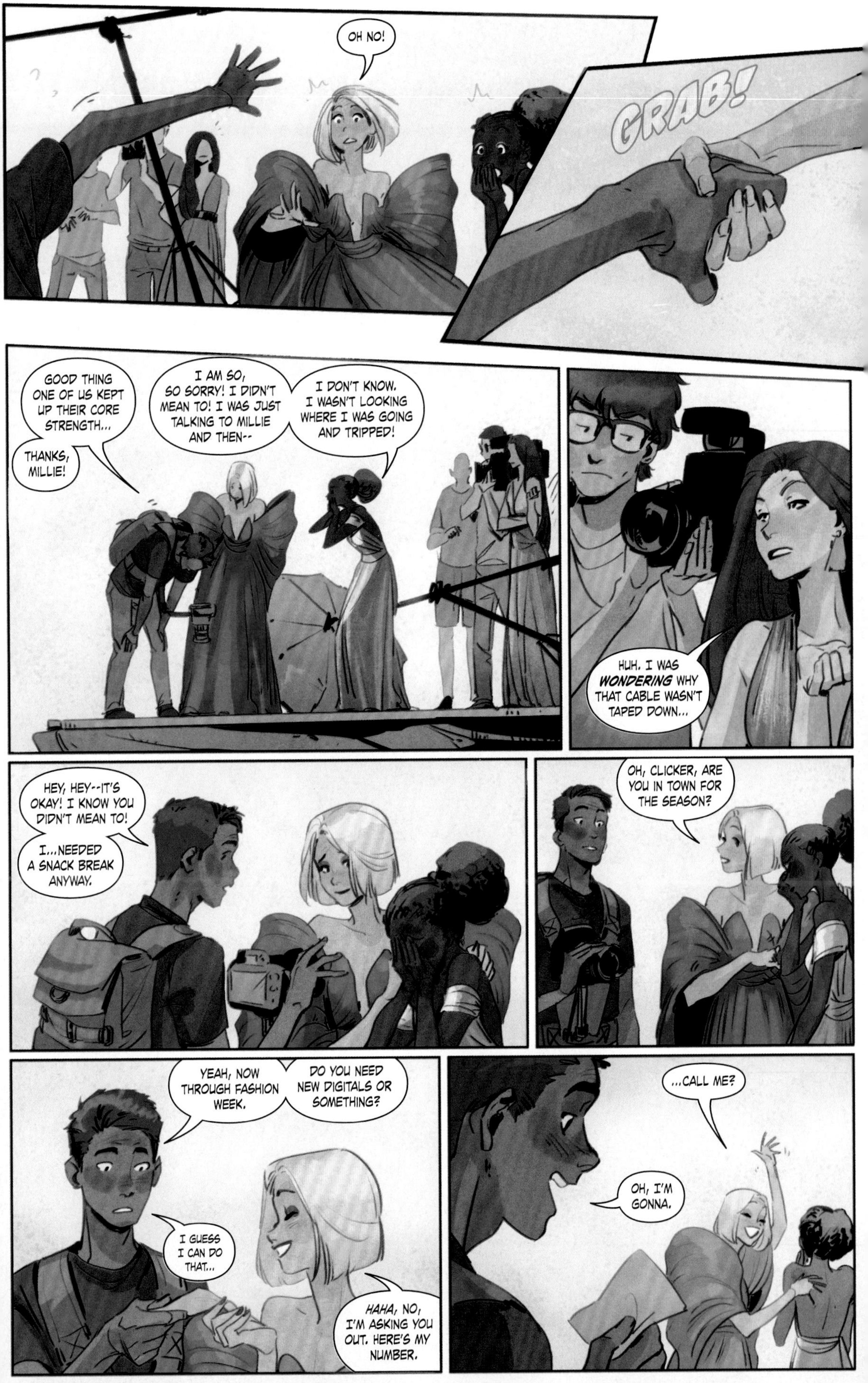
OH NO!
CRAB!
GOOD THING ONE OF US KEPT UP THEIR CORE STRENGTH...
THANKS, MILLIE!
I AM SO, SO SORRY! I DIDN'T MEAN TO! I WAS JUST TALKING TO MILLIE AND THEN--
I DON'T KNOW. I WASN'T LOOKING WHERE I WAS GOING AND TRIPPED!
HUH. I WAS *WONDERING* WHY THAT CABLE WASN'T TAPED DOWN...
HEY, HEY--IT'S OKAY! I KNOW YOU DIDN'T MEAN TO!
I...NEEDED A SNACK BREAK ANYWAY.
OH, CLICKER, ARE YOU IN TOWN FOR THE SEASON?
YEAH, NOW THROUGH FASHION WEEK.
DO YOU NEED NEW DIGITALS OR SOMETHING?
I GUESS I CAN DO THAT...
HAHA, NO, I'M ASKING YOU OUT. HERE'S MY NUMBER.
...CALL ME?
OH, I'M GONNA.

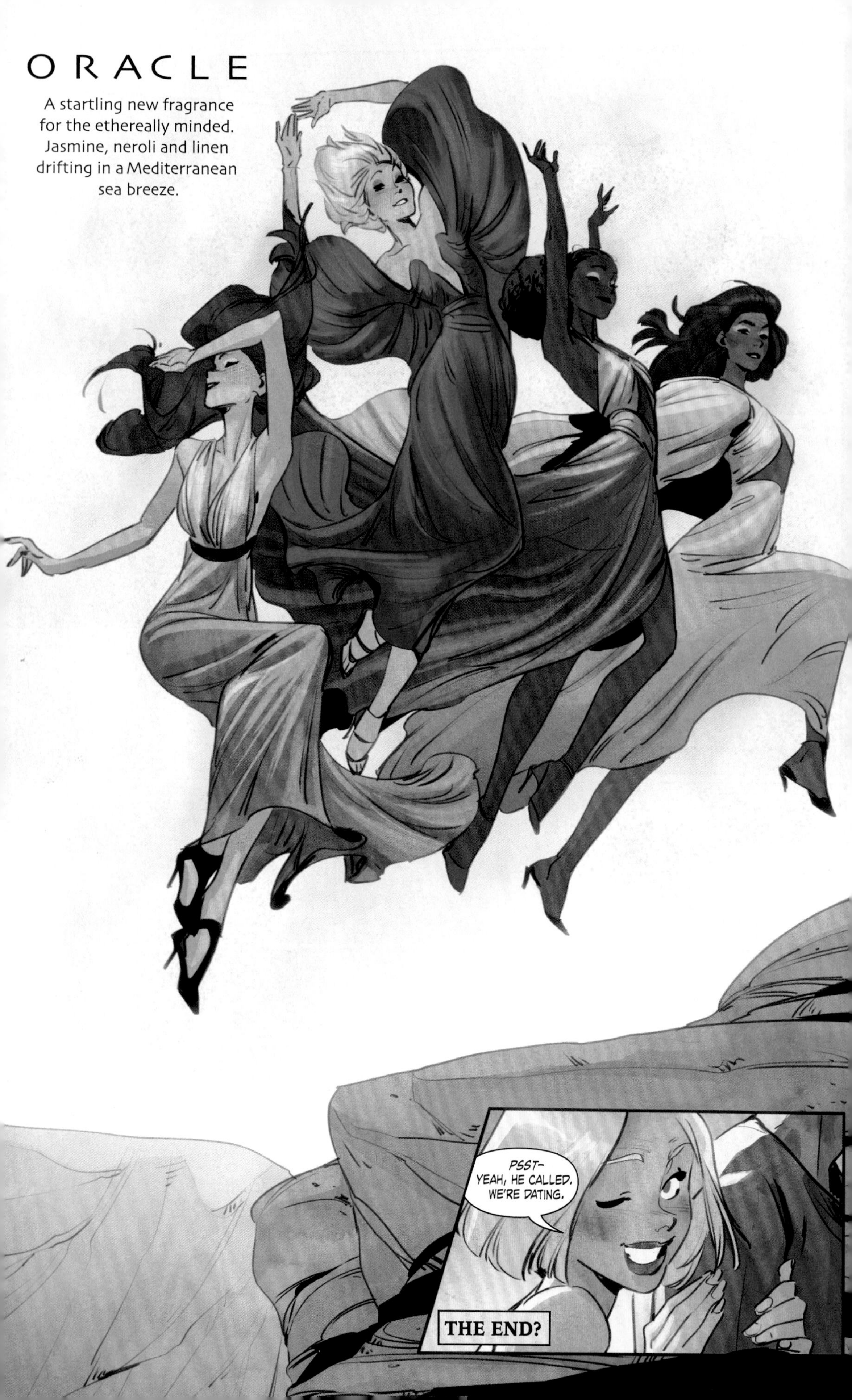
ORACLE
A startling new fragrance for the ethereally minded. Jasmine, neroli and linen drifting in a Mediterranean sea breeze.
PSST-
YEAH, HE CALLED. WE'RE DATING.
THE END?

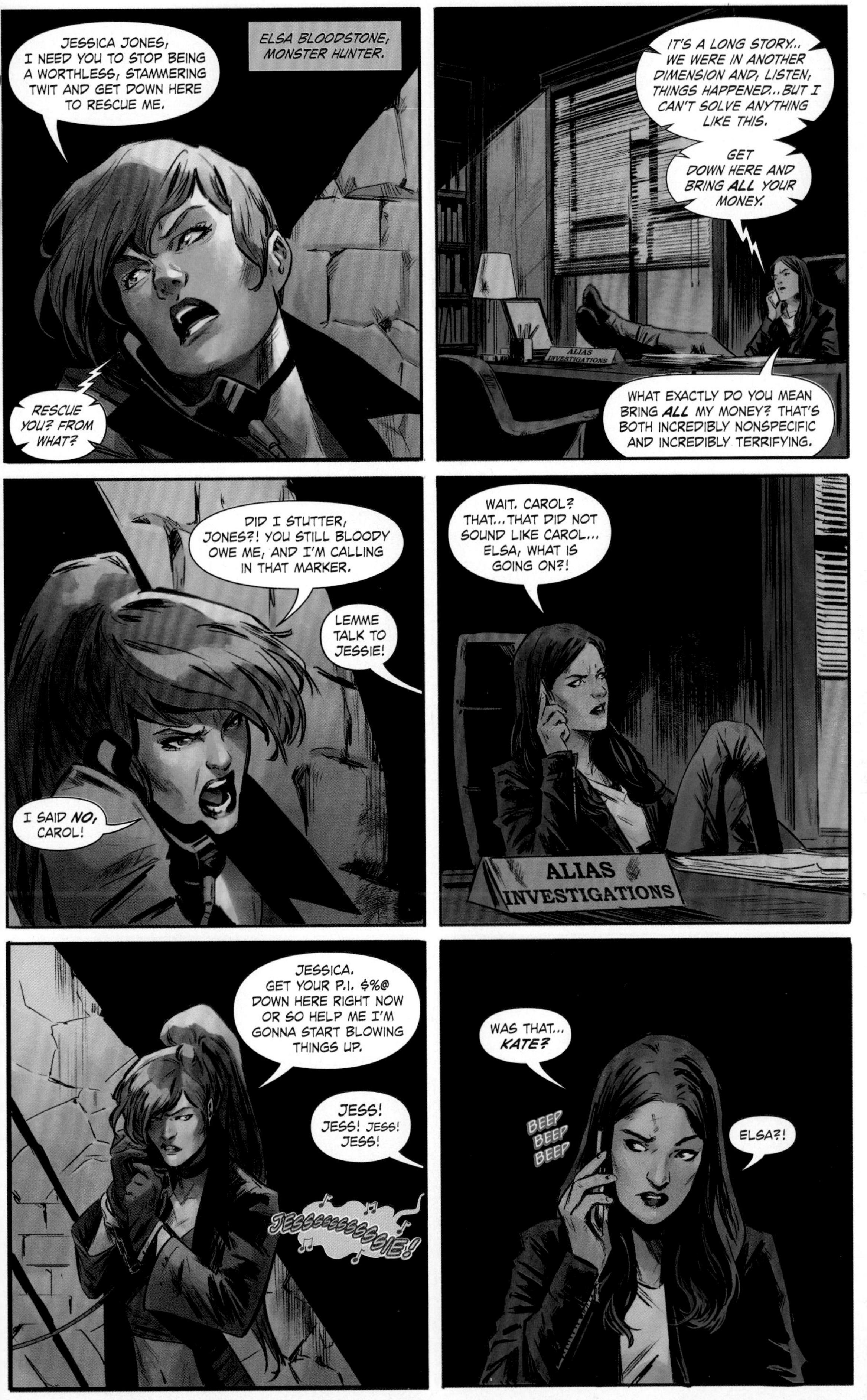

ELSA BLOODSTONE, MONSTER HUNTER.
JESSICA JONES, I NEED YOU TO STOP BEING A WORTHLESS, STAMMERING TWIT AND GET DOWN HERE TO RESCUE ME.
RESCUE YOU? FROM WHAT?
IT'S A LONG STORY... WE WERE IN ANOTHER DIMENSION AND, LISTEN, THINGS HAPPENED...BUT I CAN'T SOLVE ANYTHING LIKE THIS.
GET DOWN HERE AND BRING ALL YOUR MONEY.
ALIAS INVESTIGATIONS
WHAT EXACTLY DO YOU MEAN BRING ALL MY MONEY? THAT'S BOTH INCREDIBLY NONSPECIFIC AND INCREDIBLY TERRIFYING.
DID I STUTTER, JONES?! YOU STILL BLOODY OWE ME, AND I'M CALLING IN THAT MARKER.
LEMME TALK TO JESSIE!
I SAID NO, CAROL!
WAIT. CAROL? THAT...THAT DID NOT SOUND LIKE CAROL... ELSA, WHAT IS GOING ON?!
ALIAS INVESTIGATIONS
JESSICA. GET YOUR P.I. $%@ DOWN HERE RIGHT NOW OR SO HELP ME I'M GONNA START BLOWING THINGS UP.
JESS! JESS! JESS! JESS!
JESSSSSSSSSSIE!
WAS THAT... KATE?
BEEP BEEP BEEP
ELSA?!

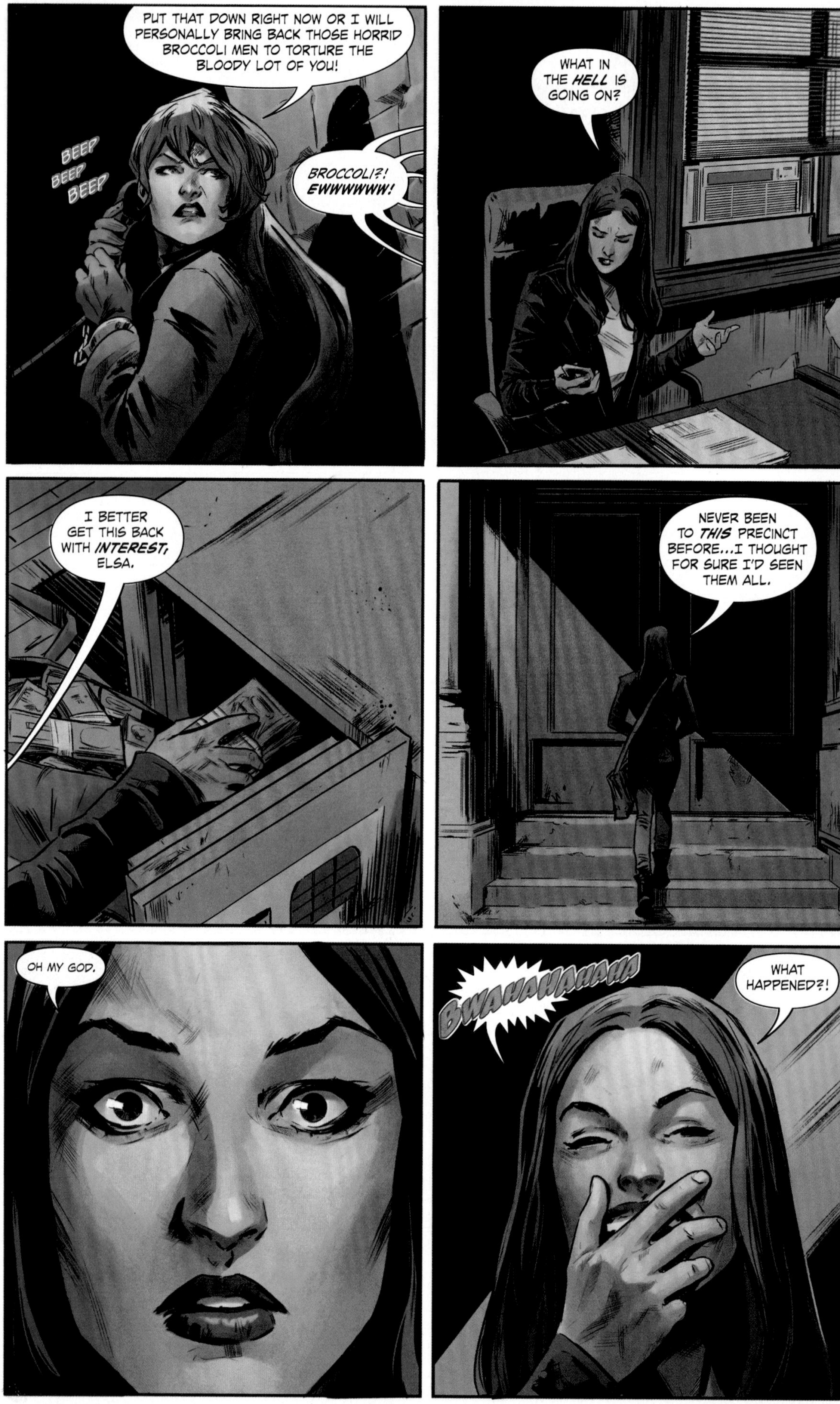
PUT THAT DOWN RIGHT NOW OR I WILL PERSONALLY BRING BACK THOSE HORRID BROCCOLI MEN TO TORTURE THE BLOODY LOT OF YOU!
BEEP BEEP BEEP
BROCCOLI?! EWWWWWW!
WHAT IN THE HELL IS GOING ON?
I BETTER GET THIS BACK WITH INTEREST, ELSA.
NEVER BEEN TO THIS PRECINCT BEFORE...I THOUGHT FOR SURE I'D SEEN THEM ALL.
OH MY GOD.
BWAHAHAHAHAHA
WHAT HAPPENED?!

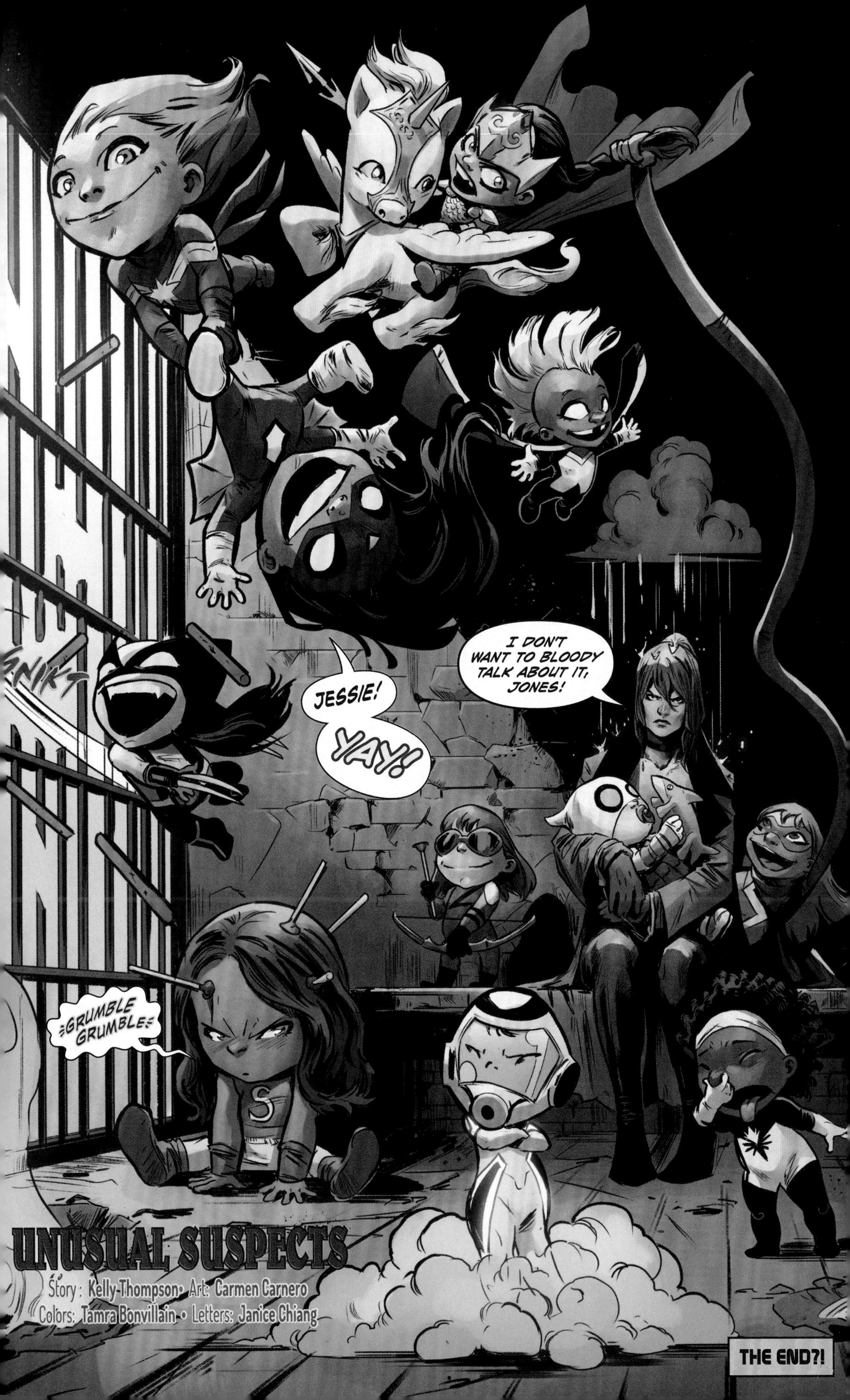
JESSIE!
YAY!
I DON'T WANT TO BLOODY TALK ABOUT IT, JONES!
GRUMBLE GRUMBLE
UNUSUAL SUSPECTS
Story: Kelly Thompson • Art: Carmen Carnero
Colors: Tamra Bonvillain • Letters: Janice Chiang
THE END?!

WRITER SPOTLIGHT
KELLY THOMPSON

DO YOU REMEMBER THE MOMENT YOU FELL IN LOVE WITH COMICS?

There were two moments early in my life, but I think both of them are really important to charting my course as a reader and, eventually, writer of comics. The first was when I found an *Archie Digest* at the supermarket when I was a kid. I didn't understand what monthly comics were or that there were actual comic book stores or even what super heroes were, but I knew I loved those comics.

Archie taught me how to understand the comics medium--and I believe that learning the language of comics early can be a huge factor in becoming a long-term comic fan. The second moment was when I discovered the X-Men comics. (And then monthly comics and comic stores and total obsession not long after!) I discovered X-Men with my brothers thanks to the *X-Men: The Animated Series* characters catching their attention on comic book covers on display at the mall. (UNCANNY X-MEN #290 and X-FORCE #3 for the record.)

The rest was history, and I was hooked. And those comics my brothers brought home that day? Well, they're in my short boxes now. Possession is nine-tenths of the law, people!

WHEN DID YOU KNOW THAT YOU WANTED TO BE A COMICS WRITER?

I wanted to be a writer since almost before I can remember. I wrote all kinds of stories (all bad I'm sure!) as a little kid, and I not only wanted to write but create--I wrote this series of stories about mermaid sisters, and in addition to writing about them, I would draw them and make my own little construction paper die-cut covers for my stories.

So when I discovered comics--this seductive mix of writing and art--everything just made sense. It was like you're listening to a fuzzy radio station all your life, and then it just suddenly clicks into clear focus. That was my brain when I found comics. I knew I had found my people...and my medium!

WHETHER IT'S A CUP OF COFFEE, A SPECIFIC TYPE OF PEN OR DESK SETUP OR EVEN AN EMOTIONAL-SUPPORT ACTION FIGURE, IS THERE AN ELEMENT IN YOUR WORK SPACE THAT YOU FEEL IS CRUCIAL TO YOUR WORK PROCESS?

It's a pretty new development--but for the last two years I've spent most of my workday covered in cats...and I wouldn't have it any other way.

FEARLESS #1: "Unusual Suspects"

PAGE ONE (6 Panels - GRID)

Panel 1. Close/tight on Elsa Bloodstone. Looking gorgeous but annoyed, as usual. She's talking on a telephone (with a cord, not a cell phone). She holds the phone with her head/shoulder – not her hands. We can't tell where she is (but she's in police precinct).

    ELSA: Jessica Jones, I need you to stop being a worthless stammering twit and get down here to rescue me.

ARTIST SPOTLIGHT
CARMEN CARNERO

WHEN DID YOU KNOW THAT YOU WANTED TO BE A COMIC ARTIST?

When I was finishing college, I was also doing a post-graduate in comics. I got some lessons from Joe Kubert (YES!), Bob Greenberger and more people who were visiting Granada Comic Con. My portfolio only had illustrations and pinups, but they pushed me to do interior pages. And if Joe Kubert tells you that you have the chops and to do pages, you just do it! ☺ And here we are!

WHAT HAS BEEN YOUR PROUDEST MOMENT IN COMICS?

Jean Grey's speech at the end of X-MEN RED #7: "The X-Men will fight for you anyway." I remember reading Tom Taylor's script and feeling shivers. It has an infinitely deep, deep meaning, and it also reflects our present times so well. I drew this during a very intense personal time, and reality and comic book fiction got mixed. Having the chance to work on something like that made me feel fortunate.

WHAT HAS BEEN YOUR FAVORITE PROJECT THAT YOU'VE WORKED ON SO FAR AND WHY?

CAPTAIN MARVEL. Being involved in the whole process, designing characters, shaping a postapocalyptic world in our first arc, etc....everything you have the hopes to be able to do when you get asked to do a series starting with issue #1. It's a very collaborative process, not an assembly line, and that makes me really proud to be a part of this book.

WHAT HAS BEEN YOUR FAVORITE EXPERIENCE WITH A FAN?

I remember during one of my few visits to the U.S. a 10- or 11-year-old girl was trying to find me around artist alley, and when she did she told her father in front of me, "See? I was right! She's a girl and she draws too!" Honestly, that made me so happy and proud, and I hope that helped her and that she's still drawing.

WHETHER IT'S A CUP OF COFFEE, A SPECIFIC TYPE OF PEN OR DESK SETUP OR EVEN AN EMOTIONAL-SUPPORT ACTION FIGURE, IS THERE AN ELEMENT IN YOUR WORKSPACE THAT YOU FEEL IS CRUCIAL TO YOUR WORK PROCESS?

My chair. It may sound silly, but when you start working in comics, you are not ready for the amount of hours you're going to spend drawing, or I wasn't, at least. That's why I recommend purchasing the best chair you can afford.

WHAT HAS BEEN YOUR FAVORITE MARVEL CHARACTER TO WORK WITH?

Easy and biased: Captain Marvel. Her personality, the "always get up." The fact that she's so powerful, such a great leader in our first arc, the story we're telling in the second arc I'm drawing as I answer this. If we add to all that the fact that we're living all this while we just had her own movie being a massive hit, everybody is looking at Carol, so this is a huge responsibility but also very special to me.

COLOR ARTIST SPOTLIGHT
TAMRA BONVILLAIN

WHEN DID YOU KNOW THAT YOU WANTED TO BE A COMICS COLORIST?

I had a few random comics when I was really young, before starting school, maybe, and I think those really stuck with me. I loved to draw and do art in general from a young age, and I'd make my own little comics.

I tried to take any art classes I could growing up, and I eventually went to a local arts high school. I majored in art at a local college for a while, then left to get more specific, comic-related art training at the Kubert School. The whole time, my goal was to eventually do something in comics.

WHAT WAS AN IMPORTANT LESSON ABOUT YOUR CHOSEN FIELD THAT YOU LEARNED EARLY ON THAT HAS STUCK WITH YOU THROUGHOUT YOUR CAREER?

Starting out, people would often give directions for how to color a project based on other, popular colorists working. I never wanted to be an imitation of someone else, so usually I just did my own thing.

I think you can still use that information to get sort of a vague idea of the direction they want, but I always made it a point to never try to completely emulate any other person's style, and instead developed my own approach to things.

Hey there, True Believers!

For each issue of **FEARLESS**, we'll be profiling the witty, wondrous women who help make Marvel marvelous, and what better place to start than with the all-star, all-female creative team of **CAPTAIN MARVEL** doing what they do best?

You can follow the dynamite team of Kelly, Carmen and Tamra into the pages of **CAPTAIN MARVEL #8**, on sale now--it's the start of a brand-new arc, so it's the perfect time to join the fun! And come back next month for more candor with can't-miss creators!

Stay fearless!
Sarah, Annalise, Lauren, Kathleen, Shannon, Alanna & Lindsey.

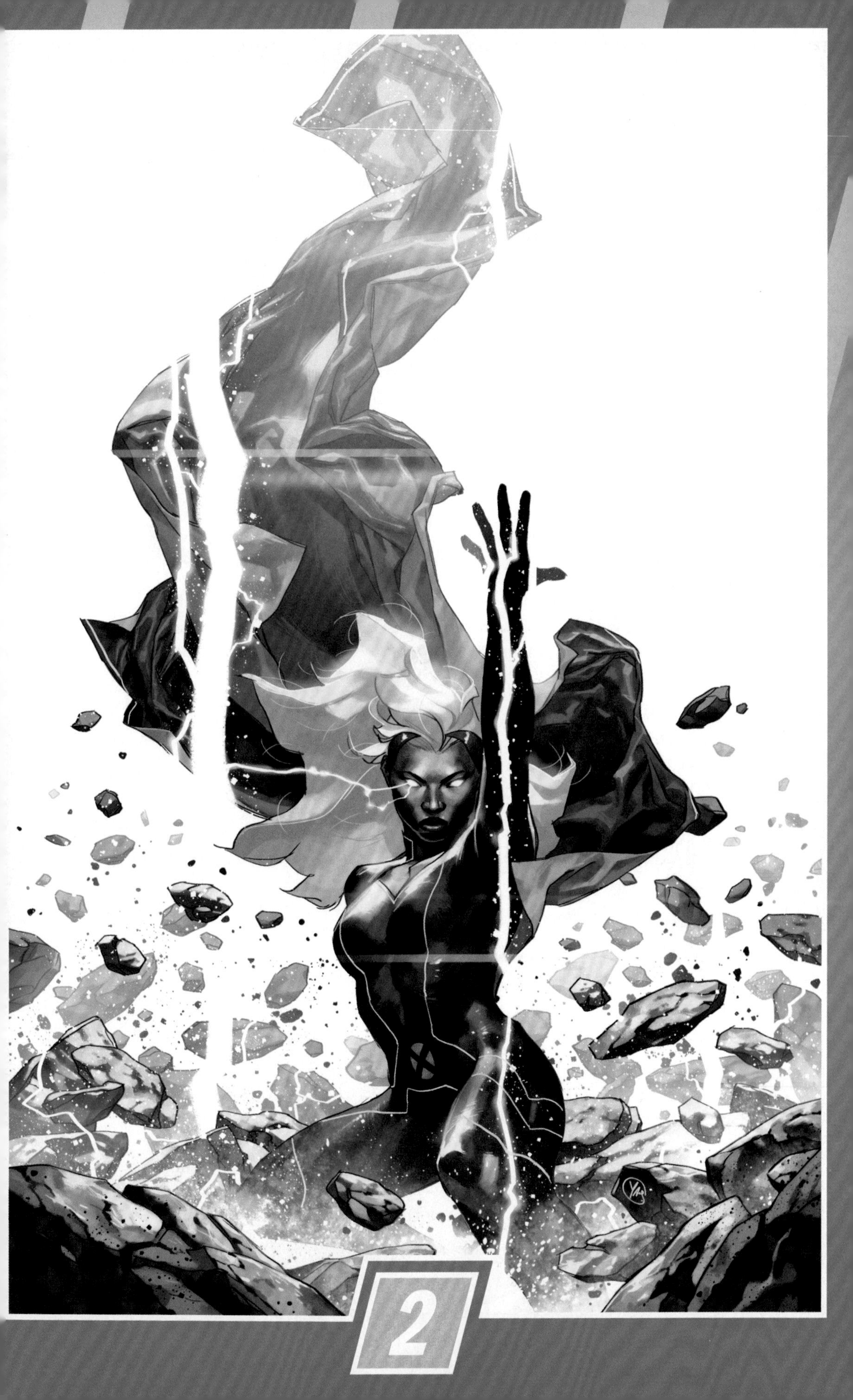
2

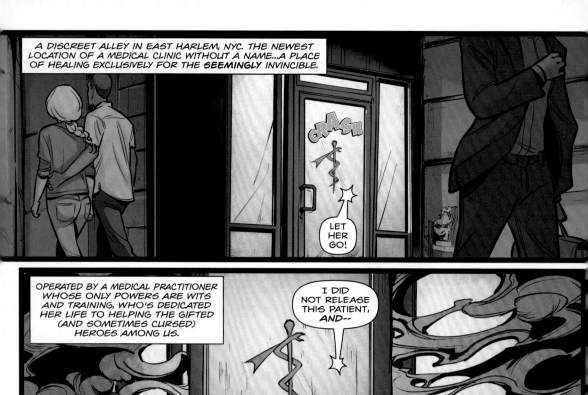

A DISCREET ALLEY IN EAST HARLEM, NYC. THE NEWEST LOCATION OF A MEDICAL CLINIC WITHOUT A NAME...A PLACE OF HEALING EXCLUSIVELY FOR THE *SEEMINGLY* INVINCIBLE.

CRASH

LET HER GO!

OPERATED BY A MEDICAL PRACTITIONER WHOSE ONLY POWERS ARE WITS AND TRAINING, WHO'S DEDICATED HER LIFE TO HELPING THE GIFTED (AND SOMETIMES CURSED) HEROES AMONG US.

I DID NOT RELEASE THIS PATIENT, AND--

SKRAAASH!!

YOU NEED AN APPOINTMENT!!!

THIS IS...
LINDA CARTER
NIGHT NURSE

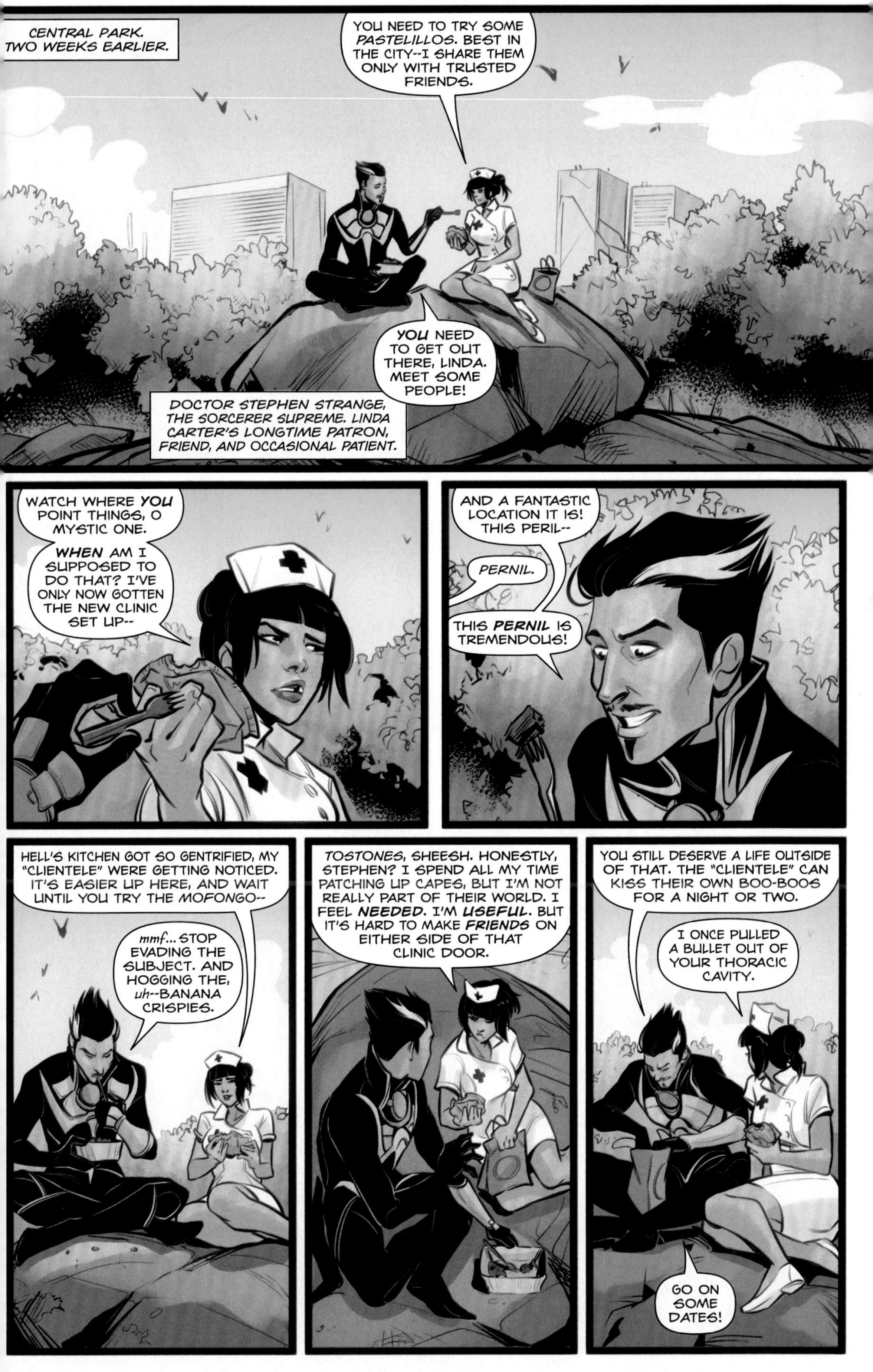
CENTRAL PARK. TWO WEEKS EARLIER.
YOU NEED TO TRY SOME PASTELILLOS. BEST IN THE CITY--I SHARE THEM ONLY WITH TRUSTED FRIENDS.
YOU NEED TO GET OUT THERE, LINDA. MEET SOME PEOPLE!
DOCTOR STEPHEN STRANGE, THE SORCERER SUPREME. LINDA CARTER'S LONGTIME PATRON, FRIEND, AND OCCASIONAL PATIENT.
WATCH WHERE YOU POINT THINGS, O MYSTIC ONE.
WHEN AM I SUPPOSED TO DO THAT? I'VE ONLY NOW GOTTEN THE NEW CLINIC SET UP--
AND A FANTASTIC LOCATION IT IS! THIS PERIL--
PERNIL.
THIS PERNIL IS TREMENDOUS!
HELL'S KITCHEN GOT SO GENTRIFIED, MY "CLIENTELE" WERE GETTING NOTICED. IT'S EASIER UP HERE, AND WAIT UNTIL YOU TRY THE MOFONGO--
mmf... STOP EVADING THE SUBJECT. AND HOGGING THE, uh--BANANA CRISPIES.
TOSTONES, SHEESH. HONESTLY, STEPHEN? I SPEND ALL MY TIME PATCHING UP CAPES, BUT I'M NOT REALLY PART OF THEIR WORLD. I FEEL NEEDED. I'M USEFUL. BUT IT'S HARD TO MAKE FRIENDS ON EITHER SIDE OF THAT CLINIC DOOR.
YOU STILL DESERVE A LIFE OUTSIDE OF THAT. THE "CLIENTELE" CAN KISS THEIR OWN BOO-BOOS FOR A NIGHT OR TWO.
I ONCE PULLED A BULLET OUT OF YOUR THORACIC CAVITY.
GO ON SOME DATES!

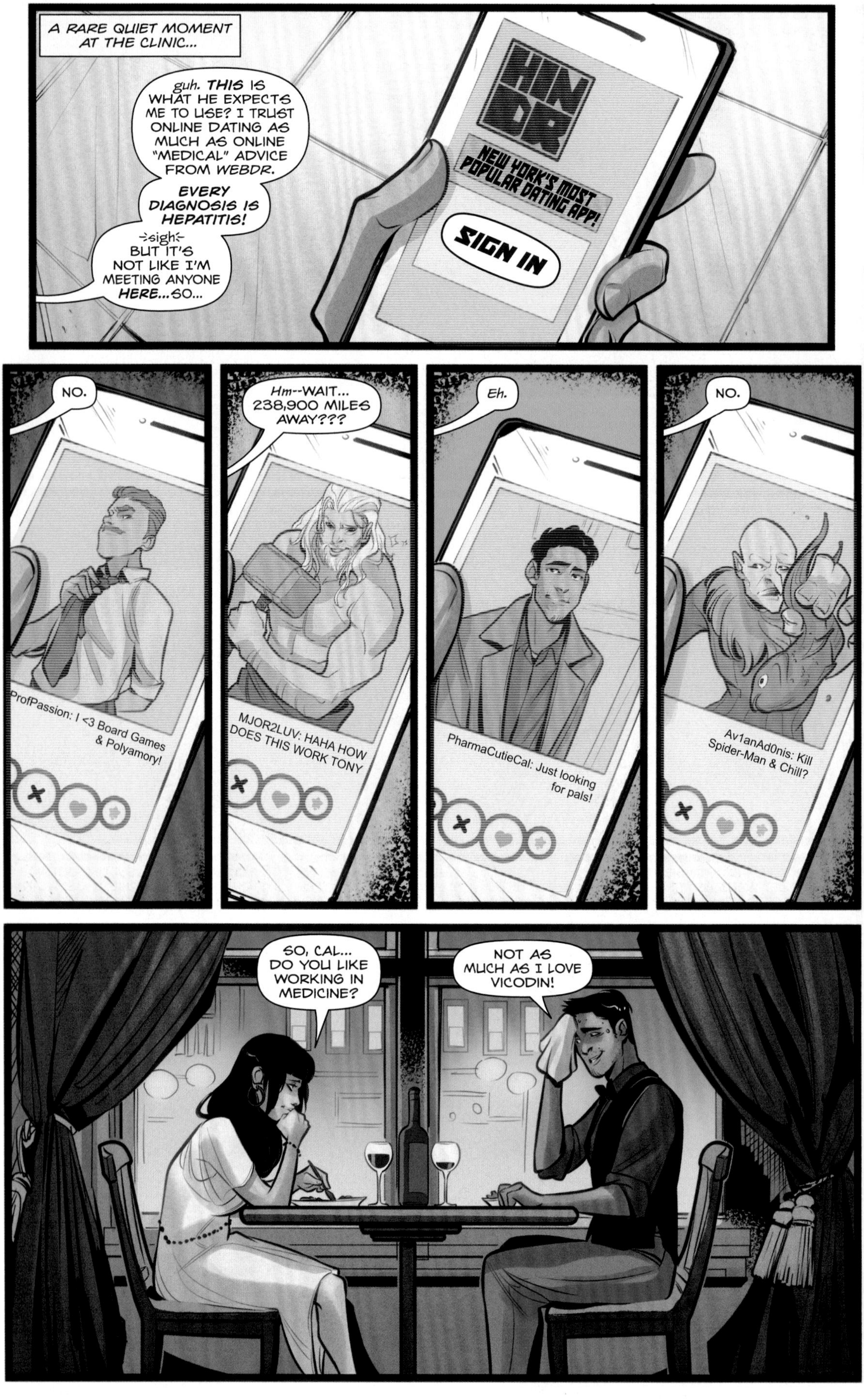
A RARE QUIET MOMENT AT THE CLINIC...
guh. THIS IS WHAT HE EXPECTS ME TO USE? I TRUST ONLINE DATING AS MUCH AS ONLINE "MEDICAL" ADVICE FROM WEBDR.
EVERY DIAGNOSIS IS HEPATITIS!
-sigh- BUT IT'S NOT LIKE I'M MEETING ANYONE HERE...SO...
HINDR
NEW YORK'S MOST POPULAR DATING APP!
SIGN IN
NO.
ProfPassion: I <3 Board Games & Polyamory!
Hm--WAIT... 238,900 MILES AWAY???
MJOR2LUV: HAHA HOW DOES THIS WORK TONY
Eh.
PharmaCutieCal: Just looking for pals!
NO.
Av1anAd0nis: Kill Spider-Man & Chill?
SO, CAL... DO YOU LIKE WORKING IN MEDICINE?
NOT AS MUCH AS I LOVE VICODIN!

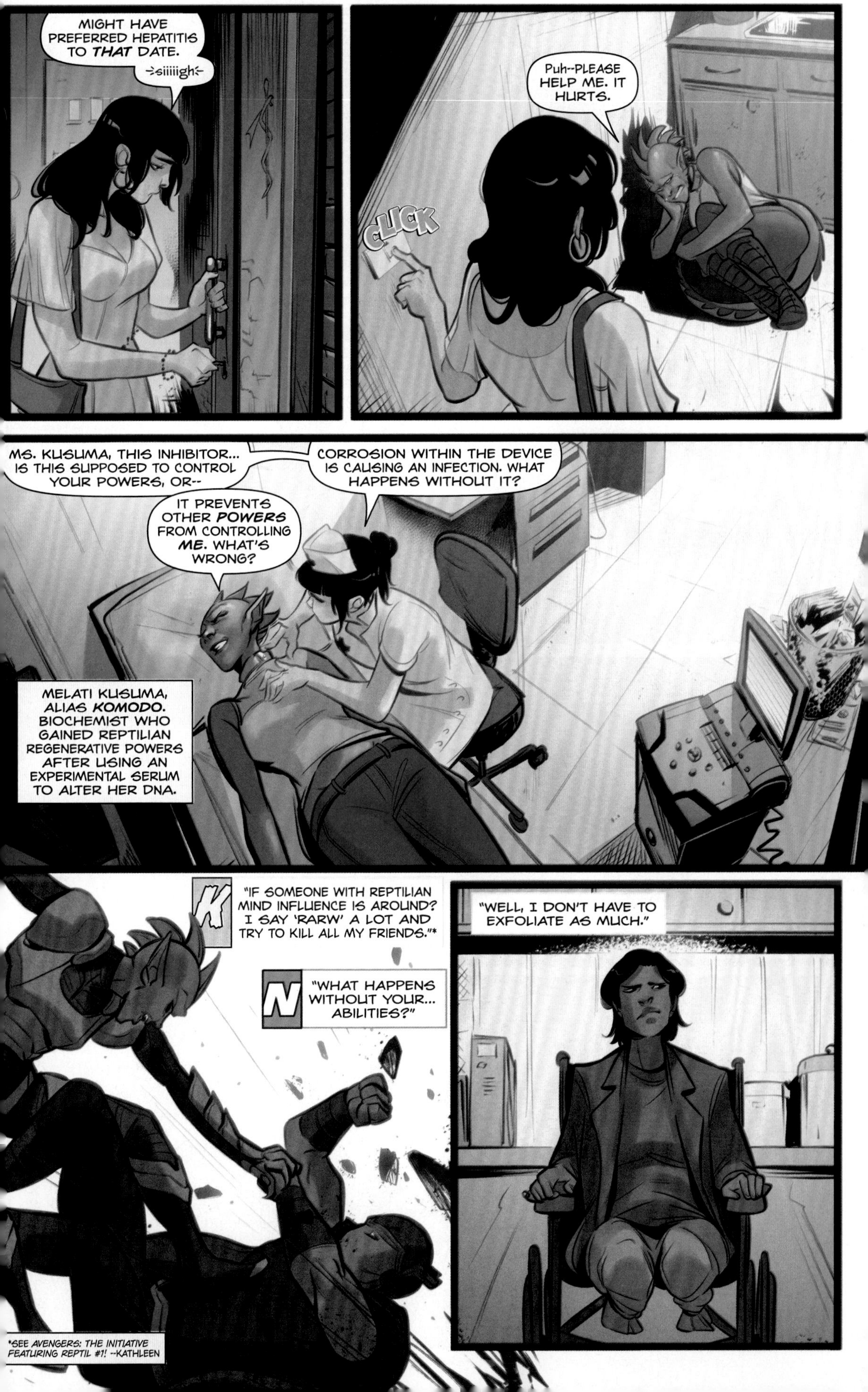
MIGHT HAVE PREFERRED HEPATITIS TO *THAT* DATE.
~siiiiigh~
Puh--PLEASE HELP ME. IT HURTS.
CLICK
MS. KUSUMA, THIS INHIBITOR... IS THIS SUPPOSED TO CONTROL YOUR POWERS, OR--
IT PREVENTS OTHER *POWERS* FROM CONTROLLING *ME*. WHAT'S WRONG?
CORROSION WITHIN THE DEVICE IS CAUSING AN INFECTION. WHAT HAPPENS WITHOUT IT?
MELATI KUSUMA, ALIAS *KOMODO*. BIOCHEMIST WHO GAINED REPTILIAN REGENERATIVE POWERS AFTER USING AN EXPERIMENTAL SERUM TO ALTER HER DNA.
K
"IF SOMEONE WITH REPTILIAN MIND INFLUENCE IS AROUND? I SAY 'RARW' A LOT AND TRY TO KILL ALL MY FRIENDS."*
N
"WHAT HAPPENS WITHOUT YOUR... ABILITIES?"
"WELL, I DON'T HAVE TO EXFOLIATE AS MUCH."
*SEE *AVENGERS: THE INITIATIVE FEATURING REPTIL #1!* --KATHLEEN

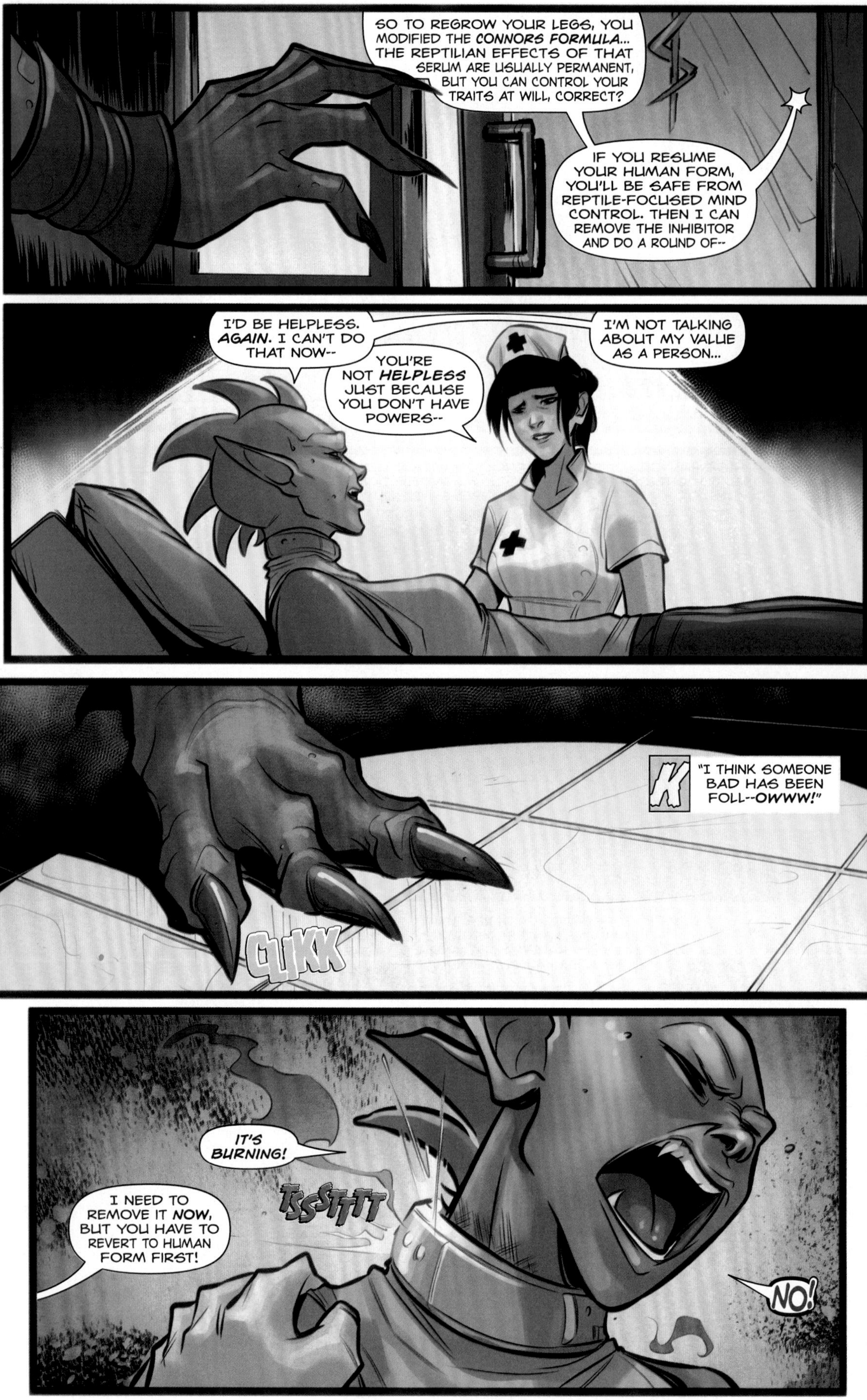

SO TO REGROW YOUR LEGS, YOU MODIFIED THE CONNORS FORMULA... THE REPTILIAN EFFECTS OF THAT SERUM ARE USUALLY PERMANENT, BUT YOU CAN CONTROL YOUR TRAITS AT WILL, CORRECT?
IF YOU RESUME YOUR HUMAN FORM, YOU'LL BE SAFE FROM REPTILE-FOCUSED MIND CONTROL. THEN I CAN REMOVE THE INHIBITOR AND DO A ROUND OF--
I'D BE HELPLESS. AGAIN. I CAN'T DO THAT NOW--
YOU'RE NOT HELPLESS JUST BECAUSE YOU DON'T HAVE POWERS--
I'M NOT TALKING ABOUT MY VALUE AS A PERSON...
"I THINK SOMEONE BAD HAS BEEN FOLL--OWWW!"
CLIKK
IT'S BURNING!
TSSSTTTT
I NEED TO REMOVE IT NOW, BUT YOU HAVE TO REVERT TO HUMAN FORM FIRST!
NO!

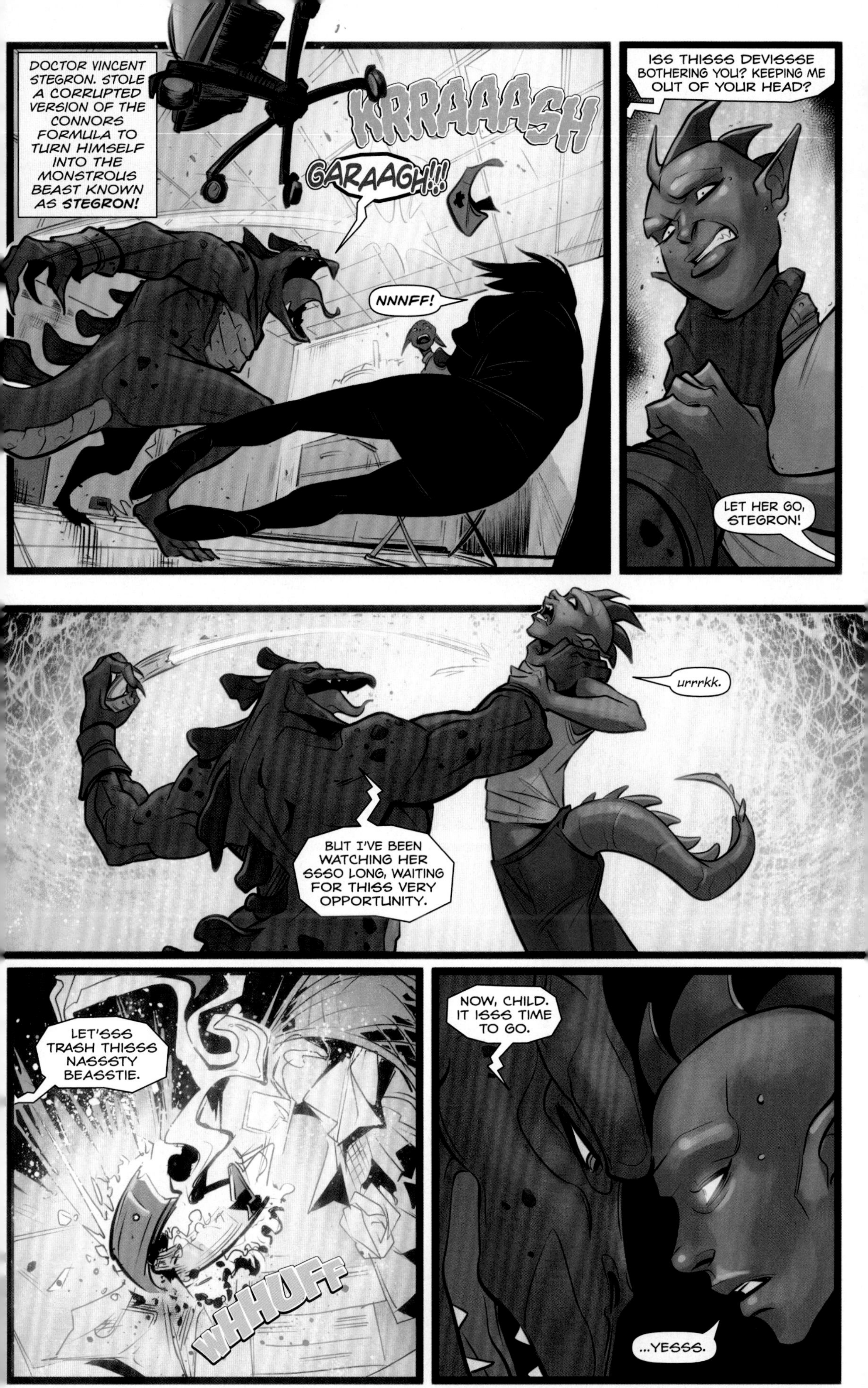
DOCTOR VINCENT STEGRON. STOLE A CORRUPTED VERSION OF THE CONNORS FORMULA TO TURN HIMSELF INTO THE MONSTROUS BEAST KNOWN AS STEGRON!
KRRAAASH
GARAAGH!!!
NNNFF!
ISS THISSS DEVISSSE BOTHERING YOU? KEEPING ME OUT OF YOUR HEAD?
LET HER GO, STEGRON!
urrrkk.
BUT I'VE BEEN WATCHING HER SSSO LONG, WAITING FOR THISS VERY OPPORTUNITY.
LET'SSS TRASH THISSS NASSSTY BEASSTIE.
WHHUFF
NOW, CHILD. IT ISSS TIME TO GO.
...YESSS.

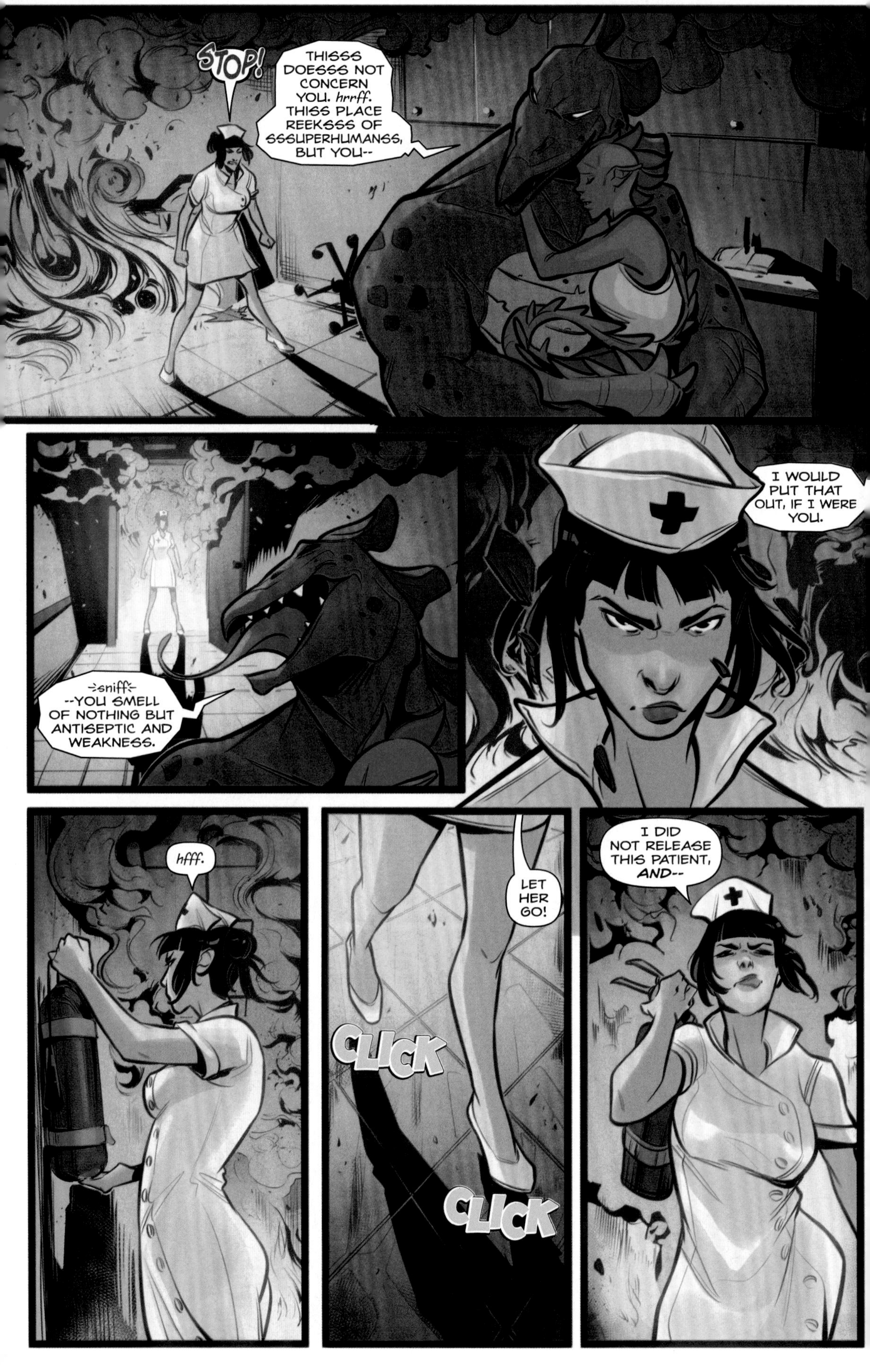
STOP!
THISSS DOESSS NOT CONCERN YOU. hrrff. THISS PLACE REEKSSS OF SSSUPERHUMANSS, BUT YOU--
-sniff-
--YOU SMELL OF NOTHING BUT ANTISEPTIC AND WEAKNESS.
I WOULD PUT THAT OUT, IF I WERE YOU.
hfff.
LET HER GO!
CLICK
CLICK
I DID NOT RELEASE THIS PATIENT, AND--

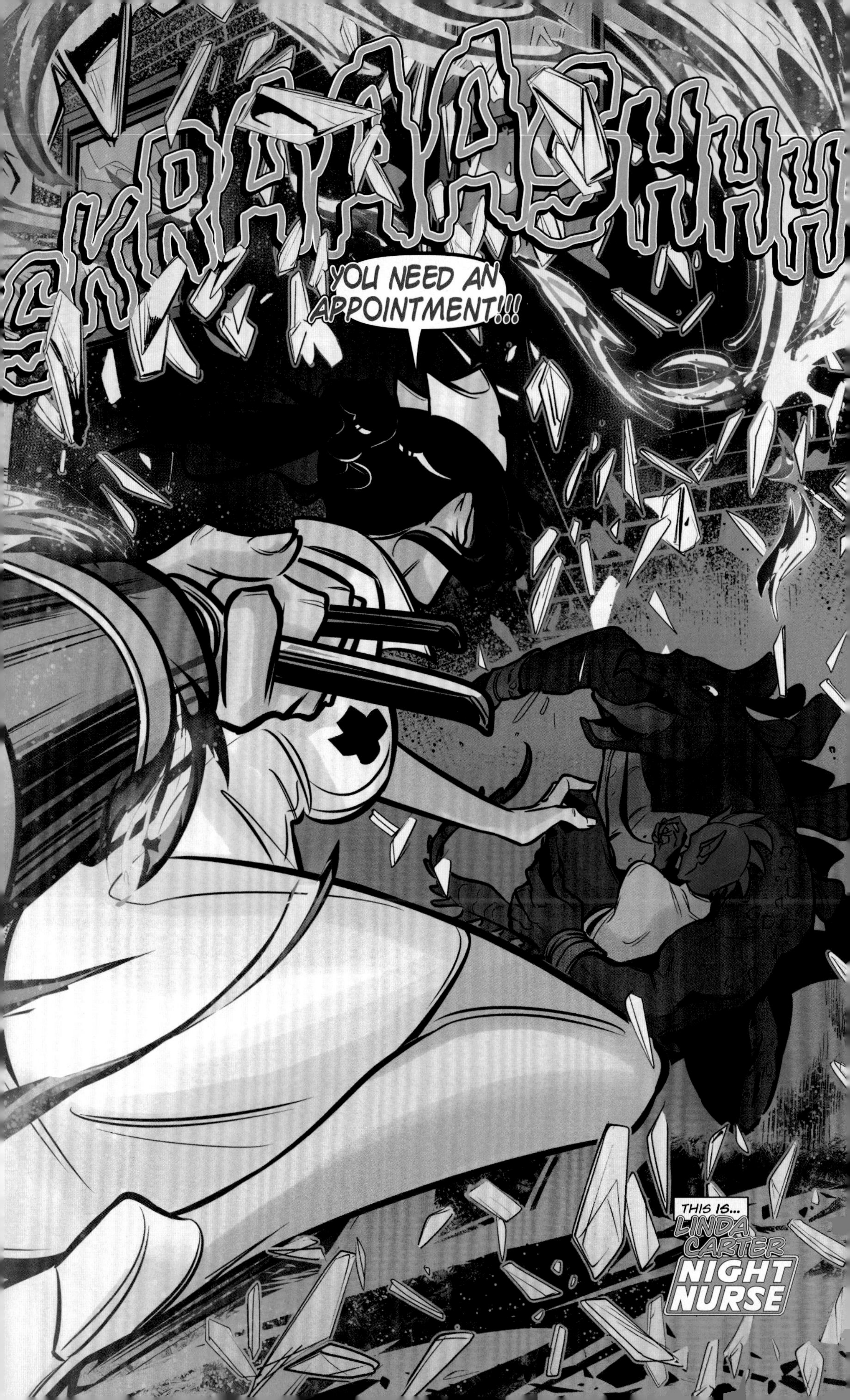
SKRAAAASHHH
YOU NEED AN APPOINTMENT!!!
THIS IS... LINDA CARTER NIGHT NURSE

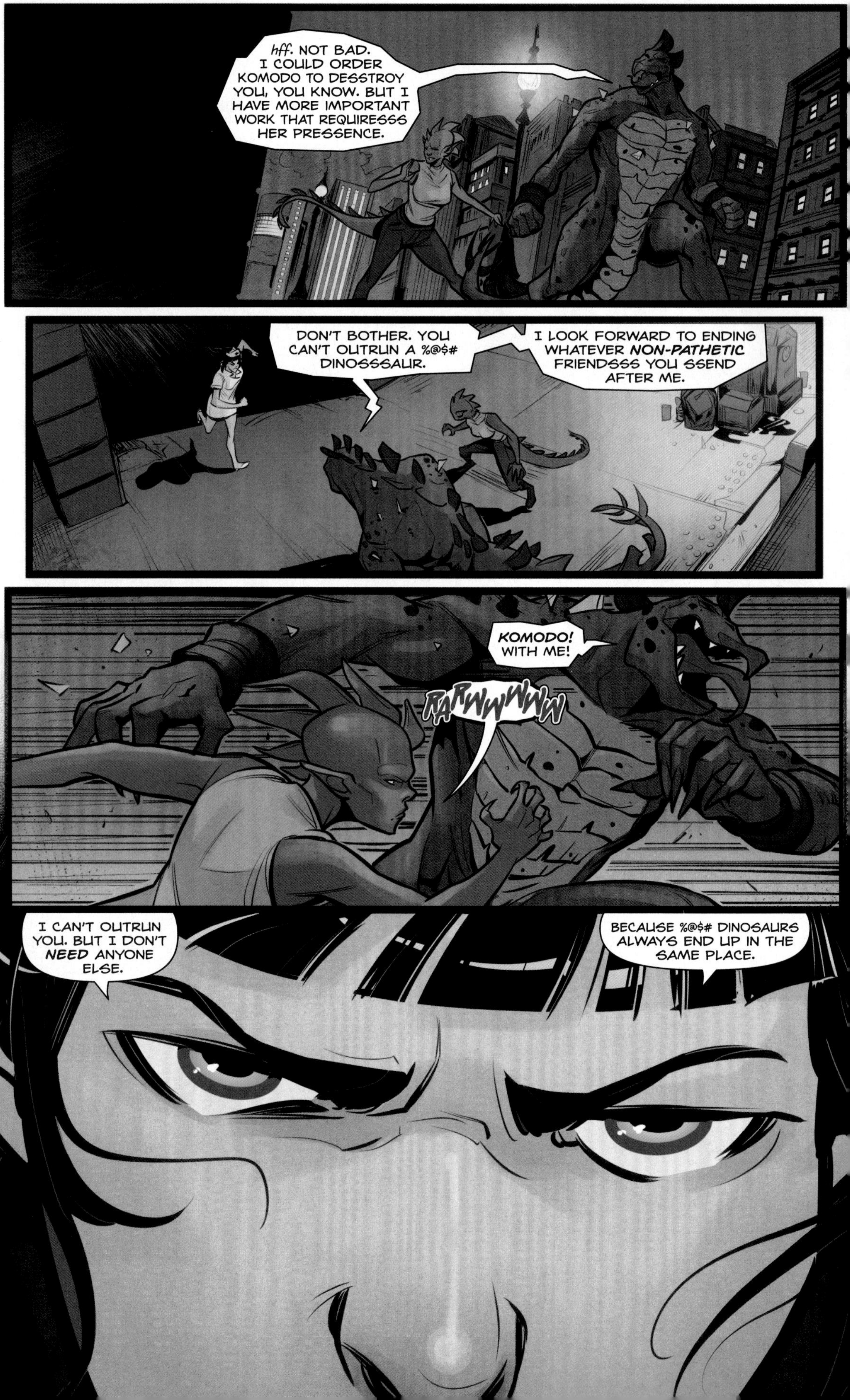
hff. NOT BAD. I COULD ORDER KOMODO TO DESSTROY YOU, YOU KNOW. BUT I HAVE MORE IMPORTANT WORK THAT REQUIRESSS HER PRESSENCE.
DON'T BOTHER. YOU CAN'T OUTRUN A %@$# DINOSSSAUR.
I LOOK FORWARD TO ENDING WHATEVER NON-PATHETIC FRIENDSSS YOU SSEND AFTER ME.
KOMODO! WITH ME!
RARWWWWW
I CAN'T OUTRUN YOU. BUT I DON'T NEED ANYONE ELSE.
BECAUSE %@$# DINOSAURS ALWAYS END UP IN THE SAME PLACE.

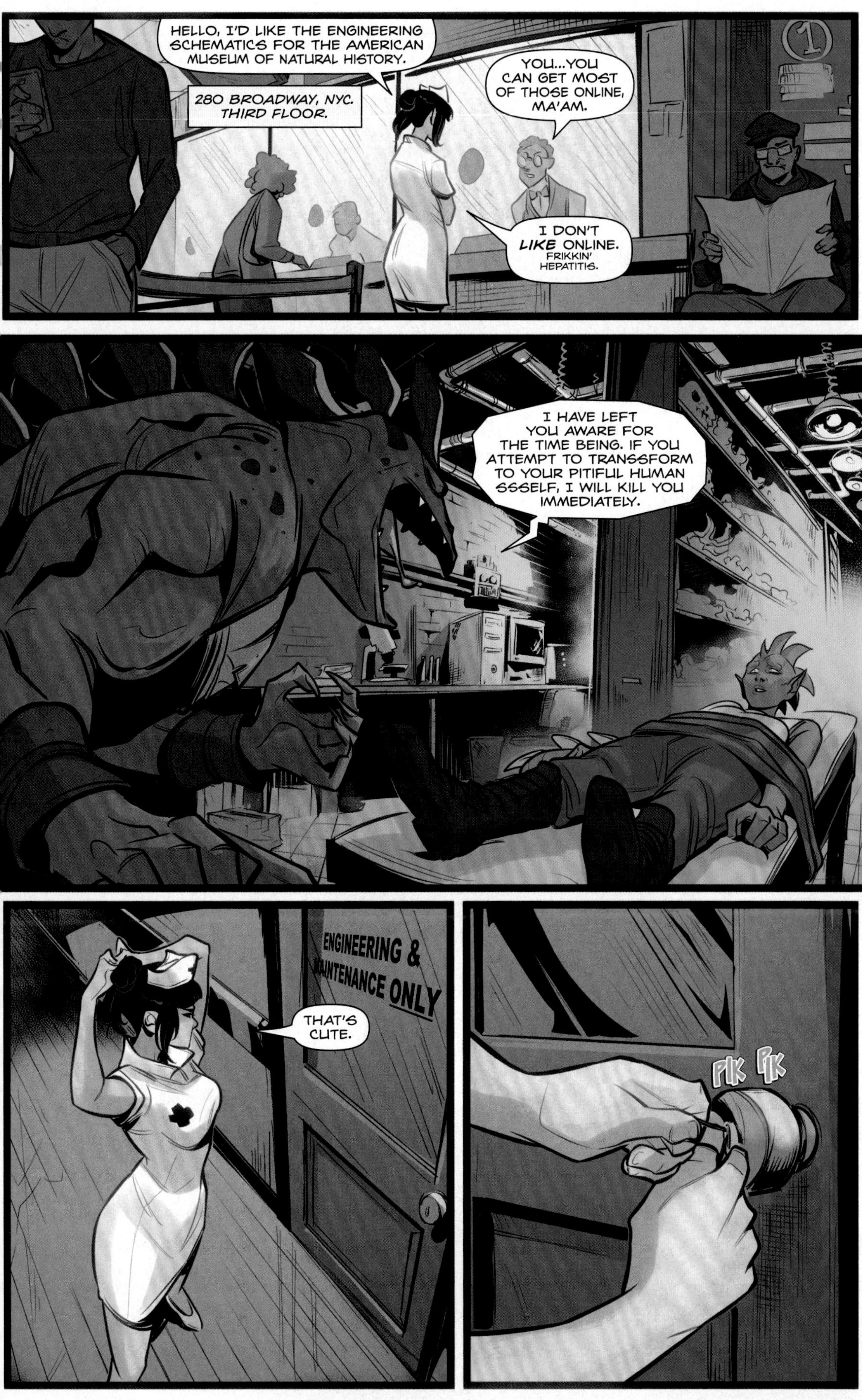
HELLO, I'D LIKE THE ENGINEERING SCHEMATICS FOR THE AMERICAN MUSEUM OF NATURAL HISTORY.
280 BROADWAY, NYC. THIRD FLOOR.
YOU...YOU CAN GET MOST OF THOSE ONLINE, MA'AM.
I DON'T LIKE ONLINE. FRIKKIN' HEPATITIS.
I HAVE LEFT YOU AWARE FOR THE TIME BEING. IF YOU ATTEMPT TO TRANSSFORM TO YOUR PITIFUL HUMAN SSSELF, I WILL KILL YOU IMMEDIATELY.
ENGINEERING & MAINTENANCE ONLY
THAT'S CUTE.
PIK PIK

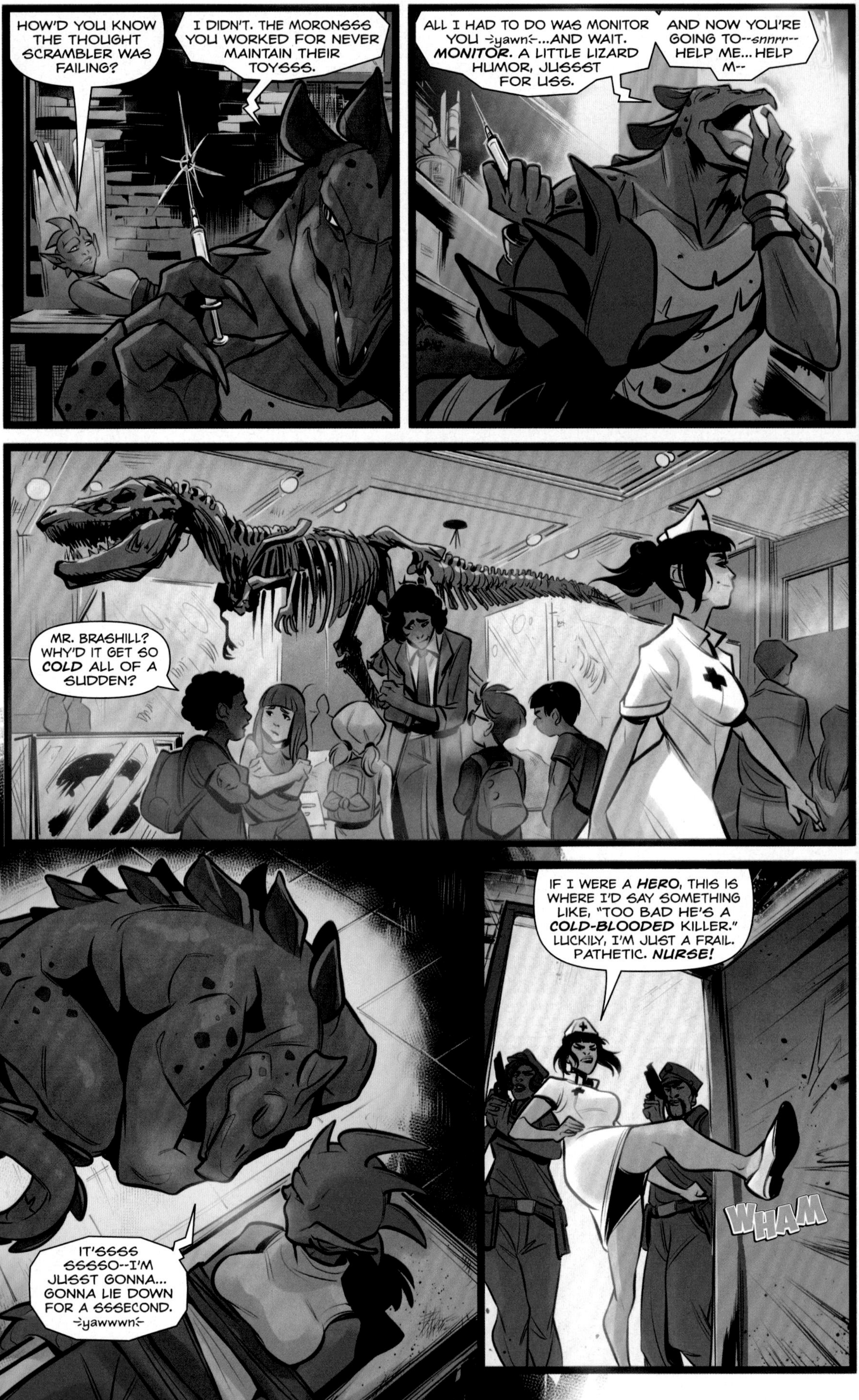
HOW'D YOU KNOW THE THOUGHT SCRAMBLER WAS FAILING?
I DIDN'T. THE MORONSSS YOU WORKED FOR NEVER MAINTAIN THEIR TOYSSS.
ALL I HAD TO DO WAS MONITOR YOU -yawn- ...AND WAIT. MONITOR. A LITTLE LIZARD HUMOR, JUSSST FOR USS.
AND NOW YOU'RE GOING TO--snnrr-- HELP ME... HELP M--
MR. BRASHILL? WHY'D IT GET SO COLD ALL OF A SUDDEN?
IT'SSSS SSSSO--I'M JUSST GONNA... GONNA LIE DOWN FOR A SSSECOND. -yawwwn-
IF I WERE A HERO, THIS IS WHERE I'D SAY SOMETHING LIKE, "TOO BAD HE'S A COLD-BLOODED KILLER." LUCKILY, I'M JUST A FRAIL. PATHETIC. NURSE!
WHAM

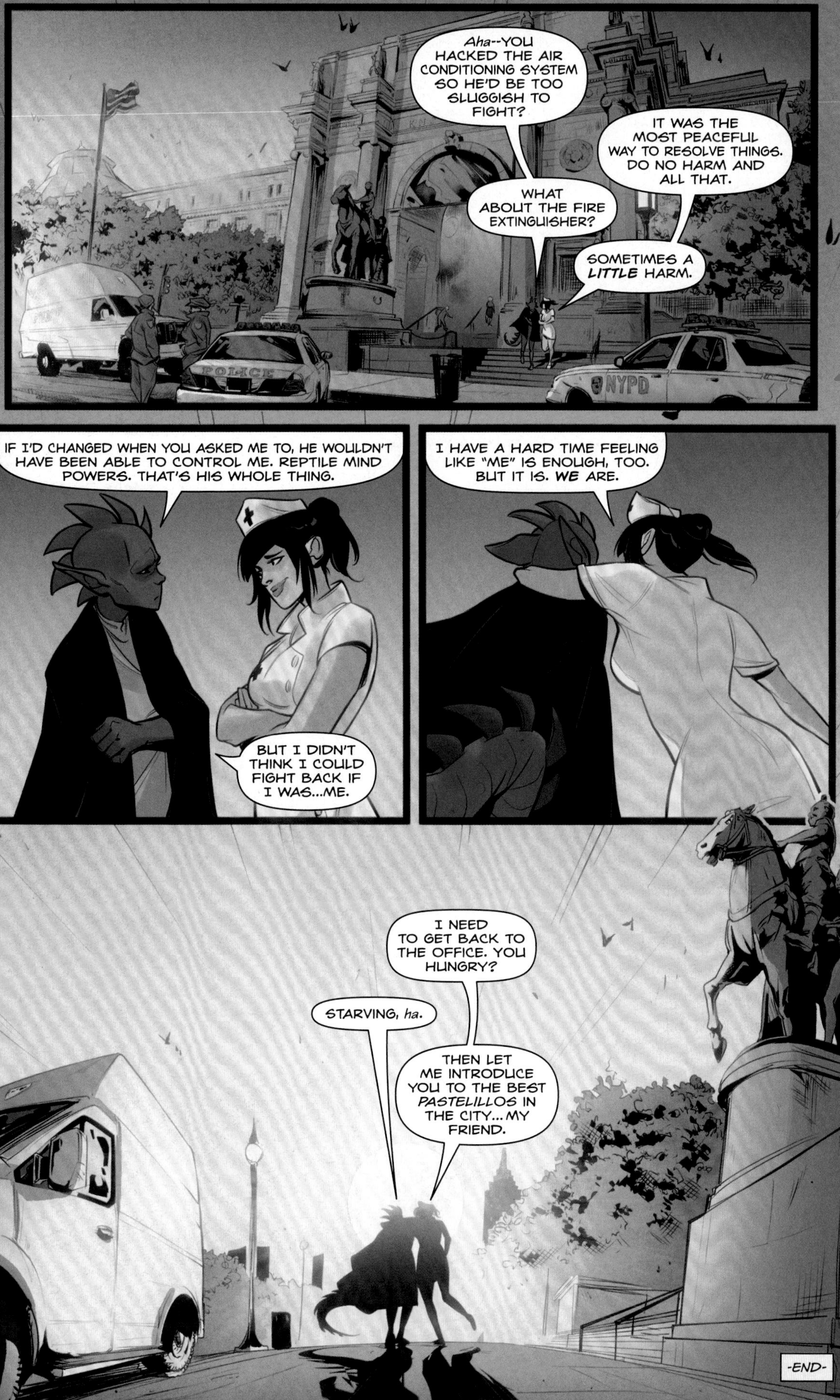
Aha--YOU HACKED THE AIR CONDITIONING SYSTEM SO HE'D BE TOO SLUGGISH TO FIGHT?
IT WAS THE MOST PEACEFUL WAY TO RESOLVE THINGS. DO NO HARM AND ALL THAT.
WHAT ABOUT THE FIRE EXTINGUISHER?
SOMETIMES A *LITTLE* HARM.
POLICE
NYPD
IF I'D CHANGED WHEN YOU ASKED ME TO, HE WOULDN'T HAVE BEEN ABLE TO CONTROL ME. REPTILE MIND POWERS. THAT'S HIS WHOLE THING.
BUT I DIDN'T THINK I COULD FIGHT BACK IF I WAS...ME.
I HAVE A HARD TIME FEELING LIKE "ME" IS ENOUGH, TOO. BUT IT IS. *WE* ARE.
I NEED TO GET BACK TO THE OFFICE. YOU HUNGRY?
STARVING, *ha*.
THEN LET ME INTRODUCE YOU TO THE BEST *PASTELILLOS* IN THE CITY... MY FRIEND.
-END-

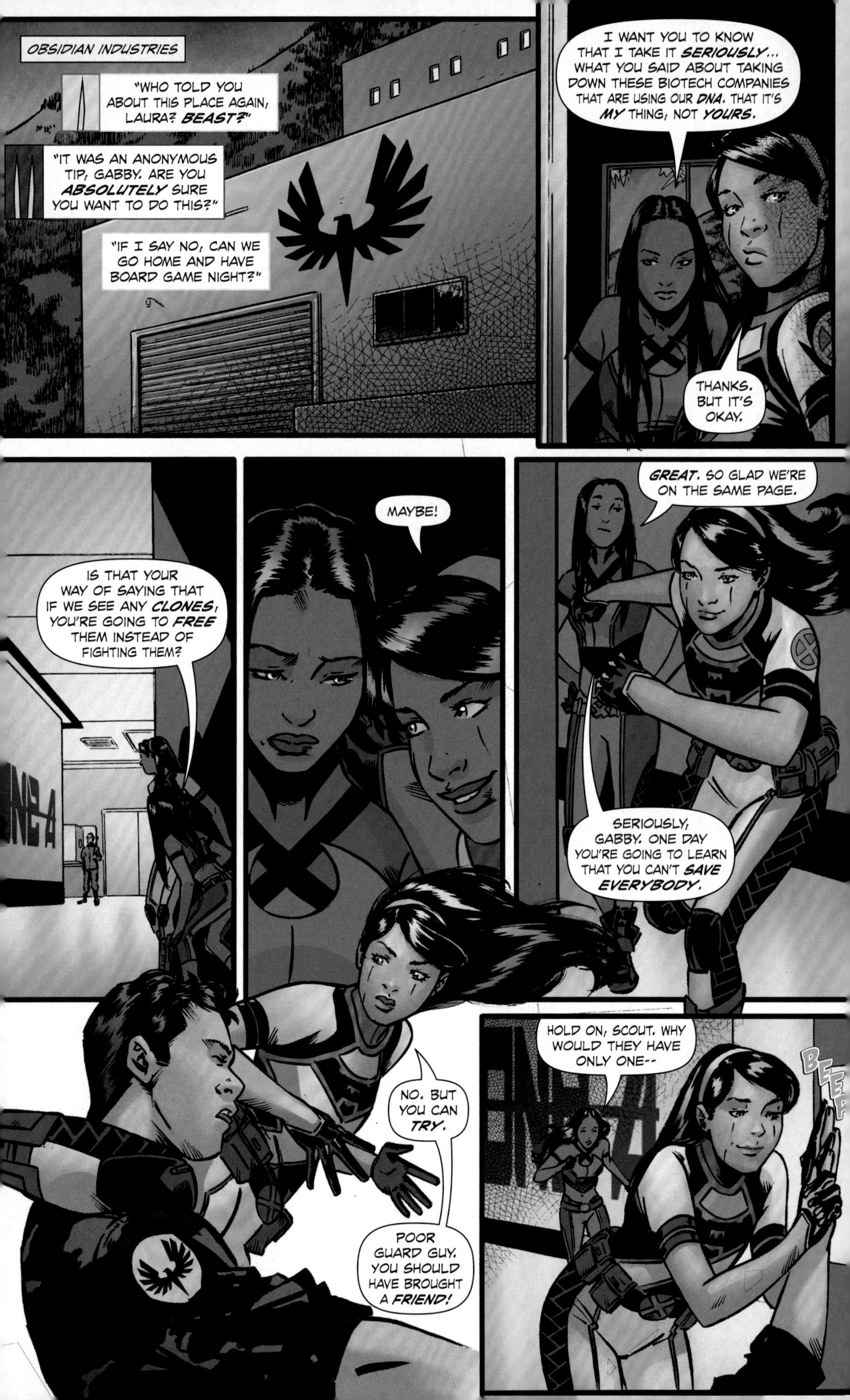
OBSIDIAN INDUSTRIES
"WHO TOLD YOU ABOUT THIS PLACE AGAIN, LAURA? BEAST?"
"IT WAS AN ANONYMOUS TIP, GABBY. ARE YOU ABSOLUTELY SURE YOU WANT TO DO THIS?"
"IF I SAY NO, CAN WE GO HOME AND HAVE BOARD GAME NIGHT?"
I WANT YOU TO KNOW THAT I TAKE IT SERIOUSLY... WHAT YOU SAID ABOUT TAKING DOWN THESE BIOTECH COMPANIES THAT ARE USING OUR DNA. THAT IT'S MY THING, NOT YOURS.
THANKS. BUT IT'S OKAY.
IS THAT YOUR WAY OF SAYING THAT IF WE SEE ANY CLONES, YOU'RE GOING TO FREE THEM INSTEAD OF FIGHTING THEM?
MAYBE!
GREAT. SO GLAD WE'RE ON THE SAME PAGE.
SERIOUSLY, GABBY. ONE DAY YOU'RE GOING TO LEARN THAT YOU CAN'T SAVE EVERYBODY.
NO. BUT YOU CAN TRY.
POOR GUARD GUY. YOU SHOULD HAVE BROUGHT A FRIEND!
HOLD ON, SCOUT. WHY WOULD THEY HAVE ONLY ONE--
BEEP

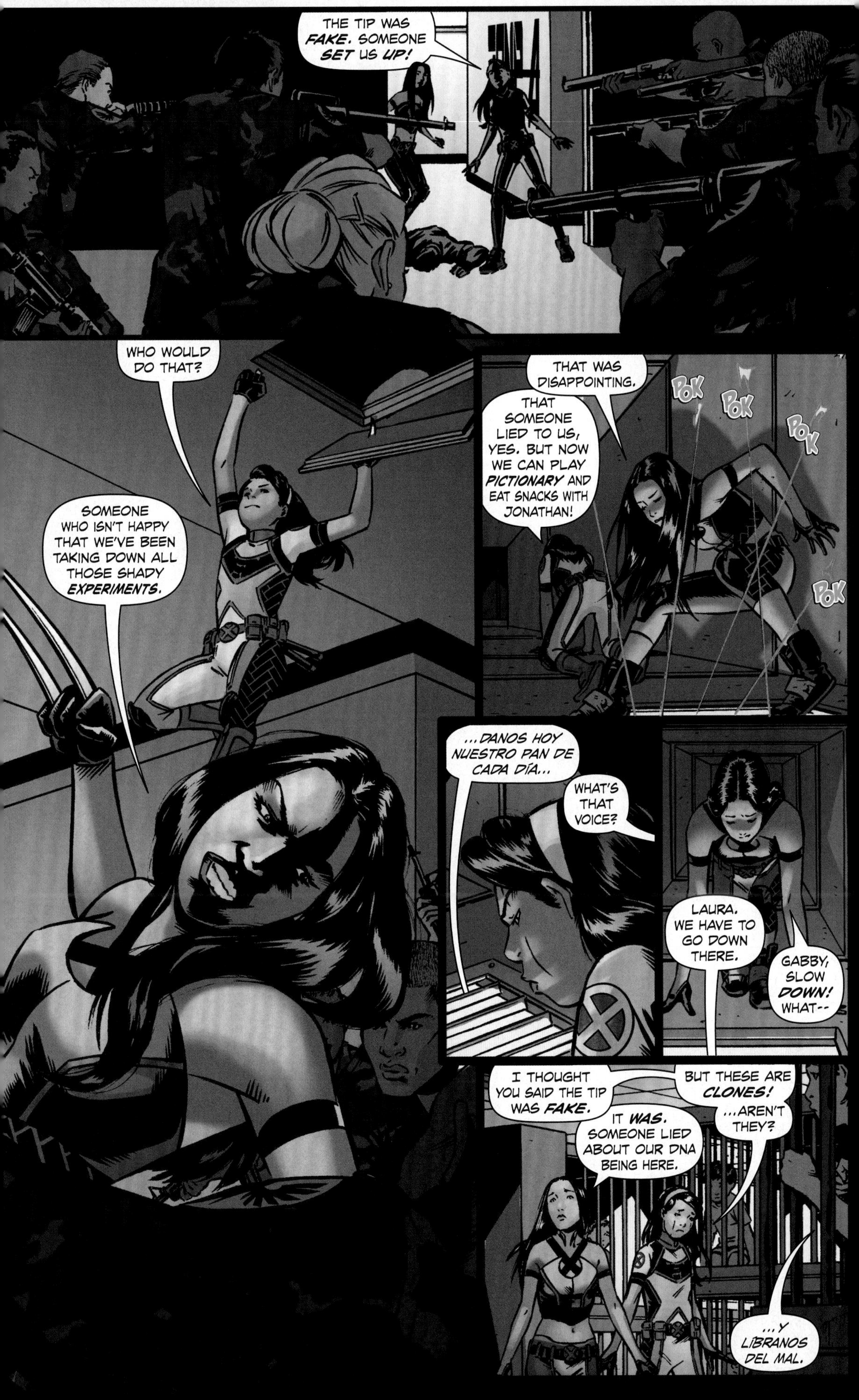

THE TIP WAS FAKE. SOMEONE SET US UP!
WHO WOULD DO THAT?
SOMEONE WHO ISN'T HAPPY THAT WE'VE BEEN TAKING DOWN ALL THOSE SHADY EXPERIMENTS.
THAT WAS DISAPPOINTING.
THAT SOMEONE LIED TO US, YES. BUT NOW WE CAN PLAY PICTIONARY AND EAT SNACKS WITH JONATHAN!
POK
POK
POK
POK
...DANOS HOY NUESTRO PAN DE CADA DÍA...
WHAT'S THAT VOICE?
LAURA. WE HAVE TO GO DOWN THERE.
GABBY, SLOW DOWN! WHAT--
I THOUGHT YOU SAID THE TIP WAS FAKE.
BUT THESE ARE CLONES! ...AREN'T THEY?
IT WAS. SOMEONE LIED ABOUT OUR DNA BEING HERE.
...Y LÍBRANOS DEL MAL.

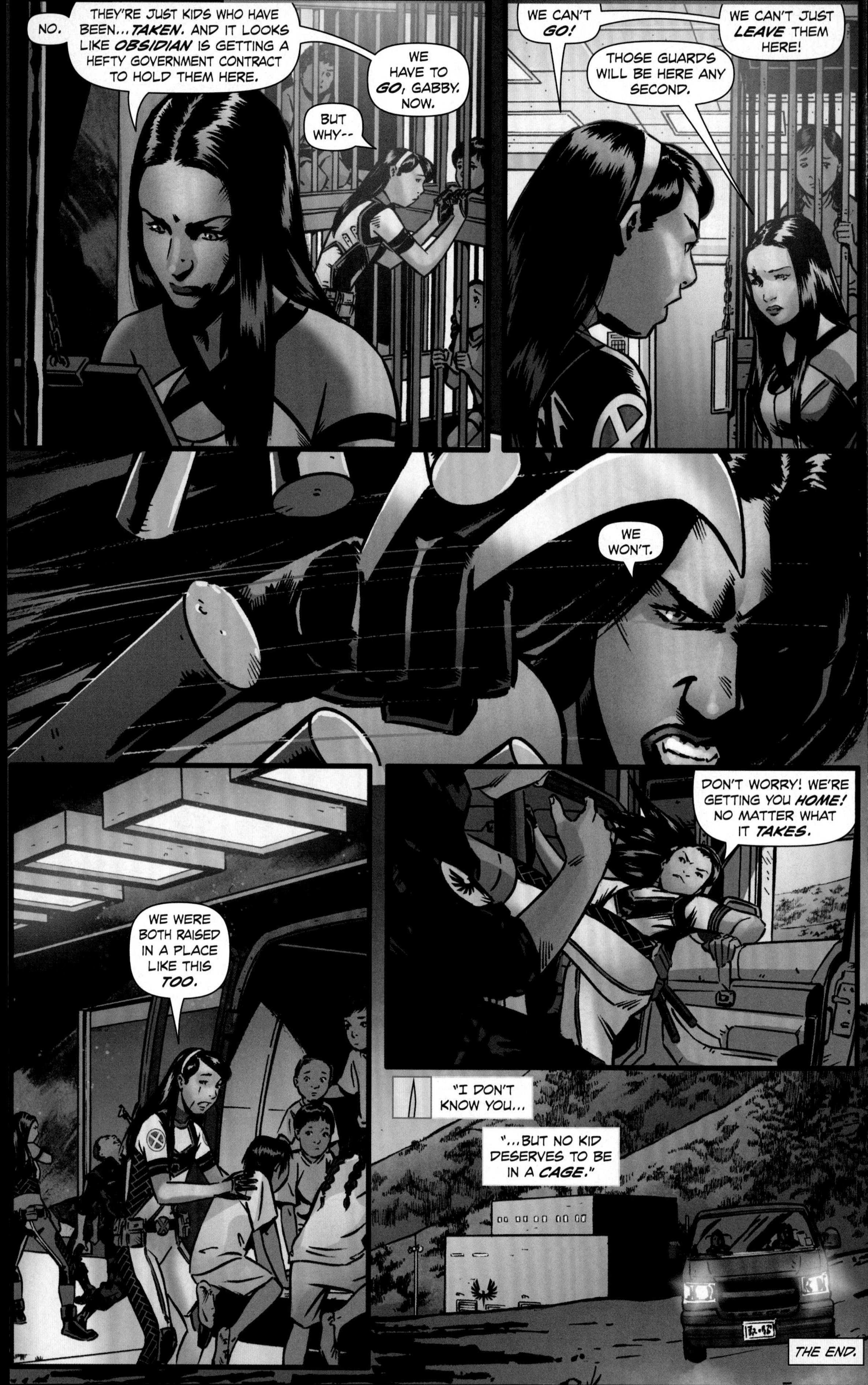
NO.
THEY'RE JUST KIDS WHO HAVE BEEN... TAKEN. AND IT LOOKS LIKE OBSIDIAN IS GETTING A HEFTY GOVERNMENT CONTRACT TO HOLD THEM HERE.
WE HAVE TO GO, GABBY. NOW.
BUT WHY--
WE CAN'T GO!
WE CAN'T JUST LEAVE THEM HERE!
THOSE GUARDS WILL BE HERE ANY SECOND.
WE WON'T.
WE WERE BOTH RAISED IN A PLACE LIKE THIS TOO.
DON'T WORRY! WE'RE GETTING YOU HOME! NO MATTER WHAT IT TAKES.
"I DON'T KNOW YOU...
"...BUT NO KID DESERVES TO BE IN A CAGE."
THE END.

WRITER SPOTLIGHT
EVE L. EWING

PHOTO BY NOLIS ANDERSON

DO YOU REMEMBER THE MOMENT THAT YOU FELL IN LOVE WITH COMICS?

When I was 5 years old, my mom brought me my first Archie comic home from the grocery store and I was hooked. Already I was obsessed with reading anything I could get my hands on--books, but also cereal boxes, paperwork at the doctor's office, literally any printed material I could get my hands on. But this unlocked something new. I think what intrigued me most was the way the same characters could recur and reappear in different iterations over the course of years.

WHAT WAS AN IMPORTANT LESSON ABOUT YOUR CHOSEN FIELD THAT YOU LEARNED EARLY ON THAT HAS STUCK WITH YOU THROUGHOUT YOUR CAREER?

Humility is one of the most important qualities you can have as a writer. Being a writer involves getting rejected a lot, and you need to be able to learn from that experience and move past it without taking it as a personal judgment on your worth. And it also involves having to take feedback and guidance from an editor without being defensive. One of my favorite parts f being a writer is working collaboratively with other people. Even in instances when I seem to be working alone, n always getting input and support from other folks, whether those are editors or peers. And to listen to that nd figure out how to grow forward requires a stance of humility or else you'll be stagnant forever.

WHAT HAS BEEN YOUR FAVORITE PROJECT THAT YOU'VE WORKED ON SO FAR, AND WHY?

f course IRONHEART is just so special. In a way it's a Cinderella story that I was asked to take on the title, and it's been oth very personally meaningful and fulfilling for me as well as inspiring to see how other people take to and respond the character. It's a once-in-a-lifetime opportunity to be able to tell that story. And in addition to the creative joy of orking on it, the artistic and editorial team is unmatched.

WHAT HAS BEEN YOUR FAVORITE EXPERIENCE WITH A FAN?

here have been so many. I really love intergenerational oments--parents bringing their kids to meet me. In articular I have met a lot of dads bringing their daughters get their comics signed, and that's just so beautiful. If I ad to pick one favorite moment, it would probably be at 2E2 where a little girl came up to me shyly and she had this wesome Ms. Marvel costume that her parents had made ovingly at home--nothing store-bought. And she had a Totoro nyard. I am a big Hayao Miyazaki fan and I was dressed as otoro for the con, and she was excited that I was also into otoro. It was just a sweet moment.

ATCH EVE'S WORK IN *IRONHEART: THOSE WITH OURAGE TPB* AND *IRONHEART #9* --ON SALE NOW!

FEARLESS #2

PAGE 2

Panel 2. Back in the hallway, Scout leaps several feet into the air and grasps an air duct with her claws, pulling the cover out of the wall while X-23 holds the assassins off momentarily.

> **SCOUT:** Who would do that?

> **X-23:** Someone who isn't happy that we've been taking down all those shady **experiments.**

ARTIST SPOTLIGHT
ALITHA E. MARTINEZ

DO YOU REMEMBER THE MOMENT THAT YOU FELL IN LOVE WITH COMICS

It wasn't so much a single moment. For most of my childhood, I didn't kno
that comic books existed. I didn't get my first comic until I was 12 years ol
after returning to this country from Curaçao. Since kindergarten I'd been tellin
stories with pictures, feeling as if it was something that I was supposed to do

WHEN DID YOU KNOW THAT YOU WANTED TO BE A COMICS ARTIST?

Literally all my life. I just didn't know that it was a profession. Then I didn't kno
that it wasn't a thing that girls did.

WHAT WAS AN IMPORTANT LESSON ABOUT YOUR CHOSEN FIELD THAT YOU LEARNED EARL
ON THAT HAS STUCK WITH YOU THROUGHOUT YOUR CAREER?

I learned to stand. Blindly stand. Work harder, longer, work through pain, work through tears, work because you mus
and work because (later on I learned this) you are the first woman of a certain color at both Marvel and DC and yo
fight so that others won't have to fight as hard. Once something is done it becomes elementary, as if it's always bee
so. Of course girls draw comics! Haven't they always?

WHAT HAS BEEN YOUR PROUDEST MOMENT IN COMICS?

I'm still working toward that. Last year BLACK PANTHER: WORLD OF WAKANDA won an Eisner. How incredible. I'm sti
wondering about that and what it means. I wasn't in attendance at SDCC, so I woke up to a flurry akin to Christma
morning. My son said, "You've earned this one, own the next one." No pressure there.

WHAT HAS BEEN YOUR FAVORITE EXPERIENCE WITH A FAN?

The moment that stuck with me was when I did a panel at SVA. I had arrived
early and I'd been sitting in the front row when the other panelists were taking
to the stage. I was slow--I had broken my tailbone, and just looking at those
metal folding chairs was making me uncomfortable. Finally as the audience
began to trickle in, I took the cue and went to the stage. Suddenly, a girl
started to cry. Her friends brought her over, and she said, "Someone who looks
like me draws comics." I saw her later on the same year at NYCC. She was
strong and confident. Not a tear in sight.

FOR MORE OF ALITHA'S WORK, CHECK OUT **BLACK PANTHER: WORLD OF
WAKANDA TPB** AND **MOON GIRL & DEVIL DINOSAUR #46**--ON SALE NOW!

COLOR ARTIST SPOTLIGHT
RACHELLE ROSENBERG

WHAT WAS AN IMPORTANT LESSON ABOUT YOUR CHOSEN FIELD THAT YOU LEARNED EARLY ON THAT HAS STUCK WITH YOU THROUGHOUT YOUR CAREER?

Always keep growing. As an artist, as a professional, as a person. I've always been a driven person, but I learned early on in my career that if I wanted to be the best, I would continually have to grow. I could never feel like I "arrived." I would continually have to push myself. Learn new things from other professionals or from just experimenting.

It's very easy to get caught up in the comics world. Deadlines can be very demanding; throw life in there and there is not a lot of time left over. But if you want to be the best, you have to keep growing.

WHAT HAS BEEN YOUR PROUDEST MOMENT IN COMICS?

I think one of my proudest moments in comics was when Marvel came to my home studio to film *Marvel Quickdraw*. It gave me a chance to go back and reflect on my journey as a comic artist: where I started, eleven years ago, working on a single book for Image, to where I am now, coloring exclusively for Marvel Comics.

My journey wasn't easy. I had several moments when I almost gave up. I went through a time when I was so broke I had to pay my mortgage with my credit card. And having kids made it even more terrifying. But I never stopped believing in myself and what I could do. And now that I work in comics and am no longer paying my mortgage with my credit card, I hope to encourage other artists to never give up on their dreams.

WHAT HAS BEEN YOUR FAVORITE EXPERIENCE WITH A FAN?

I don't know that I have ONE experience with a fan that stands out from the rest. I have to say, though, my fans are the BEST. It is truly my favorite part of attending conventions, meeting my fans. Shaking their hands, taking photos, giving hugs. It is a huge part of what inspires me to give my all.

BE SURE TO CHECK OUT MORE OF RACHELLE'S WORK IN **UNCANNY X-MEN: DISASSEMBLED TPB** --ON SALE NOW--AND **MARVEL'S SPIDER-MAN: VELOCITY #1** --ON SALE 8/28!

Hello, True Believers!

Thanks for joining us for another issue of **FEARLESS**, where we get to profile and shine a light on some of the fantastic female creators who help make Marvel marvelous! Be sure to check out the stands of your local comic book store for more of Eve's, Alitha's and Rachelle's amazing work.

And don't forget to flip to the next issue page to see what other female creative-led projects are coming out in the Marvel universe and what's in store for the next chapter of **FEARLESS**. Trust us, you're not going to want to miss out on what Ms. Marvel uncovers at Camp Gloriana--or on an all-new adventure with none other than Patsy Walker, A.K.A. Hellcat!!!

Until next time, stay Fearless!
Sarah, Annalise, Lauren, Kathleen, Shannon, Alanna & Lindsey.

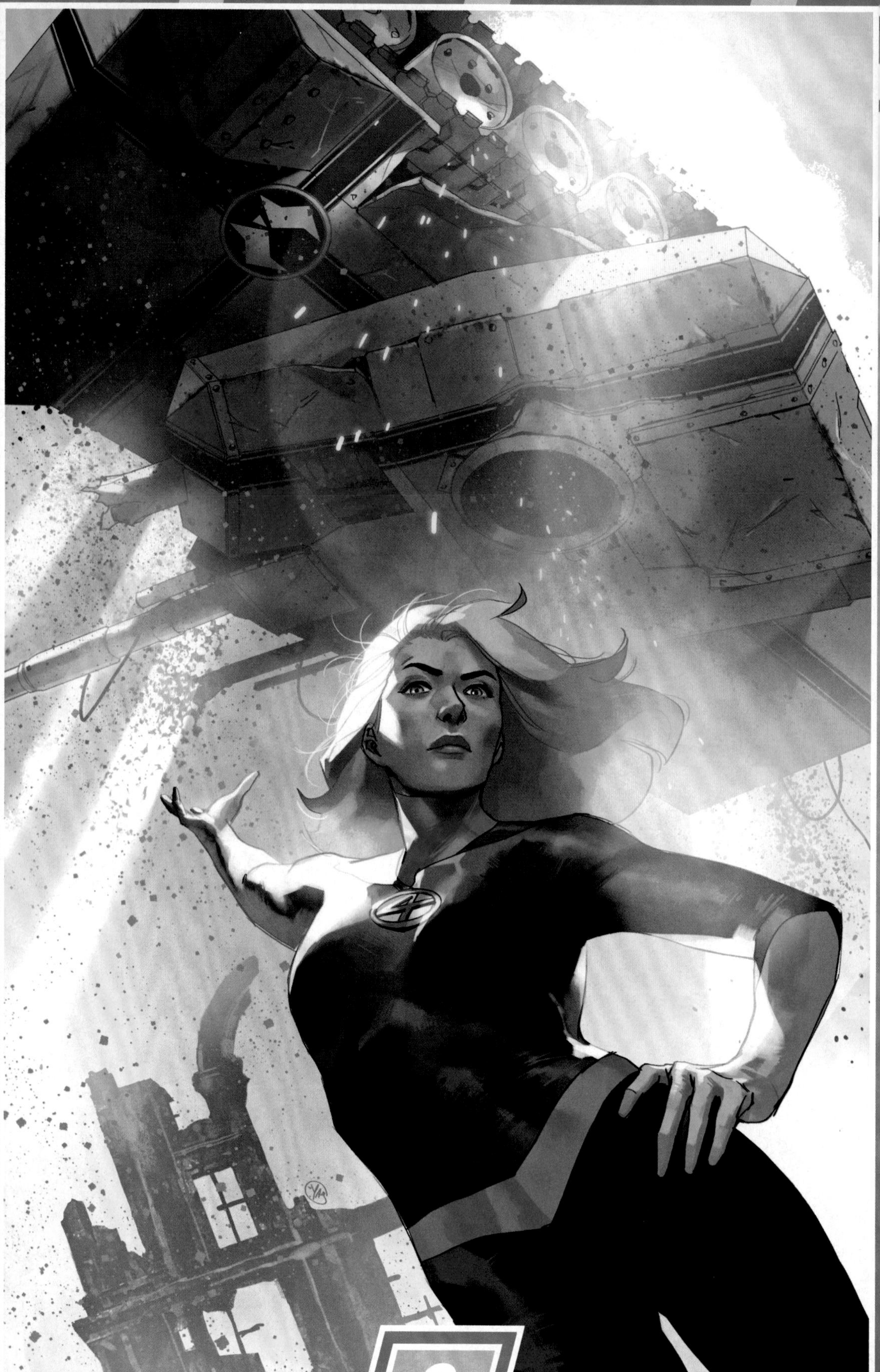

3

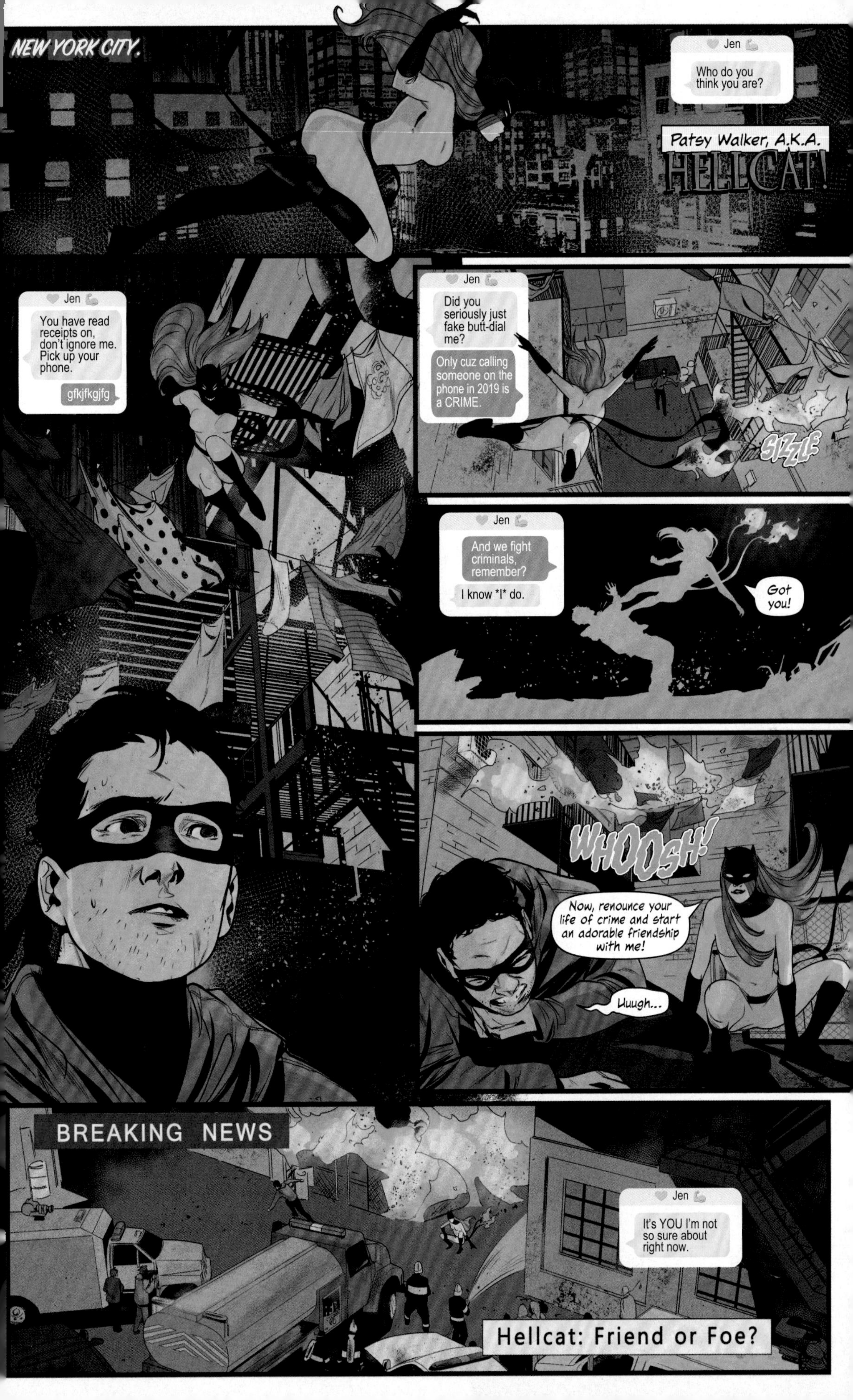
NEW YORK CITY.
Jen
Who do you think you are?
Patsy Walker, A.K.A. HELLCAT!
Jen
You have read receipts on, don't ignore me. Pick up your phone.
gfkjfkgjfg
Jen
Did you seriously just fake butt-dial me?
Only cuz calling someone on the phone in 2019 is a CRIME.
SIZZLE
Jen
And we fight criminals, remember?
I know *I* do.
Got you!
WHOOSH!
Now, renounce your life of crime and start an adorable friendship with me!
Uuugh...
BREAKING NEWS
Jen
It's YOU I'm not so sure about right now.
Hellcat: Friend or Foe?

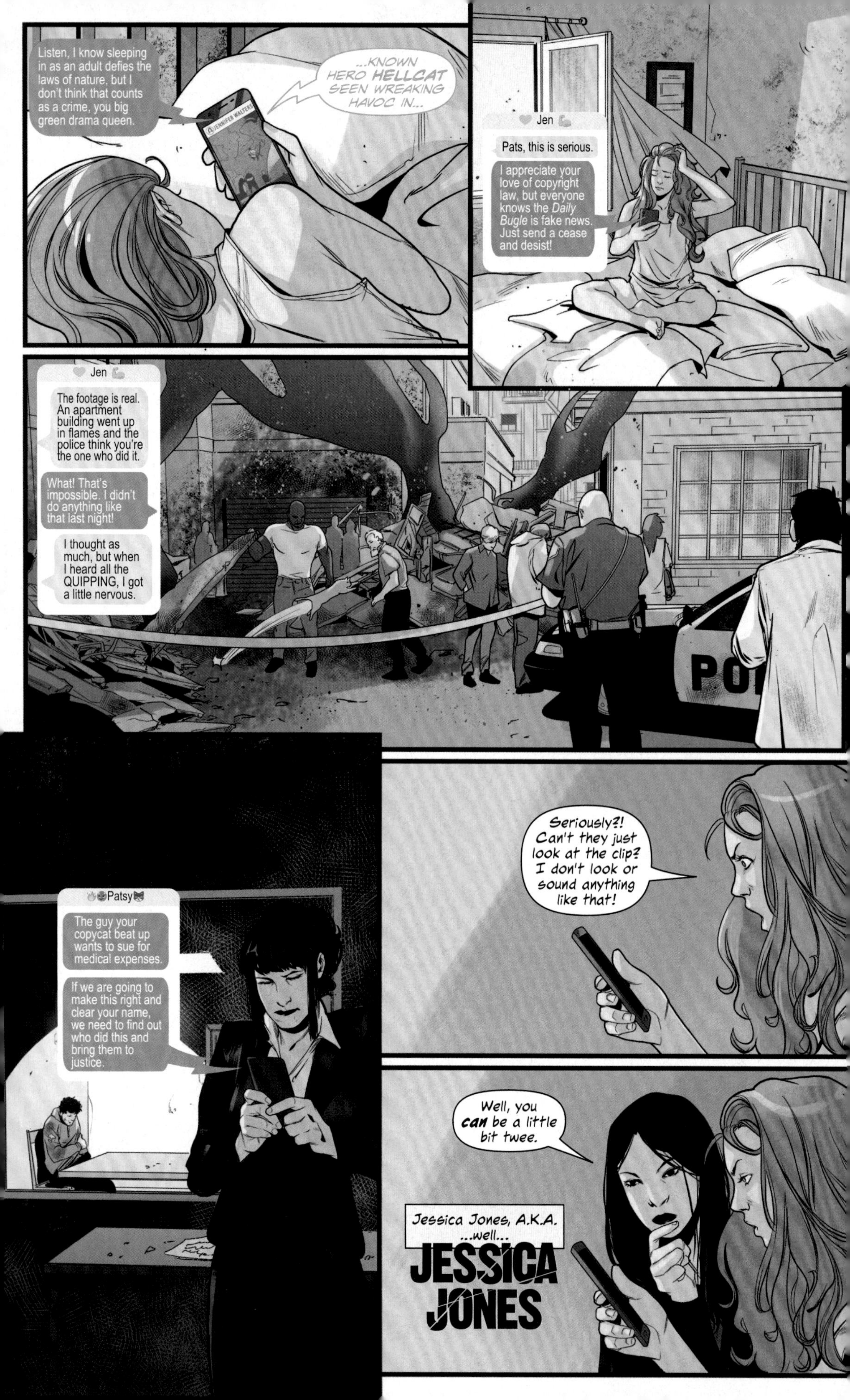

Listen, I know sleeping in as an adult defies the laws of nature, but I don't think that counts as a crime, you big green drama queen.
...KNOWN HERO HELLCAT SEEN WREAKING HAVOC IN...
JENNIFER WALTERS
Jen
Pats, this is serious.
I appreciate your love of copyright law, but everyone knows the Daily Bugle is fake news. Just send a cease and desist!
Jen
The footage is real. An apartment building went up in flames and the police think you're the one who did it.
What! That's impossible. I didn't do anything like that last night!
I thought as much, but when I heard all the QUIPPING, I got a little nervous.
POL
Patsy
The guy your copycat beat up wants to sue for medical expenses.
If we are going to make this right and clear your name, we need to find out who did this and bring them to justice.
Seriously?! Can't they just look at the clip? I don't look or sound anything like that!
Well, you can be a little bit twee.
Jessica Jones, A.K.A. ...well...
JESSICA JONES

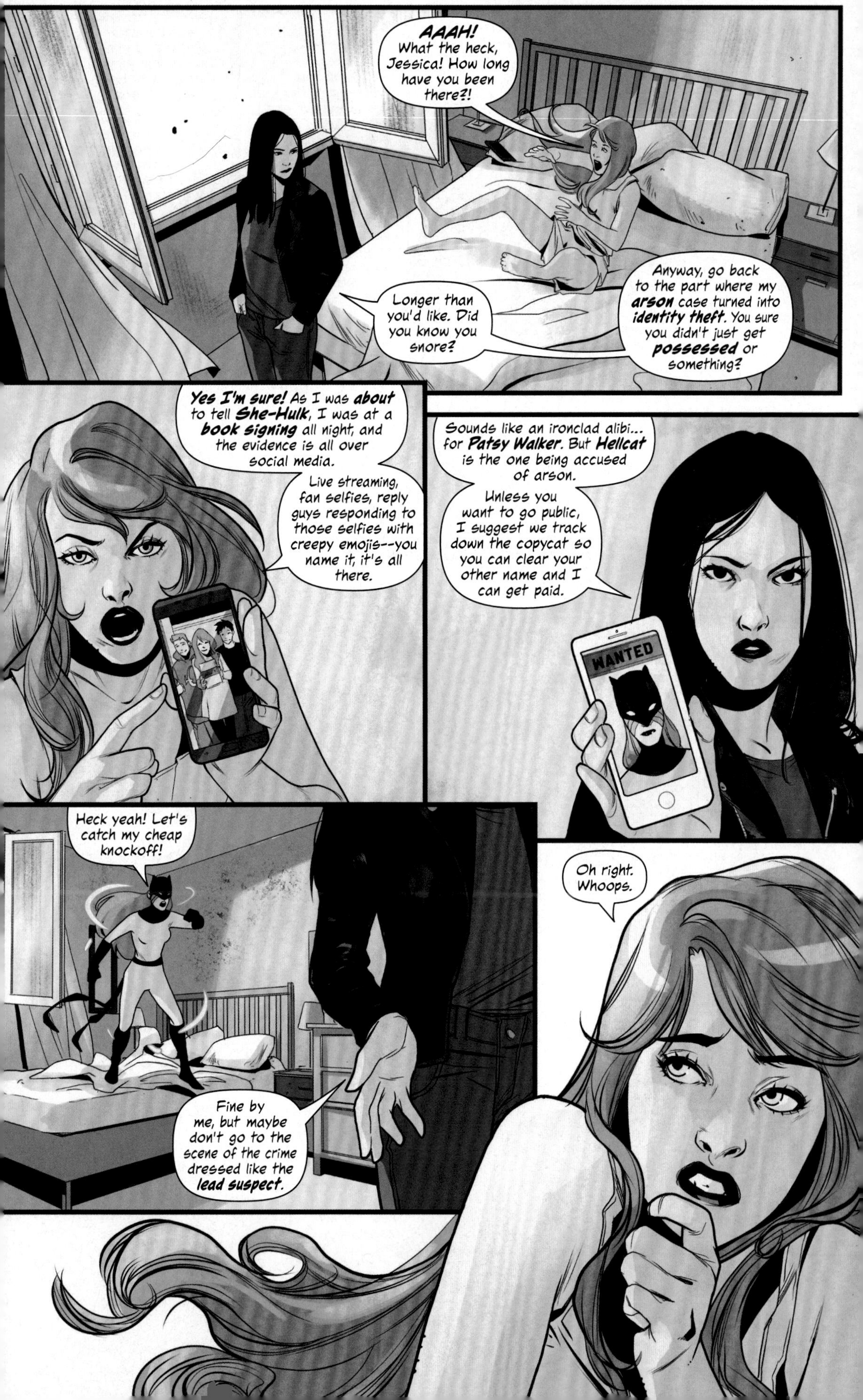
AAAH! What the heck, Jessica! How long have you been there?!
Longer than you'd like. Did you know you snore?
Anyway, go back to the part where my arson case turned into identity theft. You sure you didn't just get possessed or something?
Yes I'm sure! As I was about to tell She-Hulk, I was at a book signing all night, and the evidence is all over social media.
Live streaming, fan selfies, reply guys responding to those selfies with creepy emojis--you name it, it's all there.
Sounds like an ironclad alibi... for Patsy Walker. But Hellcat is the one being accused of arson.
Unless you want to go public, I suggest we track down the copycat so you can clear your other name and I can get paid.
WANTED
Heck yeah! Let's catch my cheap knockoff!
Fine by me, but maybe don't go to the scene of the crime dressed like the lead suspect.
Oh right. Whoops.

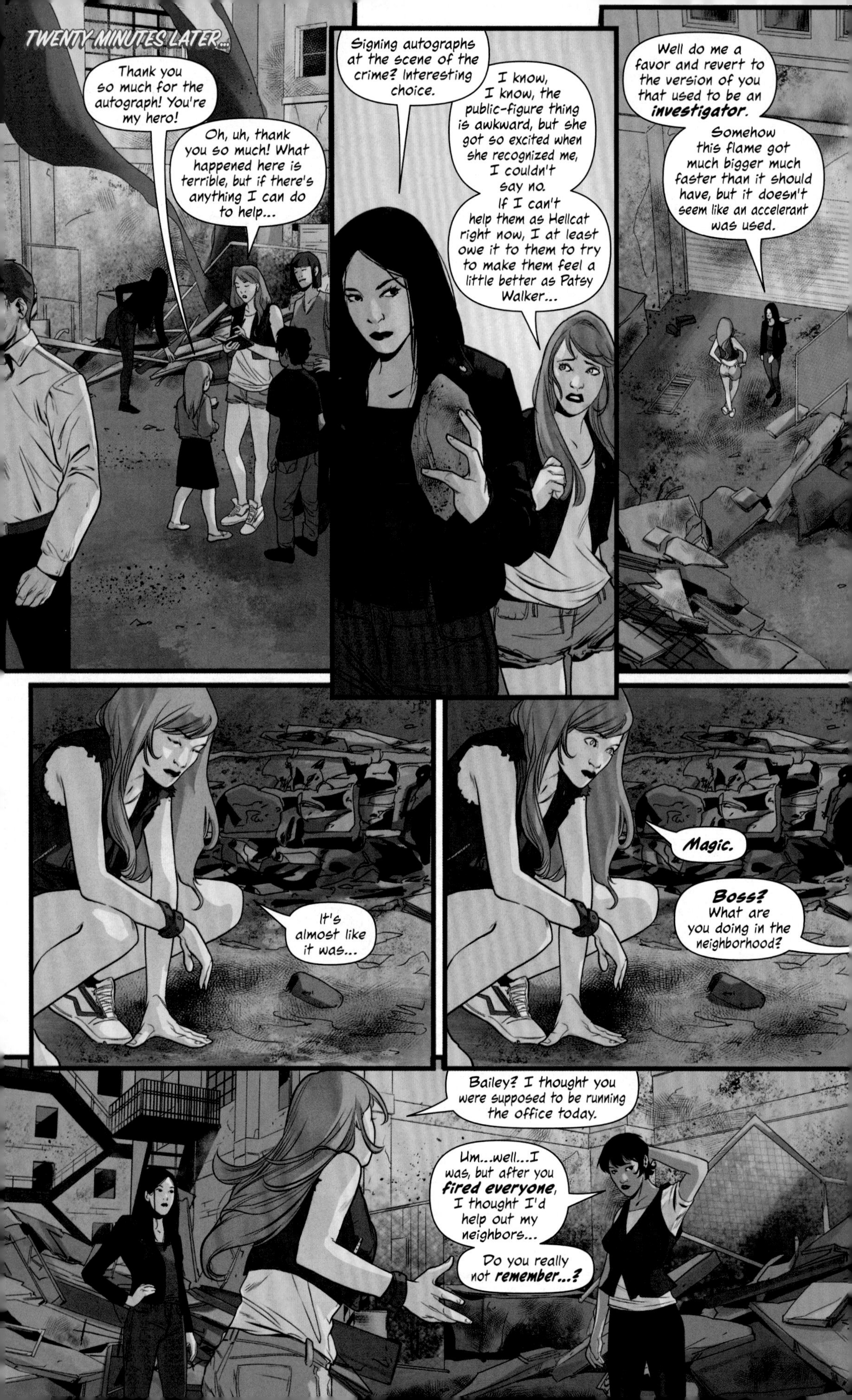
TWENTY MINUTES LATER...
Thank you so much for the autograph! You're my hero!
Oh, uh, thank you so much! What happened here is terrible, but if there's anything I can do to help...
Signing autographs at the scene of the crime? Interesting choice.
I know, I know, the public-figure thing is awkward, but she got so excited when she recognized me, I couldn't say no.
If I can't help them as Hellcat right now, I at least owe it to them to try to make them feel a little better as Patsy Walker...
Well do me a favor and revert to the version of you that used to be an investigator.
Somehow this flame got much bigger much faster than it should have, but it doesn't seem like an accelerant was used.
It's almost like it was...
Magic.
Boss? What are you doing in the neighborhood?
Bailey? I thought you were supposed to be running the office today.
Um...well...I was, but after you fired everyone, I thought I'd help out my neighbors...
Do you really not remember...?

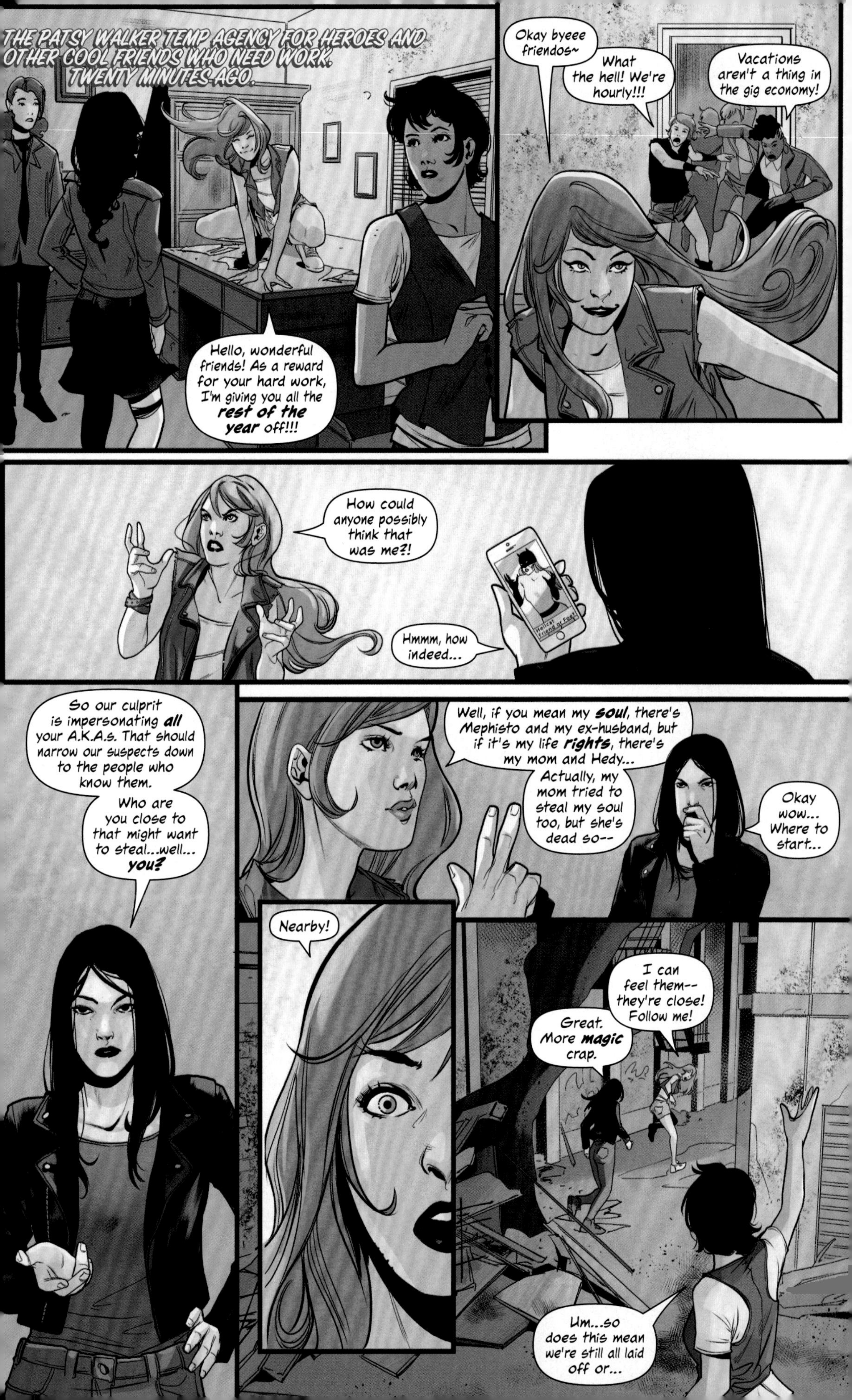
THE PATSY WALKER TEMP AGENCY FOR HEROES AND OTHER COOL FRIENDS WHO NEED WORK. TWENTY MINUTES AGO.
Hello, wonderful friends! As a reward for your hard work, I'm giving you all the **rest of the year** off!!!
Okay byeee friendos~
What the hell! We're hourly!!!
Vacations aren't a thing in the gig economy!
How could anyone possibly think that was me?!
Hellcat Friend or Foe?
Hmmm, how indeed...
So our culprit is impersonating **all** your A.K.A.s. That should narrow our suspects down to the people who know them.
Who are you close to that might want to steal...well... **you?**
Well, if you mean my **soul**, there's Mephisto and my ex-husband, but if it's my life **rights**, there's my mom and Hedy...
Actually, my mom tried to steal my soul too, but she's dead so--
Okay wow... Where to start...
Nearby!
I can feel them--they're close! Follow me!
Great. More **magic** crap.
Um...so does this mean we're still all laid off or...

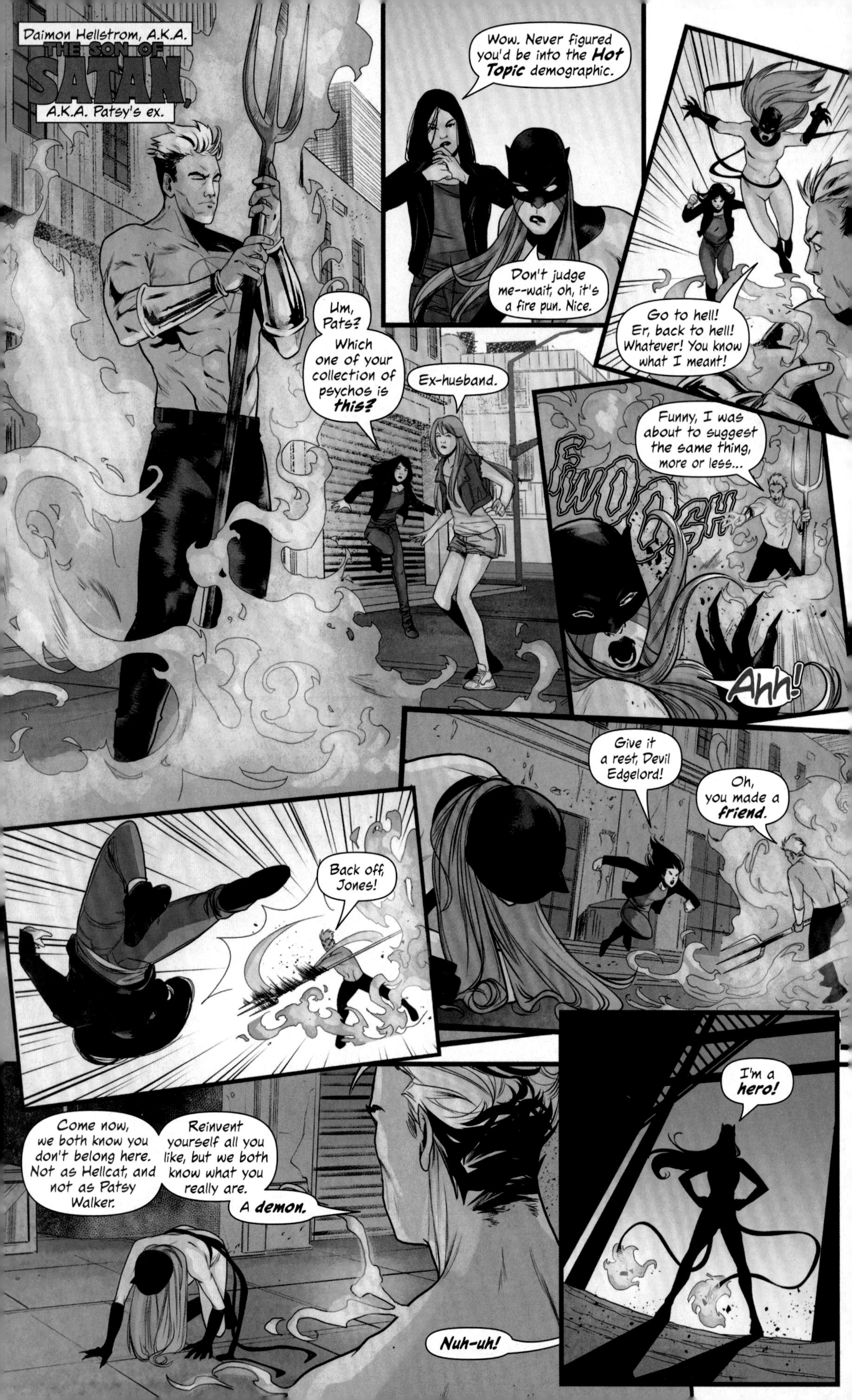

Daimon Hellstrom, A.K.A.
THE SON OF SATAN,
A.K.A. Patsy's ex.
Wow. Never figured you'd be into the Hot Topic demographic.
Don't judge me--wait, oh, it's a fire pun. Nice.
Go to hell! Er, back to hell! Whatever! You know what I meant!
Um, Pats? Which one of your collection of psychos is this?
Ex-husband.
Funny, I was about to suggest the same thing, more or less...
FWOOSH
Ahh!
Give it a rest, Devil Edgelord!
Oh, you made a friend.
Back off, Jones!
Come now, we both know you don't belong here. Not as Hellcat, and not as Patsy Walker.
Reinvent yourself all you like, but we both know what you really are.
A demon.
Nuh-uh!
I'm a hero!

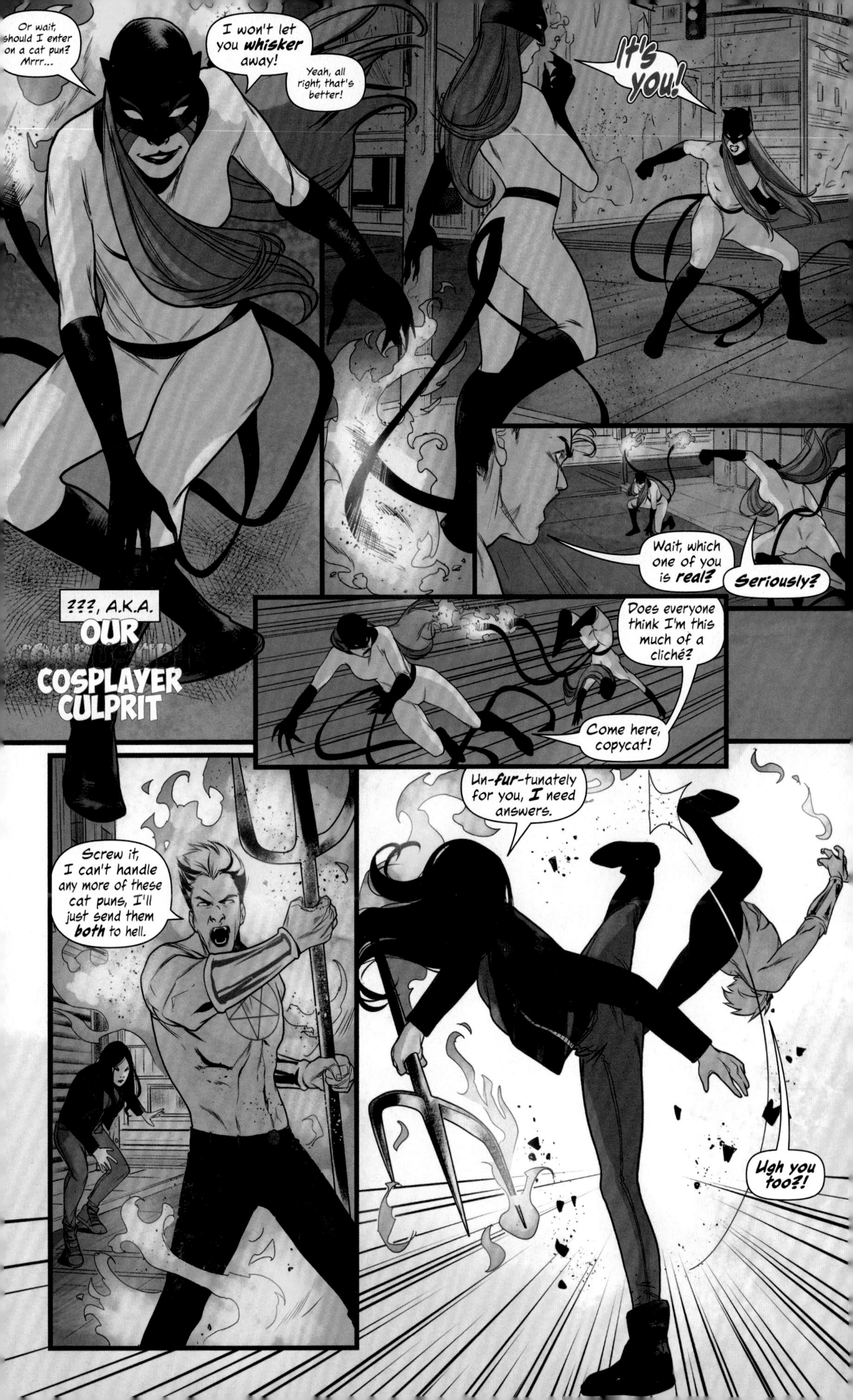
Or wait, should I enter on a cat pun? Mrrr...
I won't let you whisker away!
Yeah, all right, that's better!
It's you!
Wait, which one of you is real?
Seriously?
???, A.K.A.
OUR
COSPLAYER CULPRIT
Does everyone think I'm this much of a cliché?
Come here, copycat!
Screw it, I can't handle any more of these cat puns, I'll just send them both to hell.
Un-fur-tunately for you, I need answers.
Ugh you too?!

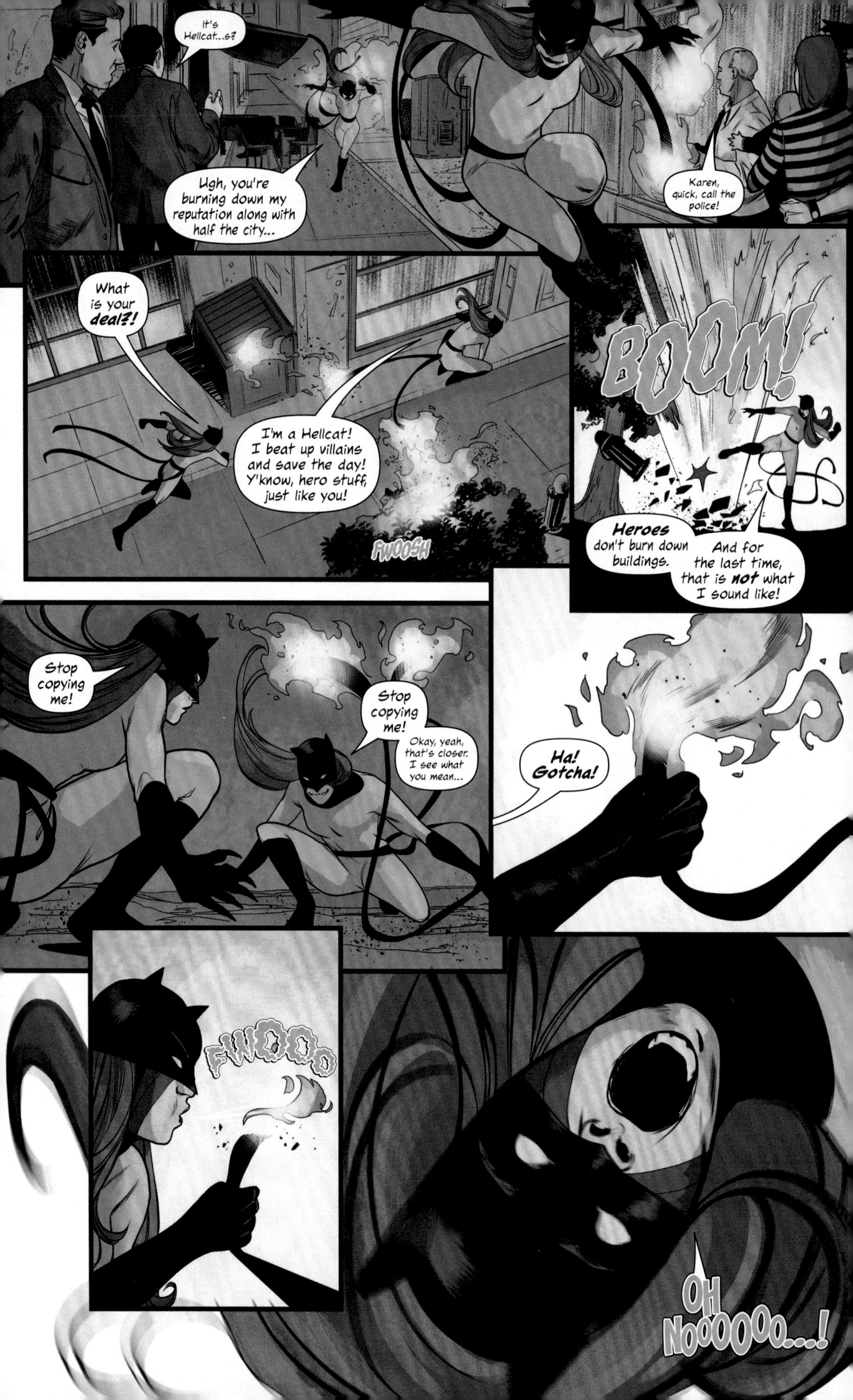

It's Hellcat...s?
Ugh, you're burning down my reputation along with half the city...
Karen, quick, call the police!
What is your deal?!
I'm a Hellcat! I beat up villains and save the day! Y'know, hero stuff, just like you!
FWOOSH
BOOM!
Heroes don't burn down buildings.
And for the last time, that is not what I sound like!
Stop copying me!
Stop copying me!
Okay, yeah, that's closer. I see what you mean...
Ha! Gotcha!
FWOOO
OH NOOOOOO...!

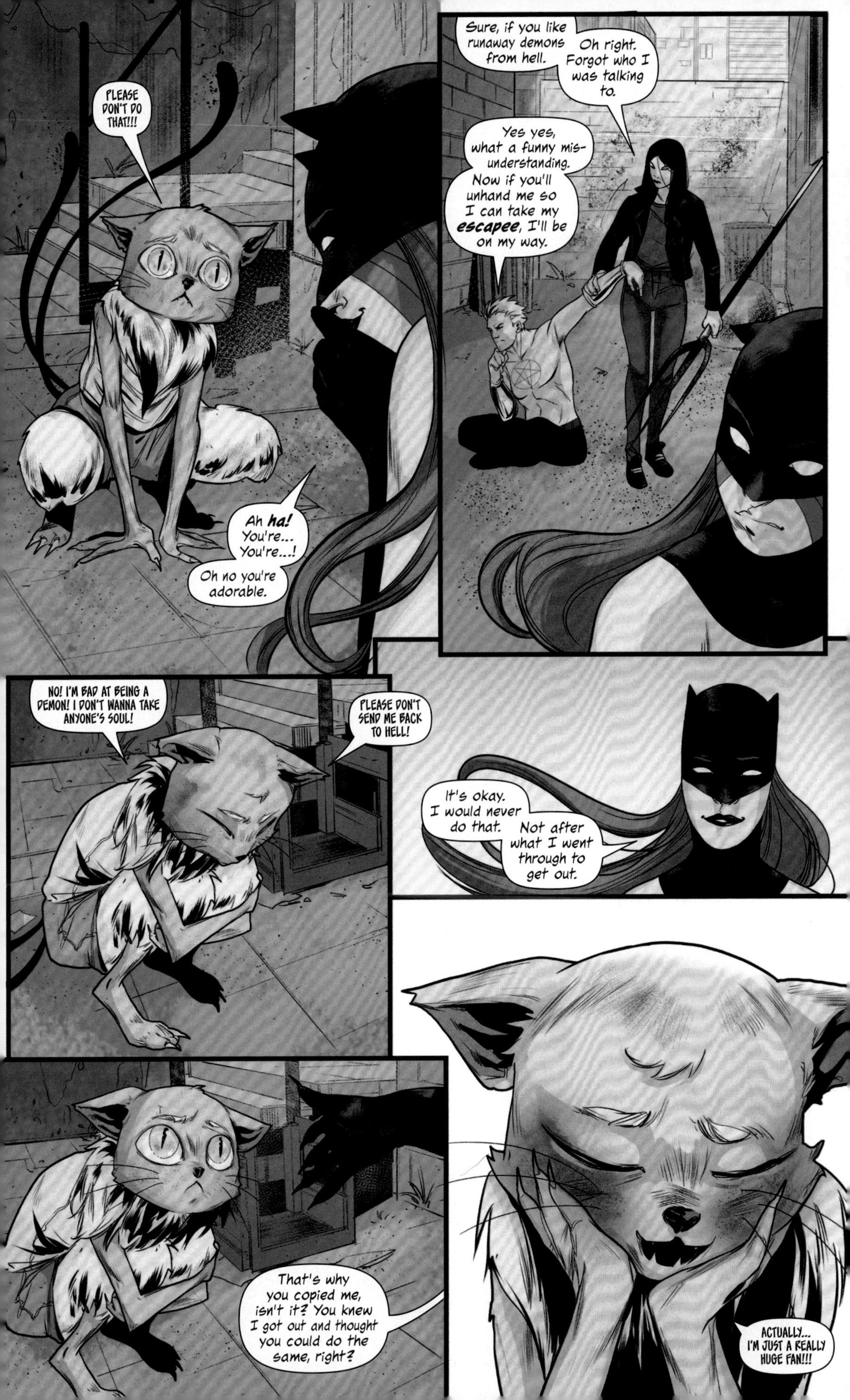

PLEASE DON'T DO THAT!!!
Ah ha! You're... You're...!
Oh no you're adorable.
Sure, if you like runaway demons from hell.
Oh right. Forgot who I was talking to.
Yes yes, what a funny mis-understanding. Now if you'll unhand me so I can take my escapee, I'll be on my way.
NO! I'M BAD AT BEING A DEMON! I DON'T WANNA TAKE ANYONE'S SOUL!
PLEASE DON'T SEND ME BACK TO HELL!
It's okay. I would never do that.
Not after what I went through to get out.
That's why you copied me, isn't it? You knew I got out and thought you could do the same, right?
ACTUALLY... I'M JUST A REALLY HUGE FAN!!!

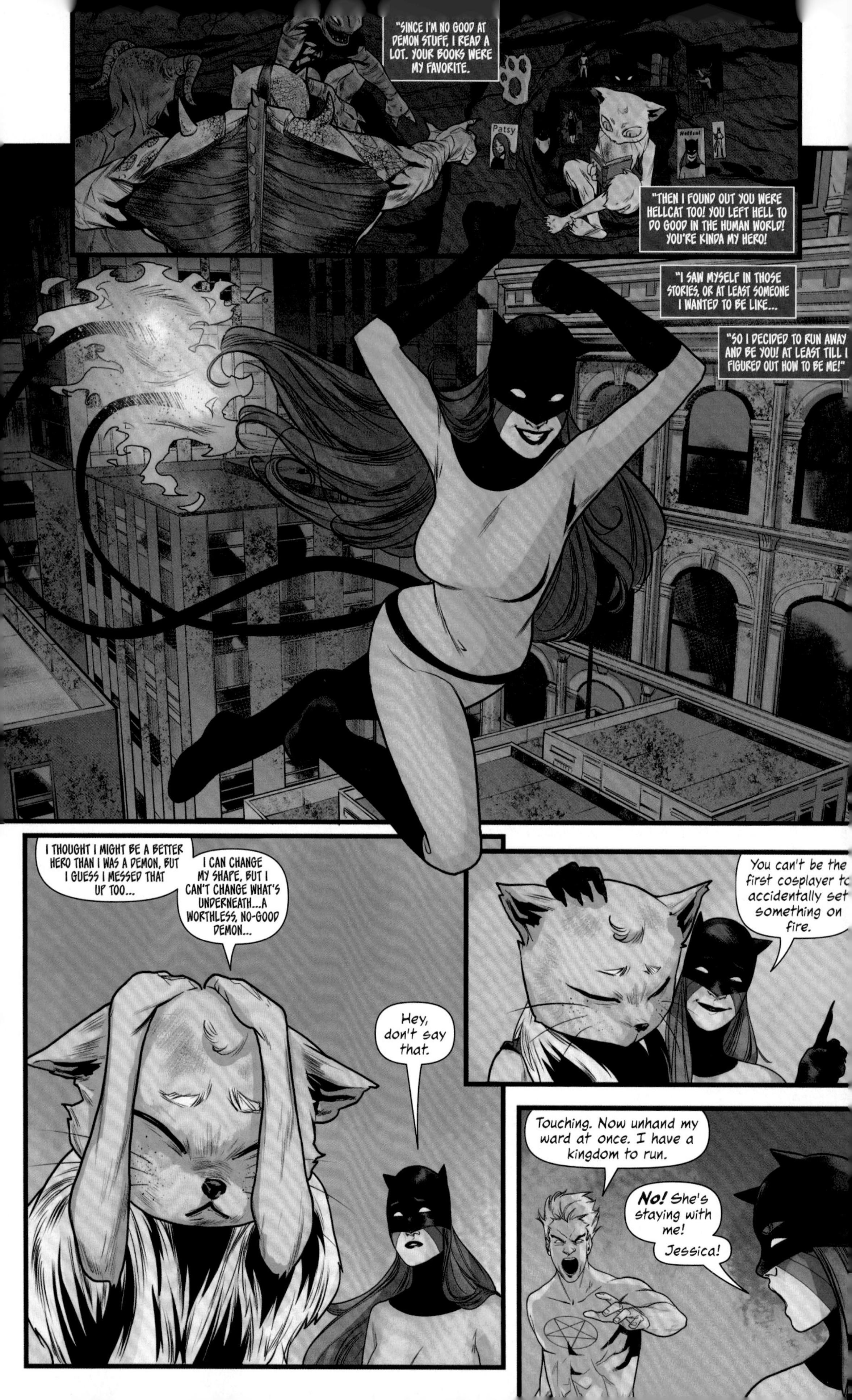
"SINCE I'M NO GOOD AT DEMON STUFF, I READ A LOT. YOUR BOOKS WERE MY FAVORITE.
Patsy
Hellcat
"THEN I FOUND OUT YOU WERE HELLCAT TOO! YOU LEFT HELL TO DO GOOD IN THE HUMAN WORLD! YOU'RE KINDA MY HERO!
"I SAW MYSELF IN THOSE STORIES, OR AT LEAST SOMEONE I WANTED TO BE LIKE...
"SO I DECIDED TO RUN AWAY AND BE YOU! AT LEAST TILL I FIGURED OUT HOW TO BE ME!"
I THOUGHT I MIGHT BE A BETTER HERO THAN I WAS A DEMON, BUT I GUESS I MESSED THAT UP TOO...
I CAN CHANGE MY SHAPE, BUT I CAN'T CHANGE WHAT'S UNDERNEATH...A WORTHLESS, NO-GOOD DEMON...
Hey, don't say that.
You can't be the first cosplayer to accidentally set something on fire.
Touching. Now unhand my ward at once. I have a kingdom to run.
No! She's staying with me!
Jessica!

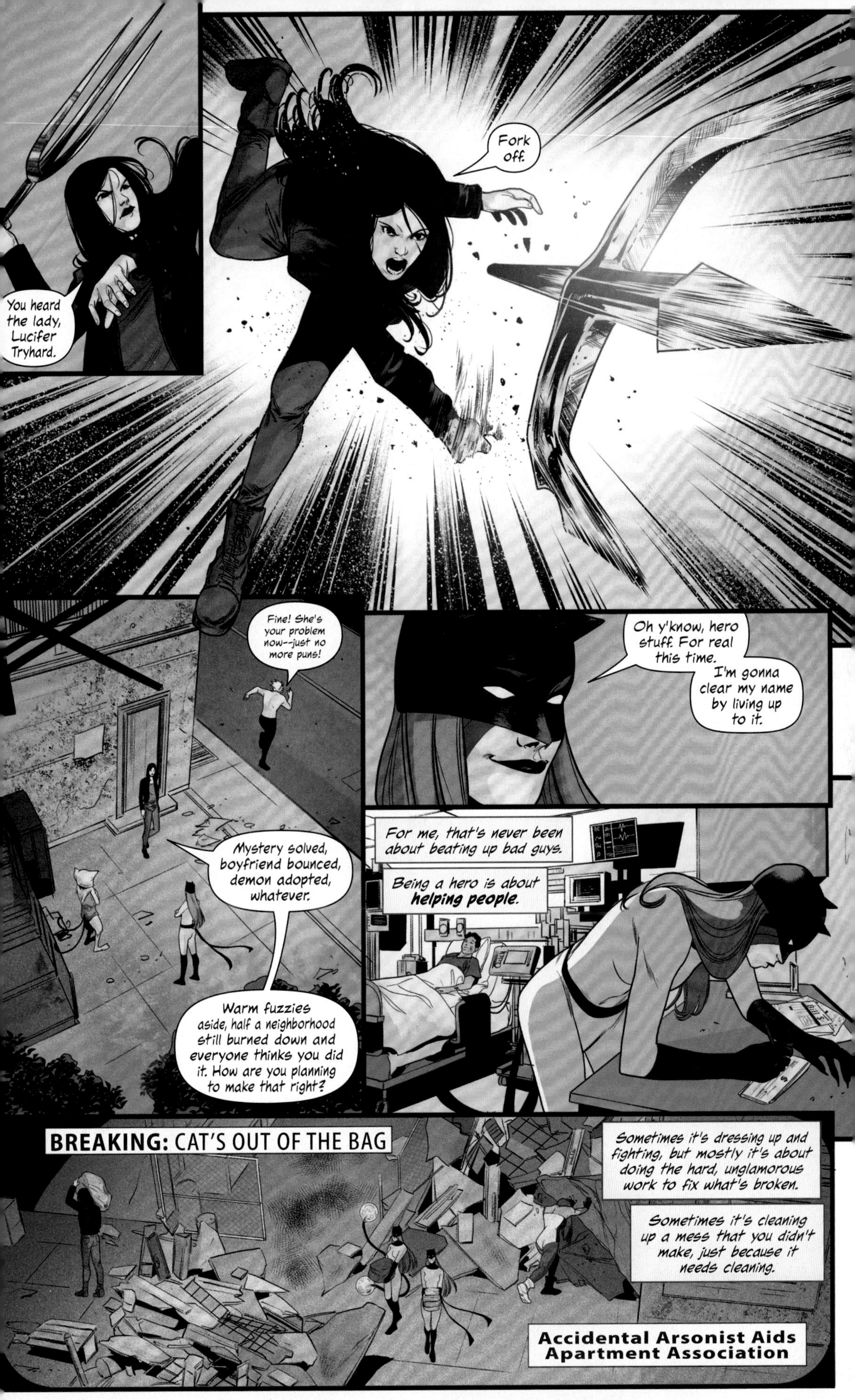

You heard the lady, Lucifer Tryhard.
Fork off.
Fine! She's your problem now--just no more puns!
Oh y'know, hero stuff. For real this time.
I'm gonna clear my name by living up to it.
Mystery solved, boyfriend bounced, demon adopted, whatever.
Warm fuzzies aside, half a neighborhood still burned down and everyone thinks you did it. How are you planning to make that right?
For me, that's never been about beating up bad guys.
Being a hero is about helping people.
BREAKING: CAT'S OUT OF THE BAG
Sometimes it's dressing up and fighting, but mostly it's about doing the hard, unglamorous work to fix what's broken.
Sometimes it's cleaning up a mess that you didn't make, just because it needs cleaning.
Accidental Arsonist Aids Apartment Association

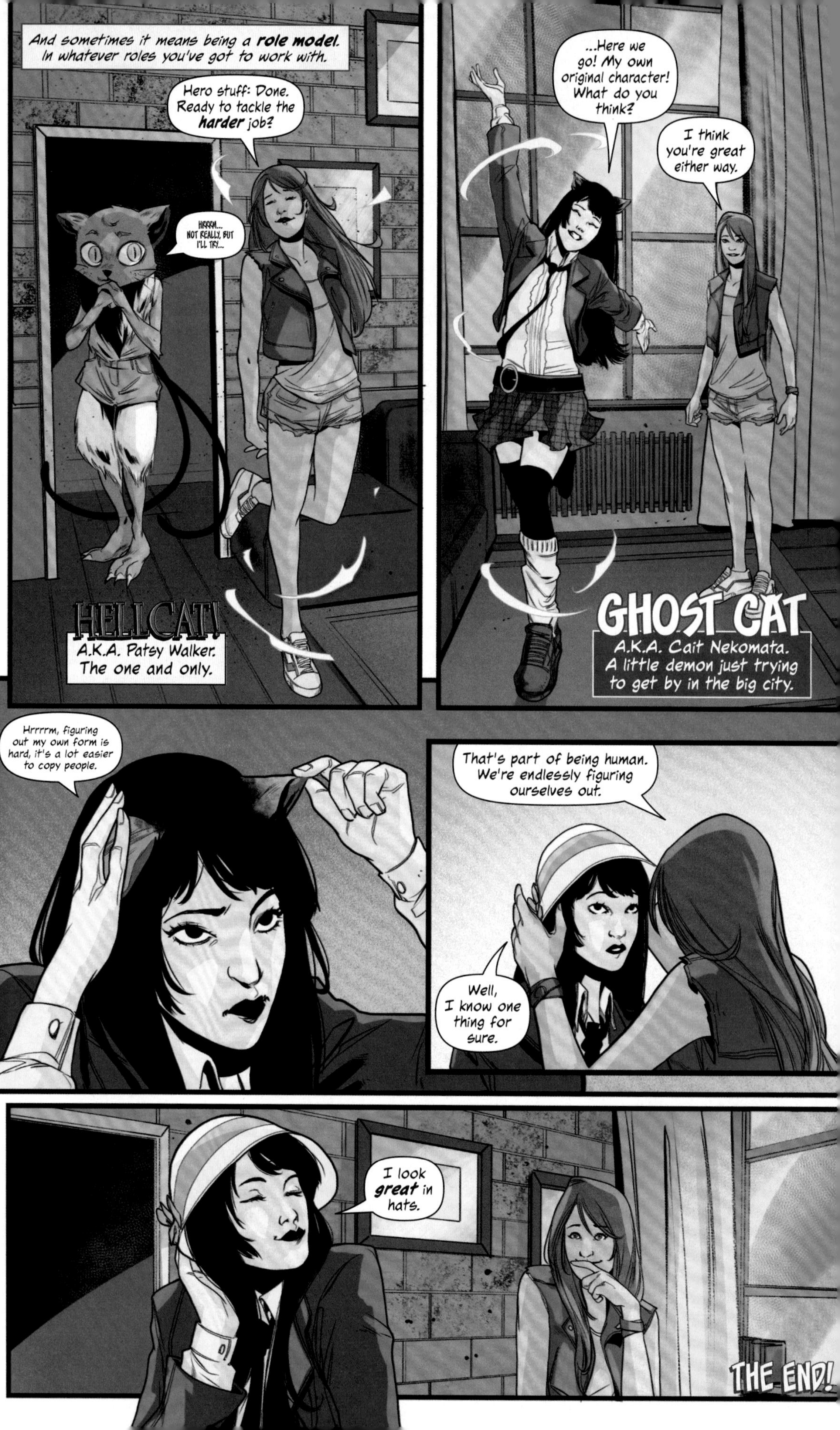
And sometimes it means being a role model. In whatever roles you've got to work with.
Hero stuff: Done. Ready to tackle the harder job?
HRRRM... NOT REALLY, BUT I'LL TRY...
HELLCAT!
A.K.A. Patsy Walker. The one and only.
...Here we go! My own original character! What do you think?
I think you're great either way.
GHOST CAT
A.K.A. Cait Nekomata. A little demon just trying to get by in the big city.
Hrrrrm, figuring out my own form is hard, it's a lot easier to copy people.
That's part of being human. We're endlessly figuring ourselves out.
Well, I know one thing for sure.
I look great in hats.
THE END!

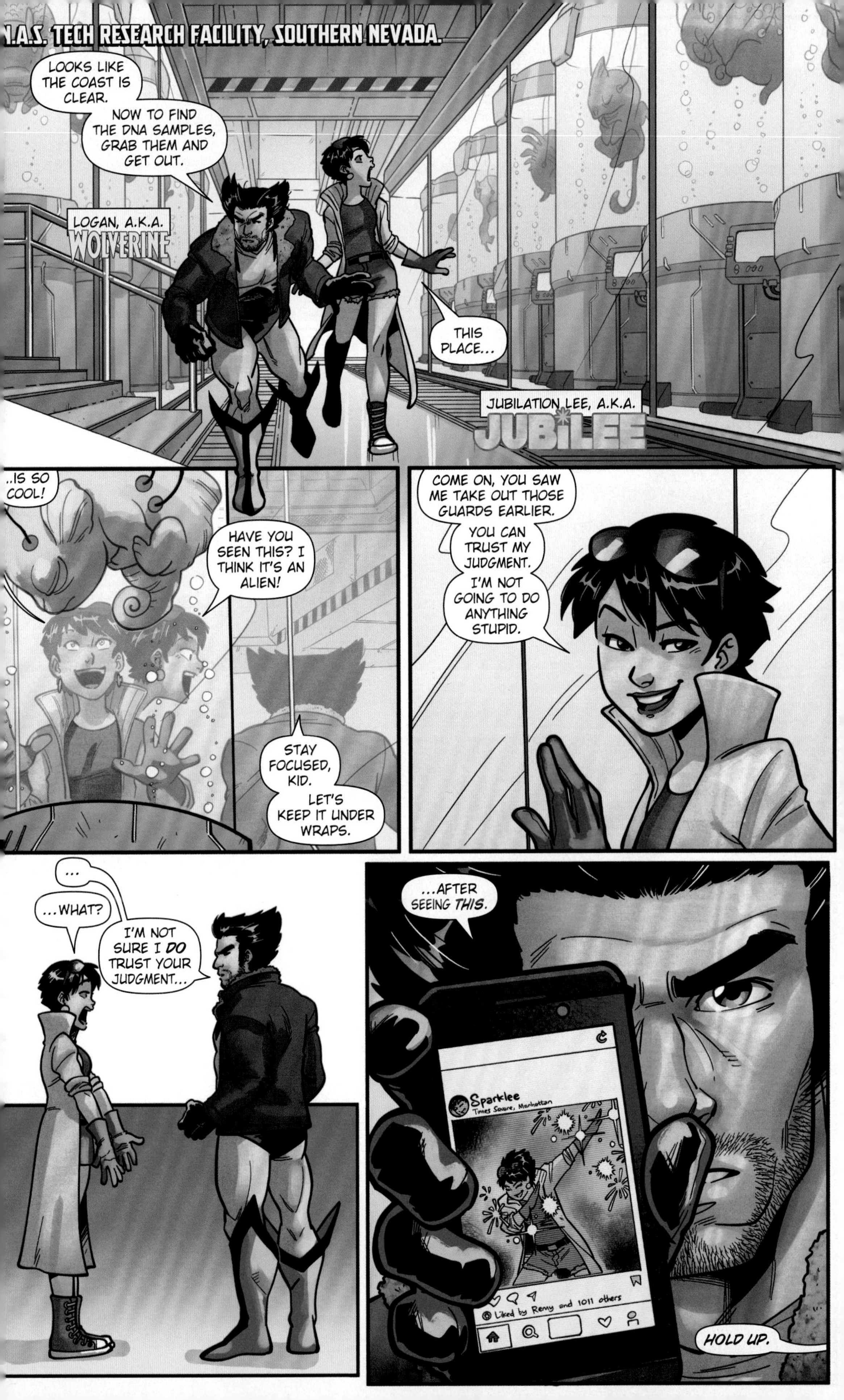

.I.A.S. TECH RESEARCH FACILITY, SOUTHERN NEVADA.
LOOKS LIKE THE COAST IS CLEAR.
NOW TO FIND THE DNA SAMPLES, GRAB THEM AND GET OUT.
LOGAN, A.K.A. WOLVERINE
THIS PLACE...
JUBILATION LEE, A.K.A. JUBILEE
..IS SO COOL!
HAVE YOU SEEN THIS? I THINK IT'S AN ALIEN!
STAY FOCUSED, KID.
LET'S KEEP IT UNDER WRAPS.
COME ON, YOU SAW ME TAKE OUT THOSE GUARDS EARLIER.
YOU CAN TRUST MY JUDGMENT.
I'M NOT GOING TO DO ANYTHING STUPID.
...
...WHAT?
I'M NOT SURE I DO TRUST YOUR JUDGMENT...
...AFTER SEEING THIS.
Sparklee
Times Square, Manhattan
Liked by Remy and 1011 others
HOLD UP.

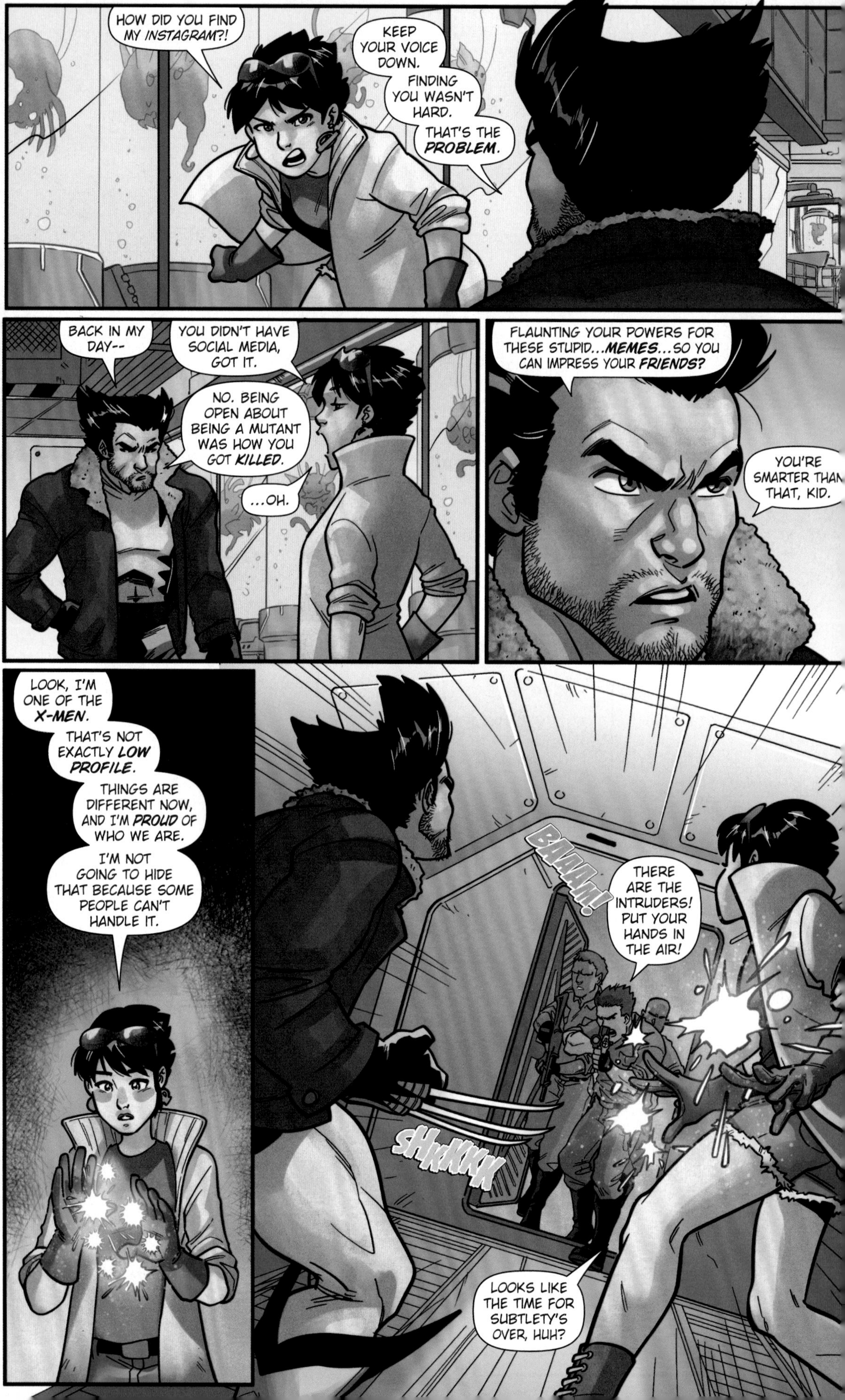
HOW DID YOU FIND MY *INSTAGRAM*?!
KEEP YOUR VOICE DOWN.
FINDING YOU WASN'T HARD.
THAT'S THE ***PROBLEM***.
BACK IN MY DAY--
YOU DIDN'T HAVE SOCIAL MEDIA, GOT IT.
NO. BEING OPEN ABOUT BEING A MUTANT WAS HOW YOU GOT ***KILLED***.
...OH.
FLAUNTING YOUR POWERS FOR THESE STUPID...***MEMES***...SO YOU CAN IMPRESS YOUR ***FRIENDS***?
YOU'RE SMARTER THAN THAT, KID.
LOOK, I'M ONE OF THE ***X-MEN***.
THAT'S NOT EXACTLY ***LOW PROFILE***.
THINGS ARE DIFFERENT NOW, AND I'M ***PROUD*** OF WHO WE ARE.
I'M NOT GOING TO HIDE THAT BECAUSE SOME PEOPLE CAN'T HANDLE IT.
BAAAAM!
THERE ARE THE INTRUDERS! PUT YOUR HANDS IN THE AIR!
SHKKKKK
LOOKS LIKE THE TIME FOR SUBTLETY'S OVER, HUH?

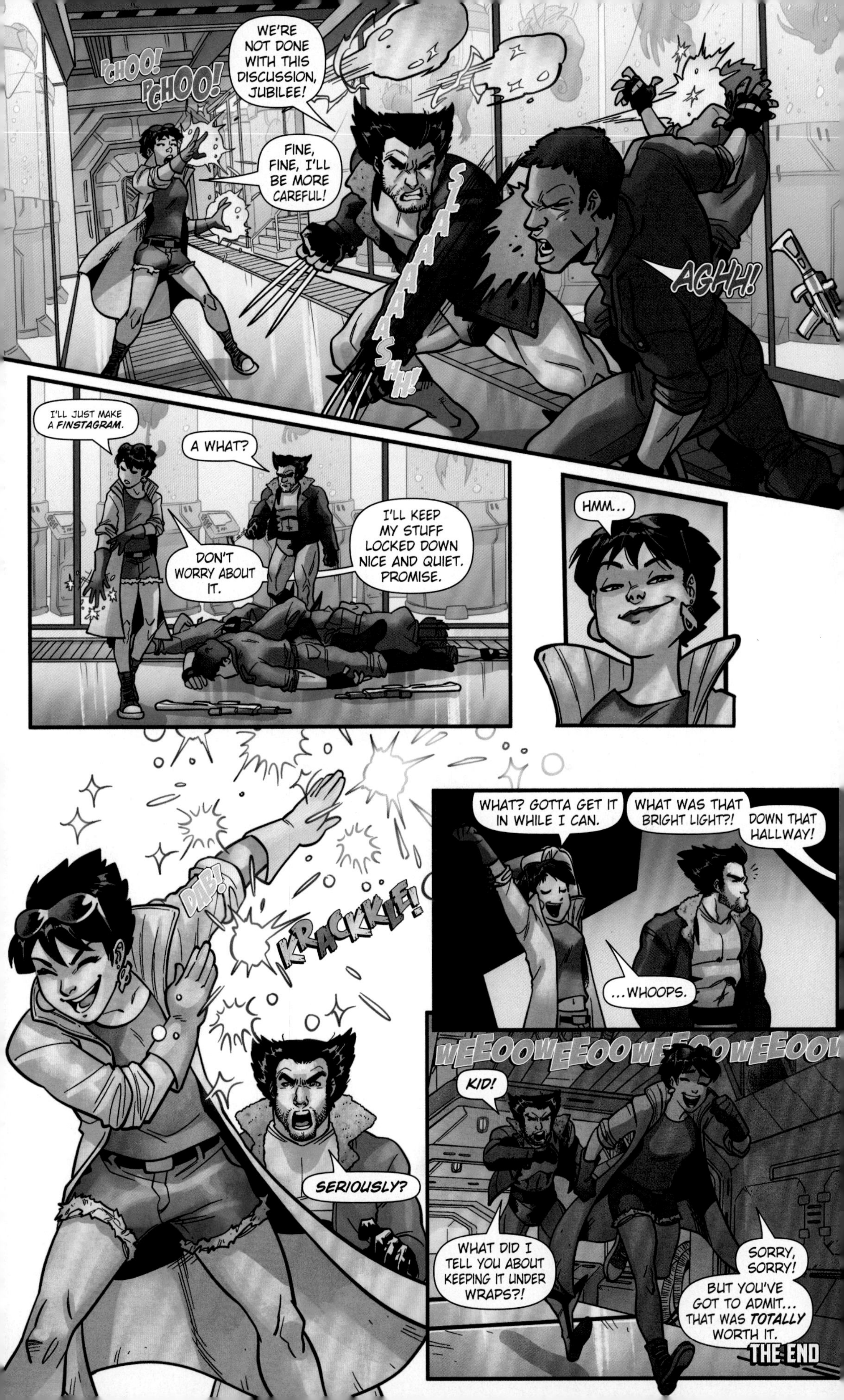

PCHOO! PCHOO!
WE'RE NOT DONE WITH THIS DISCUSSION, JUBILEE!
FINE, FINE, I'LL BE MORE CAREFUL!
SHAAAAAASHH!
AGHH!
I'LL JUST MAKE A *FINSTAGRAM*.
A WHAT?
DON'T WORRY ABOUT IT.
I'LL KEEP MY STUFF LOCKED DOWN NICE AND QUIET. PROMISE.
HMM...
DAB!
KRACKKLE!
SERIOUSLY?
WHAT? GOTTA GET IT IN WHILE I CAN.
WHAT WAS THAT BRIGHT LIGHT?!
DOWN THAT HALLWAY!
...WHOOPS.
WEEOOWEEOOWEEOOWEEOO
KID!
WHAT DID I TELL YOU ABOUT KEEPING IT UNDER WRAPS?!
SORRY, SORRY!
BUT YOU'VE GOT TO ADMIT... THAT WAS *TOTALLY* WORTH IT.
THE END

WRITER SPOTLIGHT
ALYSSA WONG

WHAT WAS AN IMPORTANT LESSON ABOUT YOUR CHOSEN FIELD THAT YOU LEARNED EARLY ON THAT HAS STUCK WITH YOU THROUGHOUT YOUR CAREER?

Chase your weird and write what inspires you. I think it's easy to get in your own head about what a story "should" be; everyone's got a different idea of what makes a story successful, and everyone thinks they're right. But I think it's important to ask yourself, "What do I want? What do I think this story is, and how can I make that happen?"

Writing can be incredibly rewarding, but if you're not enjoying it or invested in it it's just a painful, awful process. So don't be afraid to write things that you enjoy! I think you should always be a little indulgent when you're writing, because your audience can tell when you're having fun (and, conversely, when you're not into it).

WHAT IS YOUR FAVORITE THING TO WRITE?

I love to write stressed-out teens, interesting villains and monstrous girls. Most of my stories are also queer, because that's important to me. You always want to see more characters who reflect your experiences, right? That's also why I write a lot of Asian American and Asian diaspora characters.

I like characters with complicated motivations and morality, who walk that knife's edge between "What do I need to do?" and "What's the right thing to do?" It's an elemental, everyday struggle. With interesting villains, their choices are weighted more heavily toward the former...so when they choose the latter, the personal stakes are amplified.

WHAT HAS BEEN YOUR FAVORITE MARVEL CHARACTER TO WORK WITH?

I'm going to cheat a little and name two: Wave and White Fox!

Wave is really special to me because when I was a kid, I rarely, if ever, saw Filipino characters in media. (I'm Chinese Filipino American.) So getting to see a Filipina super hero is awesome, and getting to write her is a dream come true. She means a lot to me, and I know she means a lot to other Filipino fans, and I feel honored to get to tell her story with Greg Pak in the AERO books.

My other favorite is definitely White Fox! She's a kumiho, a Korean shape-shifting fox creature, and the last of her kind. So she's got this great responsibility on her shoulders and has inherited the legacy--and the grudges--of an entire species. I think there's a lot of really rich material to play with there. And her powers are super cool! FUTURE FIGHT FIRSTS: WHITE FOX #1 is also my first solo story, and that comes out in October.

FEARLESS #3

PAGE 2

Panel 4: Jubilee meets his gaze, defiant and unafraid. She cups her hand and tiny sparks of colored light dance above her fingertips, casting their colors on her face.

    11. Jubilee: Look, I'm one of the X-Men.
    12. Jubilee: That's not exactly *low profile*.
    13. Jubilee: Things are different now, and I'm *proud* of who I am.
    14. Jubilee: I'm not going to hide that because some people can't handle seeing it.

CHECK OUT ALYSSA'S WORK IN *AERO #1*, ON SALE NOW, AND *FUTURE FIGHT FIRSTS: WHITE FOX*, ON SALE NEXT WEEK!

ARTIST SPOTLIGHT
ALTI FIRMANSYAH

DO YOU REMEMBER THE MOMENT THAT YOU FELL IN LOVE WITH COMICS?

When I was in elementary school, my parents gave me a bunch of translated European comic books, such as *Asterix*, *Agent 212* and *Tintin*, and I watched Disney animations over and over. From that point on, I started to draw my own comics with a marker. No panels or frames, just papers with numbers on them.

WHEN DID YOU KNOW THAT YOU WANTED TO BE A COMICS ARTIST?

My career started as a visualizer/storyboard artist, so my job description was to visualize the art director and copywriter's idea into sequential art. After six grueling years, I thought to myself, all these panels were so flat and static, and so I challenged myself to be a comic artist where I can play with panels and layouts to be more dramatic and dynamic.

WHAT WAS AN IMPORTANT LESSON ABOUT YOUR CHOSEN FIELD THAT YOU LEARNED EARLY ON THAT HAS STUCK WITH YOU THROUGHOUT YOUR CAREER?

That I never work alone -- it is always a team, and therefore, I should keep a good communication between colleagues and never let my work be a backlog for the others.

WHETHER IT'S A CUP OF COFFEE, A SPECIFIC TYPE OF PEN OR DESK SETUP OR EVEN AN EMOTIONAL-SUPPORT ACTION FIGURE, IS THERE AN ELEMENT IN YOUR WORKSPACE THAT YOU FEEL IS CRUCIAL TO YOUR WORK PROCESS?

Music is a must! Well, any sound, actually. I used to play random Netflix movies just for the background sound or video game play-through videos. :) But since my baby boy came into the picture, I only need his photo on every lockscreen and wallpaper.

WHAT HAS BEEN YOUR PROUDEST MOMENT IN COMICS?

When C.B. Cebulski emailed me after my portfolio review in 2014 and told me that I got the project! I was so happy and proud at the same time; I promised to myself that I would do my best on every task that is given to me.

WHAT HAS BEEN YOUR FAVORITE PROJECT THAT YOU'VE WORKED ON SO FAR, AND WHY?

STAR-LORD & KITTY PRYDE written by Sam Humphries was my very first comic project that I got from Marvel, so it is very memorable. But until now, every project is so meaningful for me because all the people on the team (all the editors and writers) are SUPER NICE and very, very helpful!

WHAT HAS BEEN YOUR FAVORITE EXPERIENCE WITH A FAN?

I was so shocked when a fan from the USA sent me a hand-painted Converse shoe with Peter Quill and Kitty Pryde from my comic version! I still keep it along with my comic collection. It is so precious to me!

CATCH MORE OF ALTI'S WORK IN THE ***UNSTOPPABLE WASP: UNLIMITED VOL. 2*** AND ***THOR VS. HULK: CHAMPIONS OF THE UNIVERSE***, BOTH ON SALE NOW!

LETTERER SPOTLIGHT
CARDINAL RAE

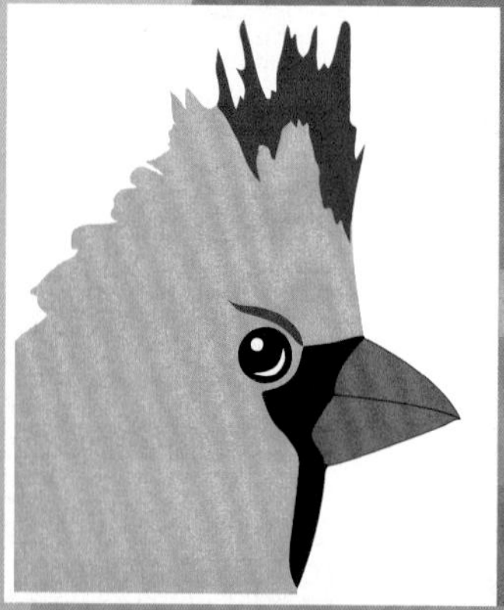

DO YOU REMEMBER THE MOMENT THAT YOU FELL IN LOVE WITH COMICS?

Like a lot of comics fans, the cartoons brought me into reading. *Spider-Man and His Amazing Friends* and *Super Friends* were the gateway, and later the *X-Men* cartoon. That opened me up to the Claremont era with Byrne, Smith, Cockrum, Romita, Adams and, of course, Jim Lee, which made for essential reading.

WHEN DID YOU KNOW THAT YOU WANTED TO BE A COMICS ARTIST?

I was always interested in storytelling through art. I originally focused mainly on advertising and graphic design but got into comics when a friend needed a letterer. Turned out I was pretty good at it.

WHAT WAS AN IMPORTANT LESSON ABOUT YOUR CHOSEN FIELD THAT YOU LEARNED EARLY ON THAT HAS STUCK WITH YOU THROUGHOUT YOUR CAREER?

You can never prepare for everything, but you can do your best. The letterer and colorist are where a lot of comics projects bottleneck, so the more work you can do on the front end -- like choosing fonts, creating the palette, etc. -- the better. That way, when you get the pages, you can just go to work!

WHETHER IT'S A CUP OF COFFEE, A SPECIFIC TYPE OF PEN OR DESK SETUP OR EVEN AN EMOTIONAL-SUPPORT ACTION FIGURE, IS THERE AN ELEMENT IN YOUR WORKSPACE THAT YOU FEEL IS CRUCIAL TO YOUR WORK PROCESS?

I have a pillow for my left elbow and a small stuffed Pusheen for my right elbow. They're pretty crucial. I'm embarrassed to say that my desk setup is "organized chaos." If I could get some antigravity shelves that just floated when I needed extra space, that'd be ideal.

WHAT IS YOUR FAVORITE TOOL OF THE TRADE?

My Wacom tablet. I know many letterers use a Cintiq, but my li'l ol' Intuos works just fine.

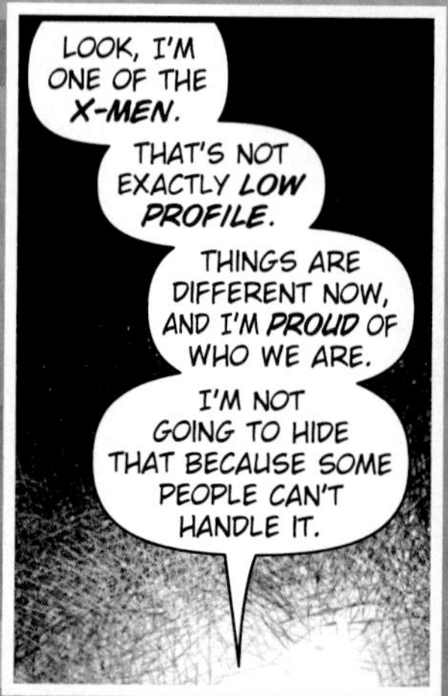

LOOK, I'M ONE OF THE X-MEN.
THAT'S NOT EXACTLY LOW PROFILE.
THINGS ARE DIFFERENT NOW, AND I'M PROUD OF WHO WE ARE.
I'M NOT GOING TO HIDE THAT BECAUSE SOME PEOPLE CAN'T HANDLE IT.

WHAT IS YOUR FAVORITE THING TO WRITE/DRAW/COLOR?

I guess my favorite things to letter are indie books because you see so many terrific indie stories with terrible lettering because someone did it themselves. So I like to help with the overall aesthetic of the book.

WHAT HAS BEEN YOUR PROUDEST MOMENT IN COMICS?

To be honest, lettering for Marvel is a pretty proud moment. Also when *Crowded* (Image Comics) got nominated for an Eisner this past summer.

WHAT HAS BEEN YOUR FAVORITE PROJECT THAT YOU'VE WORKED ON SO FAR, AND WHY?

Working with Meredith Finch, Ig Guara and Tríona Farrell on *Rose* (Image Comics) was a terrific experience. They're consummate professionals and do incredible work.

WHAT HAS BEEN YOUR FAVORITE EXPERIENCE WITH A FAN?

Being in an elevator with Stan Lee and him saying "Ladies first" to me when we reached the lobby.

WHAT HAS BEEN YOUR FAVORITE MARVEL CHARACTER TO WORK WITH?

Since this is my first Marvel series, I'd say Ms. Marvel. I'm a HUGE fan of G. Willow Wilson's run on that book, and the lettering is fun and really suits the character!

TO SEE MORE OF CARDINAL'S WORK, CHECK OUT YOUR LOCAL COMIC BOOK STORE TO FIND CROWDED *AND* ROSE *-- AND TO SEE THE MS. MARVEL RUN SHE MENTIONED, CHECK OUT* **MS. MARVEL VOL 10: TIME AND TIME AGAIN**. *ALL BOOKS ON SALE NOW!*

Don't forget to flip to the Next Issue page to see what other female-led creative projects are going on in the Marvel Universe -- and stay tuned for our final issue of **FEARLESS***!*

Until next time, True Believers!
Sarah, Annalise, Lauren, Kathleen, Shannon, Alanna & Lindsey

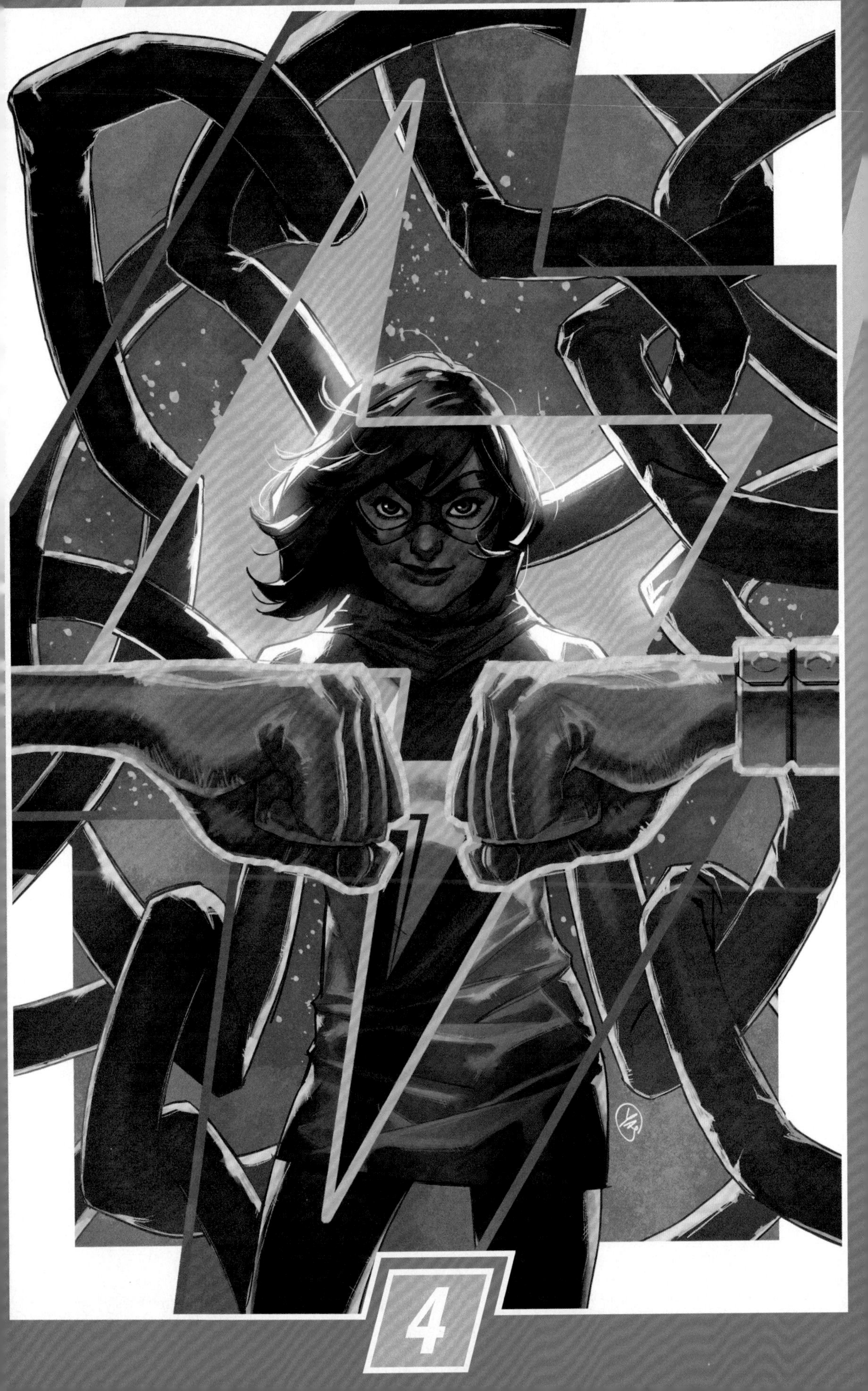
4

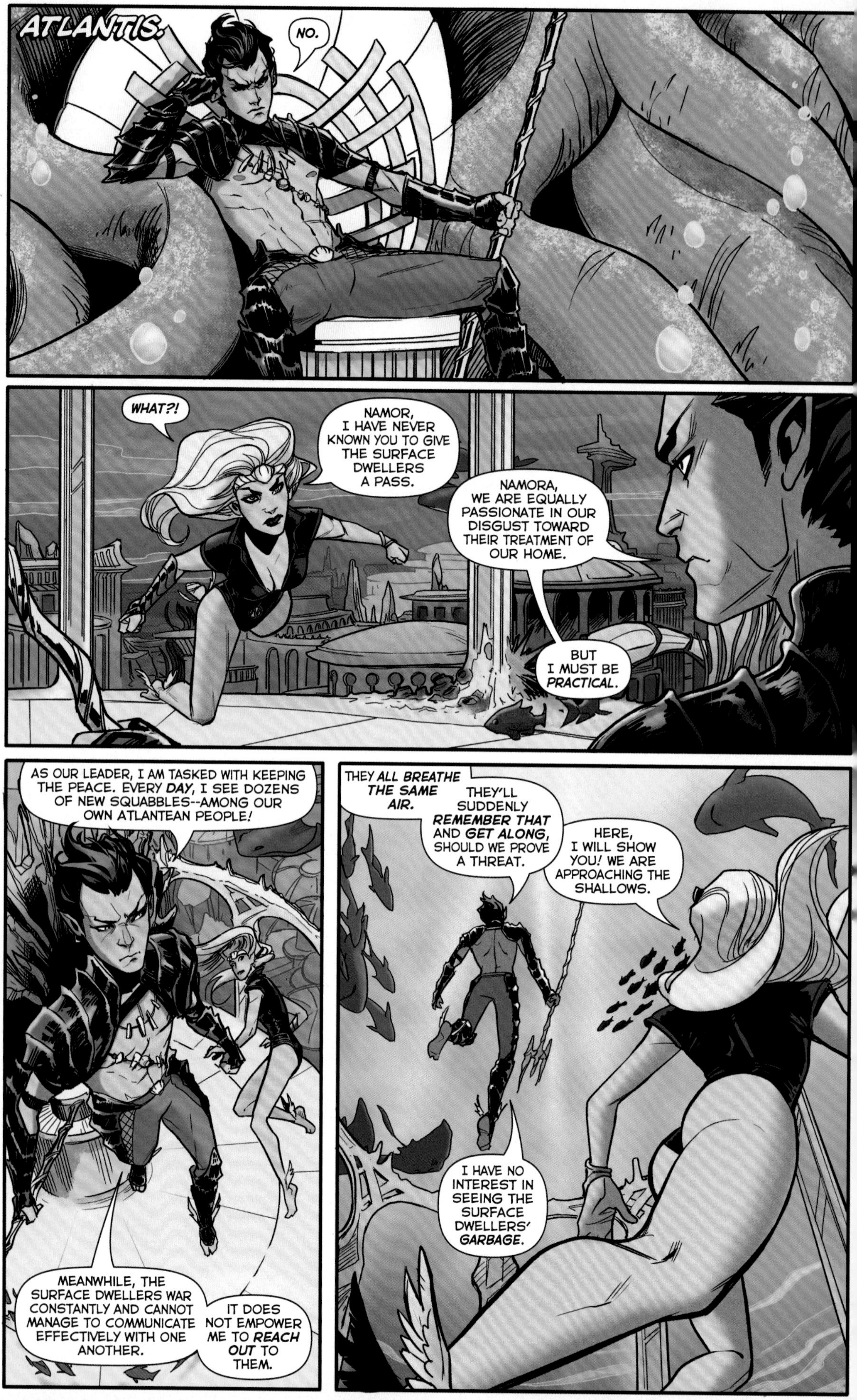
ATLANTIS.
NO.
WHAT?!
NAMOR, I HAVE NEVER KNOWN YOU TO GIVE THE SURFACE DWELLERS A PASS.
NAMORA, WE ARE EQUALLY PASSIONATE IN OUR DISGUST TOWARD THEIR TREATMENT OF OUR HOME.
BUT I MUST BE PRACTICAL.
AS OUR LEADER, I AM TASKED WITH KEEPING THE PEACE. EVERY DAY, I SEE DOZENS OF NEW SQUABBLES--AMONG OUR OWN ATLANTEAN PEOPLE!
MEANWHILE, THE SURFACE DWELLERS WAR CONSTANTLY AND CANNOT MANAGE TO COMMUNICATE EFFECTIVELY WITH ONE ANOTHER.
IT DOES NOT EMPOWER ME TO REACH OUT TO THEM.
THEY ALL BREATHE THE SAME AIR.
THEY'LL SUDDENLY REMEMBER THAT AND GET ALONG, SHOULD WE PROVE A THREAT.
HERE, I WILL SHOW YOU! WE ARE APPROACHING THE SHALLOWS.
I HAVE NO INTEREST IN SEEING THE SURFACE DWELLERS' GARBAGE.

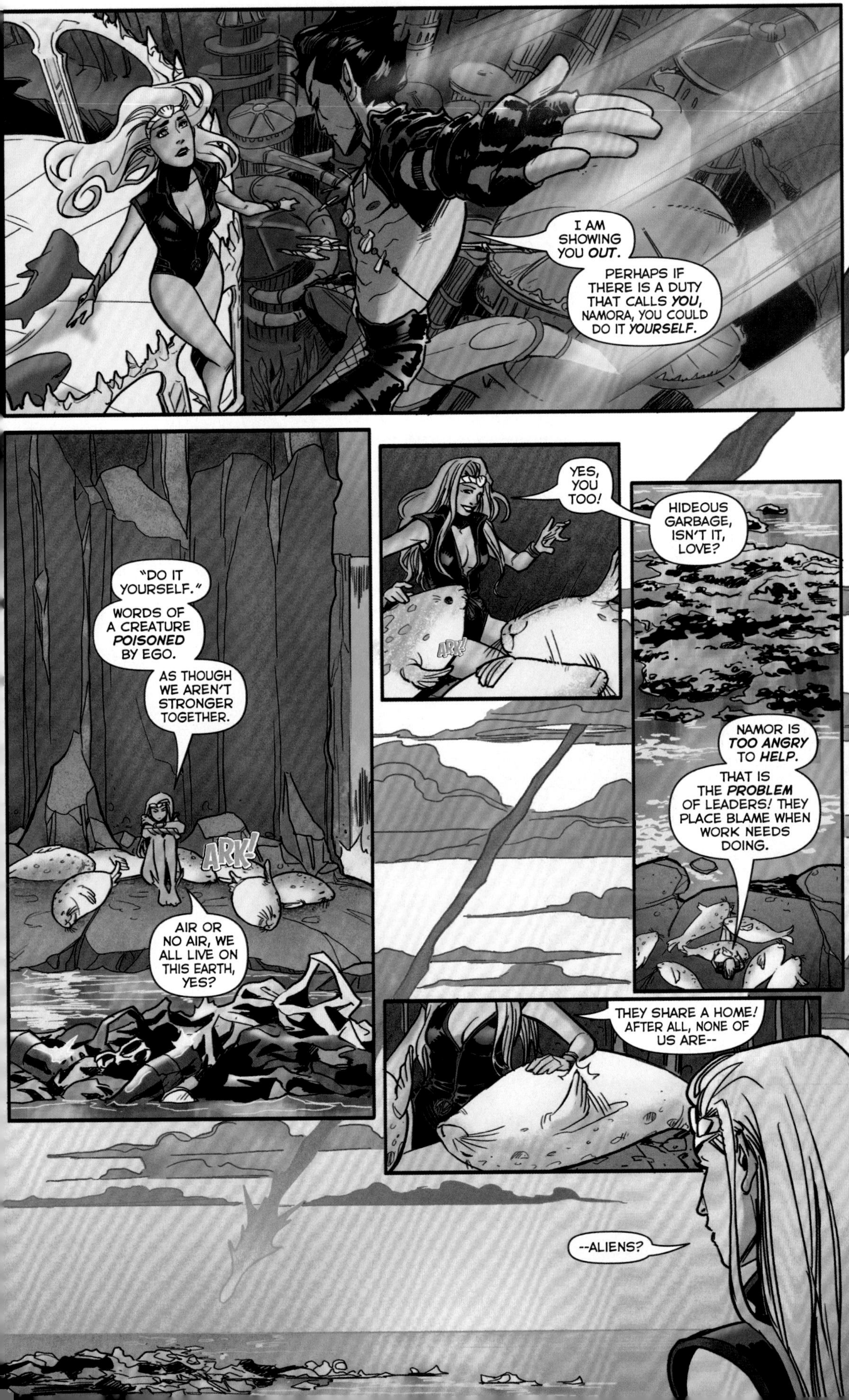
I AM SHOWING YOU OUT.
PERHAPS IF THERE IS A DUTY THAT CALLS YOU, NAMORA, YOU COULD DO IT YOURSELF.
"DO IT YOURSELF."
WORDS OF A CREATURE POISONED BY EGO.
AS THOUGH WE AREN'T STRONGER TOGETHER.
ARK!
AIR OR NO AIR, WE ALL LIVE ON THIS EARTH, YES?
YES, YOU TOO!
ARK!
HIDEOUS GARBAGE, ISN'T IT, LOVE?
NAMOR IS TOO ANGRY TO HELP.
THAT IS THE PROBLEM OF LEADERS! THEY PLACE BLAME WHEN WORK NEEDS DOING.
THEY SHARE A HOME! AFTER ALL, NONE OF US ARE--
--ALIENS?

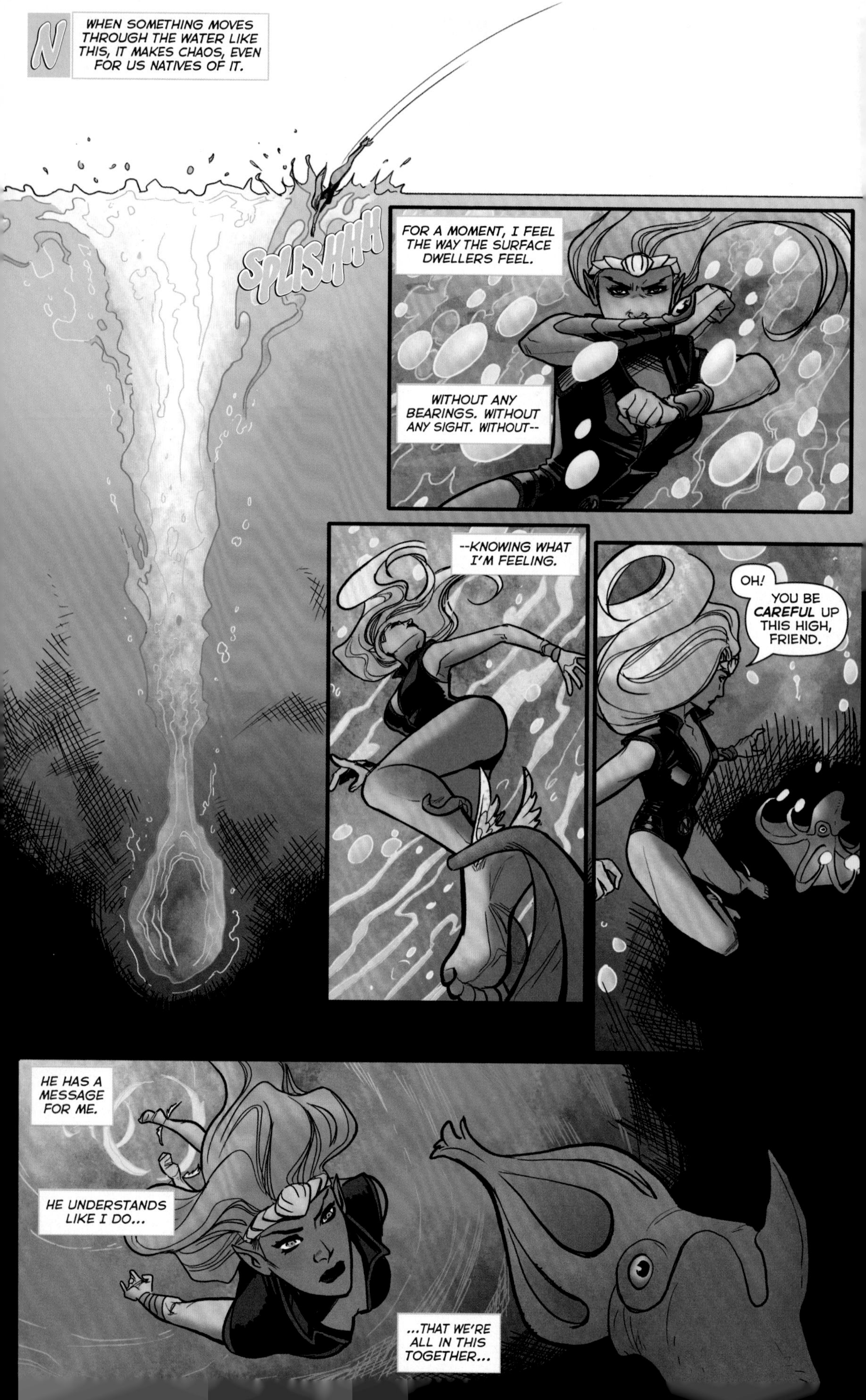

N
WHEN SOMETHING MOVES THROUGH THE WATER LIKE THIS, IT MAKES CHAOS, EVEN FOR US NATIVES OF IT.
SPLISHHH
FOR A MOMENT, I FEEL THE WAY THE SURFACE DWELLERS FEEL.
WITHOUT ANY BEARINGS. WITHOUT ANY SIGHT. WITHOUT--
--KNOWING WHAT I'M FEELING.
OH!
YOU BE CAREFUL UP THIS HIGH, FRIEND.
HE HAS A MESSAGE FOR ME.
HE UNDERSTANDS LIKE I DO...
...THAT WE'RE ALL IN THIS TOGETHER...

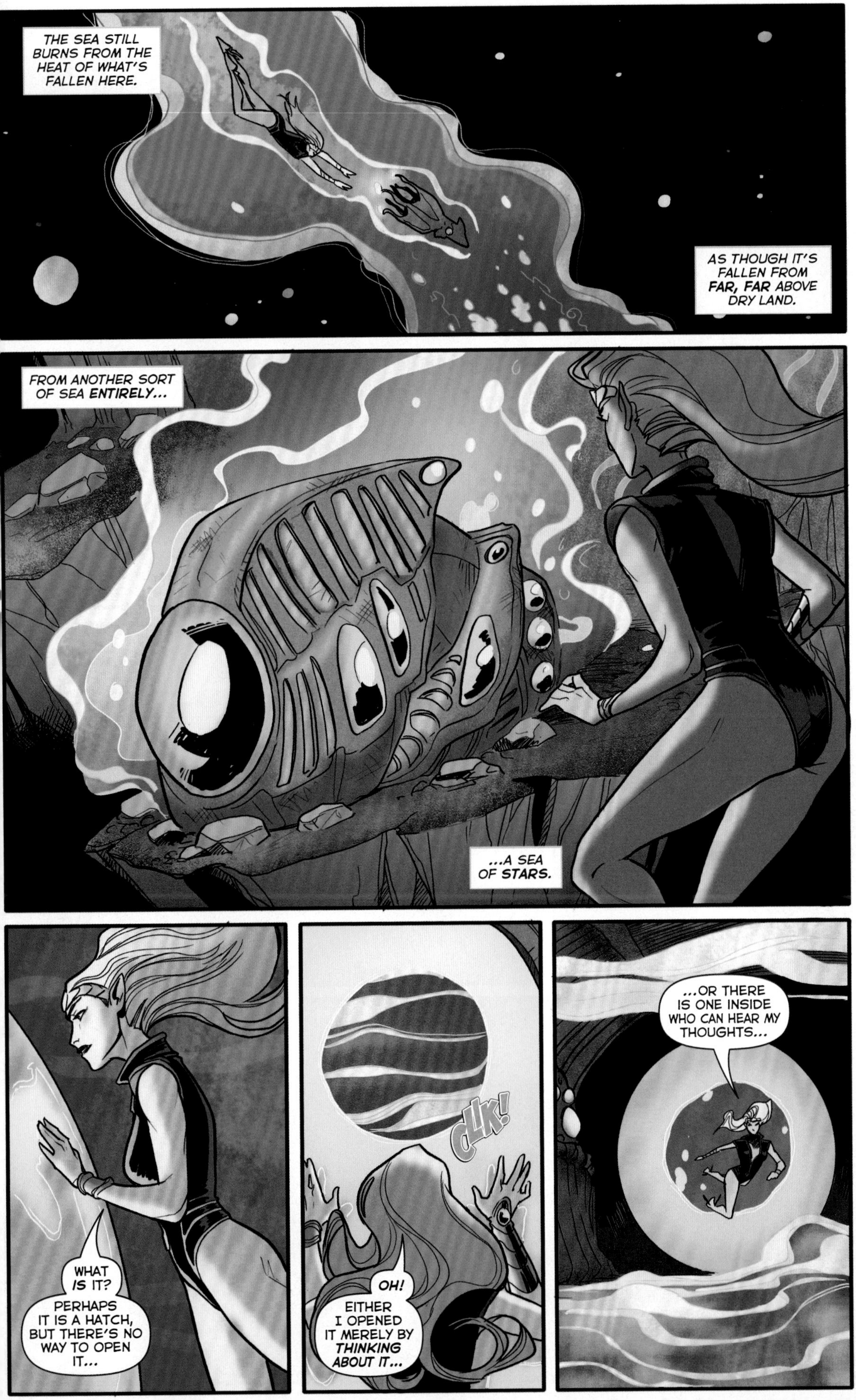
THE SEA STILL BURNS FROM THE HEAT OF WHAT'S FALLEN HERE.
AS THOUGH IT'S FALLEN FROM FAR, FAR ABOVE DRY LAND.
FROM ANOTHER SORT OF SEA ENTIRELY...
...A SEA OF STARS.
WHAT IS IT?
PERHAPS IT IS A HATCH, BUT THERE'S NO WAY TO OPEN IT...
CLIK!
OH!
EITHER I OPENED IT MERELY BY THINKING ABOUT IT...
...OR THERE IS ONE INSIDE WHO CAN HEAR MY THOUGHTS...

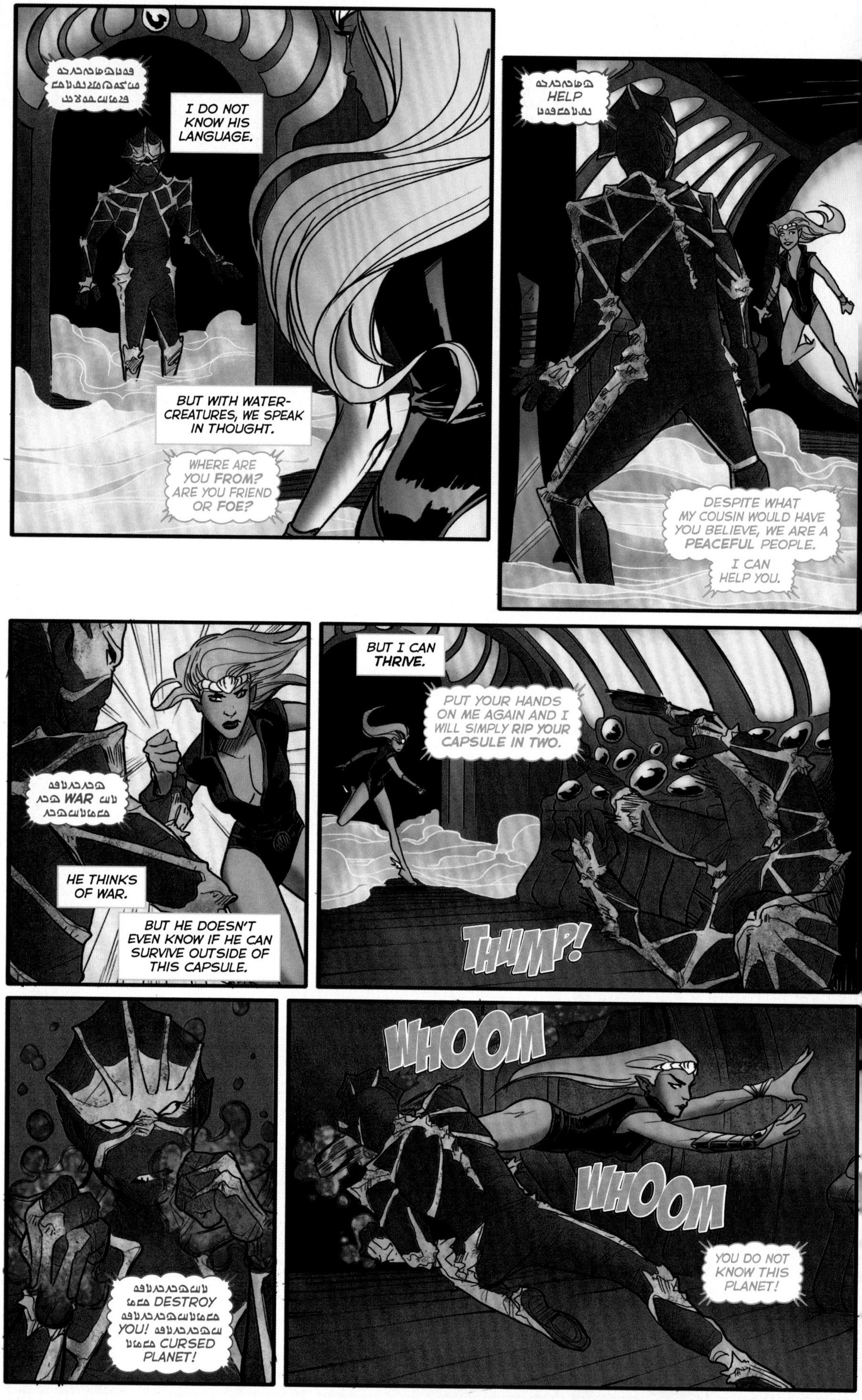
I DO NOT KNOW HIS LANGUAGE.
BUT WITH WATER-CREATURES, WE SPEAK IN THOUGHT.
WHERE ARE YOU FROM? ARE YOU FRIEND OR FOE?
HELP
DESPITE WHAT MY COUSIN WOULD HAVE YOU BELIEVE, WE ARE A PEACEFUL PEOPLE.
I CAN HELP YOU.
WAR
HE THINKS OF WAR.
BUT HE DOESN'T EVEN KNOW IF HE CAN SURVIVE OUTSIDE OF THIS CAPSULE.
BUT I CAN THRIVE.
PUT YOUR HANDS ON ME AGAIN AND I WILL SIMPLY RIP YOUR CAPSULE IN TWO.
THUMP!
DESTROY YOU! CURSED PLANET!
WHOOM
WHOOM
YOU DO NOT KNOW THIS PLANET!

I KNOW THIS PLANET LIKE SHE IS MY OWN SISTER.

I KNOW THE GRAVITY ABOVE THE WATER AND BELOW.

WITH THE POD OPEN, HE IS NAKED TO THE STANDARD PRESSURE HERE.

AND IT'S FAR TOO LOW FOR HIM.

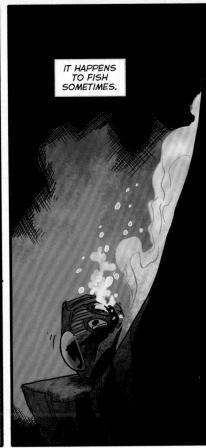

IT HAPPENS TO FISH SOMETIMES.

FISHERMEN BRING DEEP-SEA DWELLERS TO THE SURFACE...

...AND THEY FALL APART.

TRY TO BRING A DEEP-SEA FISH TO THE SURFACE...

...AND THEY MELT.

I COULD LET HIM MELT HERE.

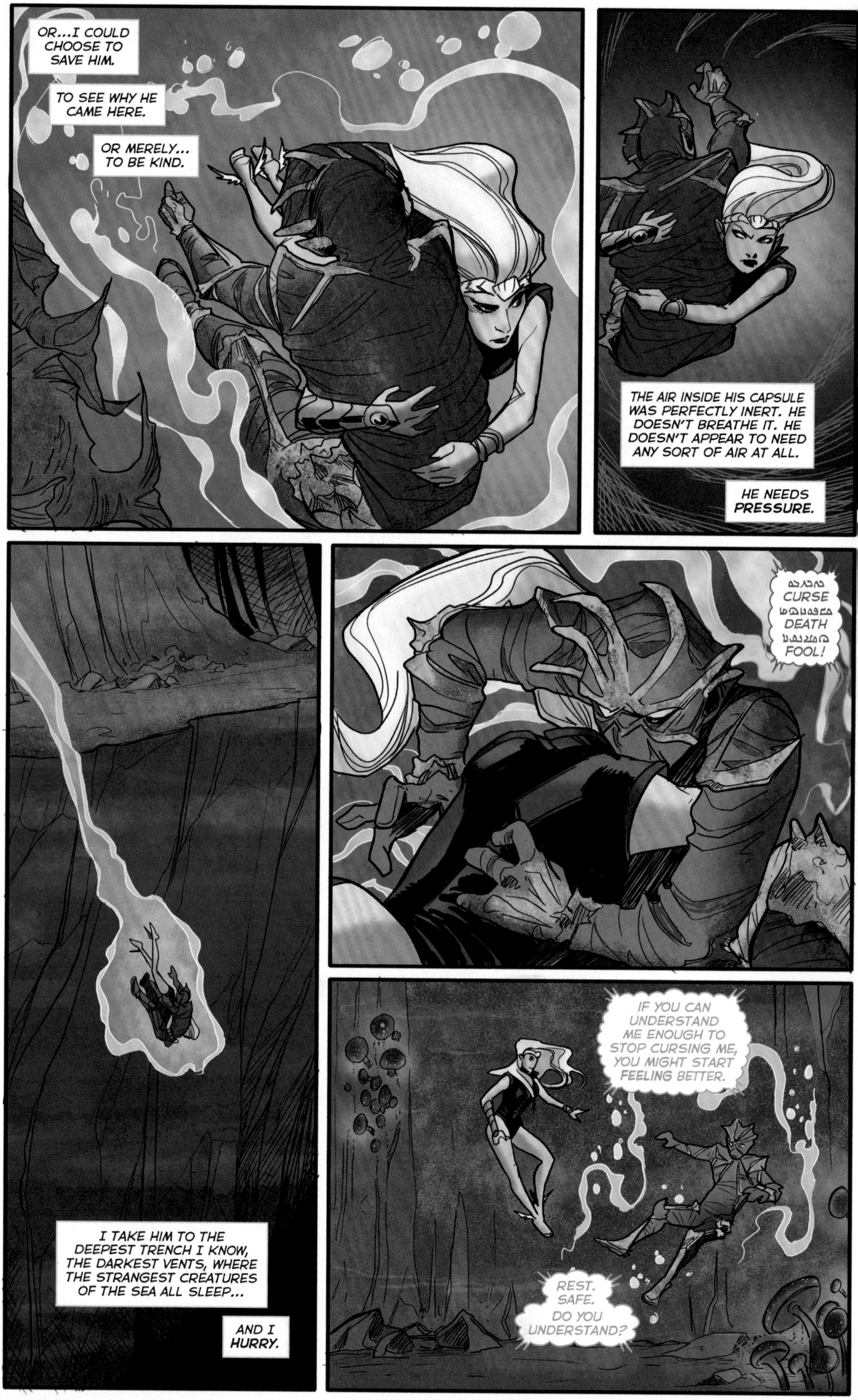
OR...I COULD CHOOSE TO SAVE HIM.
TO SEE WHY HE CAME HERE.
OR MERELY... TO BE KIND.
THE AIR INSIDE HIS CAPSULE WAS PERFECTLY INERT. HE DOESN'T BREATHE IT. HE DOESN'T APPEAR TO NEED ANY SORT OF AIR AT ALL.
HE NEEDS PRESSURE.
I TAKE HIM TO THE DEEPEST TRENCH I KNOW, THE DARKEST VENTS, WHERE THE STRANGEST CREATURES OF THE SEA ALL SLEEP...
AND I HURRY.
CURSE DEATH FOOL!
IF YOU CAN UNDERSTAND ME ENOUGH TO STOP CURSING ME, YOU MIGHT START FEELING BETTER.
REST. SAFE. DO YOU UNDERSTAND?

ᘁᒉᘁᕂᕂᗷ
WHY ᗷᗭᗭᐃᘁᕂᗷ
CAPTIVE?

NOT CAPTIVE.

WHO ARE YOU?

NO.

I'M NAMORA. YOU DON'T HAVE TO TELL ME YOUR NAME IF YOU ARE AFRAID.

NOT AFRAID!!!
ᗷᗷᗷᗭᗷᐃᗭᗷᗷ

IT IS OKAY TO BE AFRAID. I WON'T USE IT AGAINST YOU. REST NOW?

WE WILL SPEAK AGAIN WHEN YOU ARE WELL.

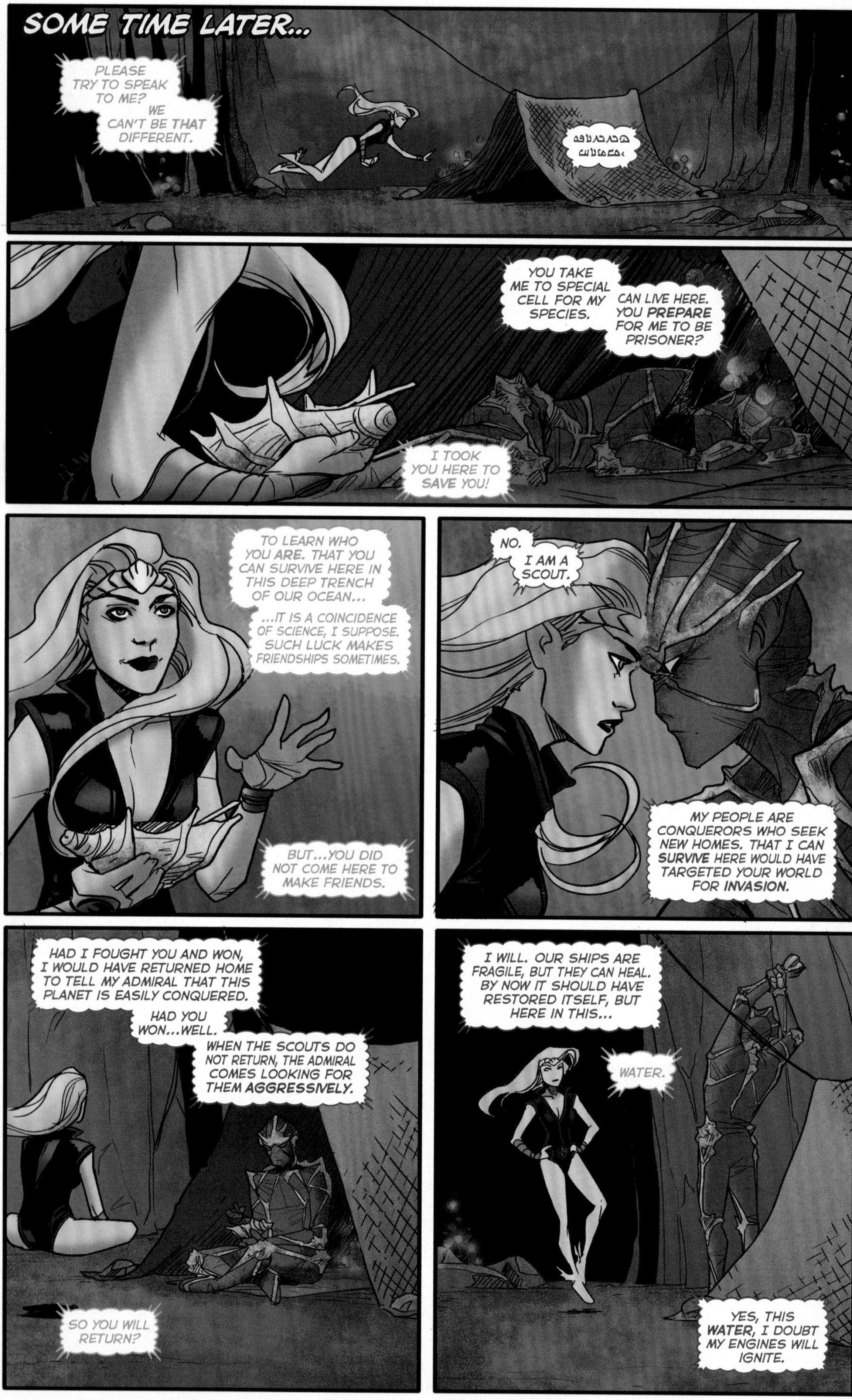
SOME TIME LATER...
PLEASE TRY TO SPEAK TO ME? WE CAN'T BE THAT DIFFERENT.
YOU TAKE ME TO SPECIAL CELL FOR MY SPECIES.
CAN LIVE HERE. YOU PREPARE FOR ME TO BE PRISONER?
I TOOK YOU HERE TO SAVE YOU!
TO LEARN WHO YOU ARE. THAT YOU CAN SURVIVE HERE IN THIS DEEP TRENCH OF OUR OCEAN...
...IT IS A COINCIDENCE OF SCIENCE, I SUPPOSE. SUCH LUCK MAKES FRIENDSHIPS SOMETIMES.
BUT...YOU DID NOT COME HERE TO MAKE FRIENDS.
NO.
I AM A SCOUT.
MY PEOPLE ARE CONQUERORS WHO SEEK NEW HOMES. THAT I CAN SURVIVE HERE WOULD HAVE TARGETED YOUR WORLD FOR INVASION.
HAD I FOUGHT YOU AND WON, I WOULD HAVE RETURNED HOME TO TELL MY ADMIRAL THAT THIS PLANET IS EASILY CONQUERED.
HAD YOU WON...WELL.
WHEN THE SCOUTS DO NOT RETURN, THE ADMIRAL COMES LOOKING FOR THEM AGGRESSIVELY.
SO YOU WILL RETURN?
I WILL. OUR SHIPS ARE FRAGILE, BUT THEY CAN HEAL. BY NOW IT SHOULD HAVE RESTORED ITSELF, BUT HERE IN THIS...
WATER.
YES, THIS WATER, I DOUBT MY ENGINES WILL IGNITE.

THEN I WILL SEE YOU TO THE SURFACE MYSELF.

ᐊᕙᐊᕙᐊᕙ
ᐊᕙᐊᕙᐊᕙᐊᕙᐊᕙ
ᐊᕙᐊᕙᐊᕙ

ARE YOU READY?

YES. PREPARING TAKEOFF PROCEDURE.

THANK YOU, NAMORA. WHEN I RETURN, I WILL TELL THE ADMIRAL THAT THERE WAS NOTHING HERE.

YOUR PEOPLE ARE HARMLESS.

WHOOSHHHHH

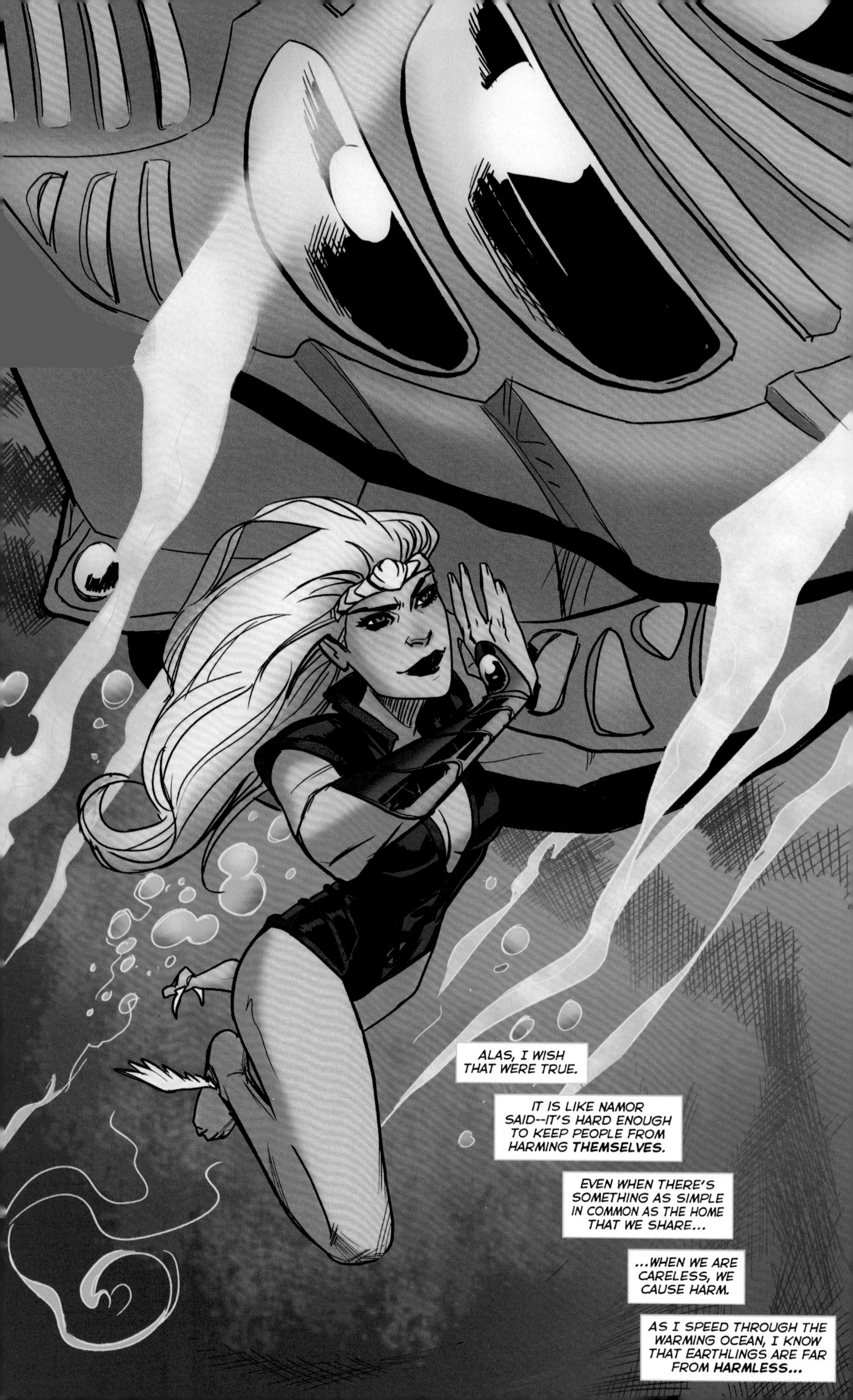
ALAS, I WISH THAT WERE TRUE.
IT IS LIKE NAMOR SAID--IT'S HARD ENOUGH TO KEEP PEOPLE FROM HARMING THEMSELVES.
EVEN WHEN THERE'S SOMETHING AS SIMPLE IN COMMON AS THE HOME THAT WE SHARE...
...WHEN WE ARE CARELESS, WE CAUSE HARM.
AS I SPEED THROUGH THE WARMING OCEAN, I KNOW THAT EARTHLINGS ARE FAR FROM HARMLESS...

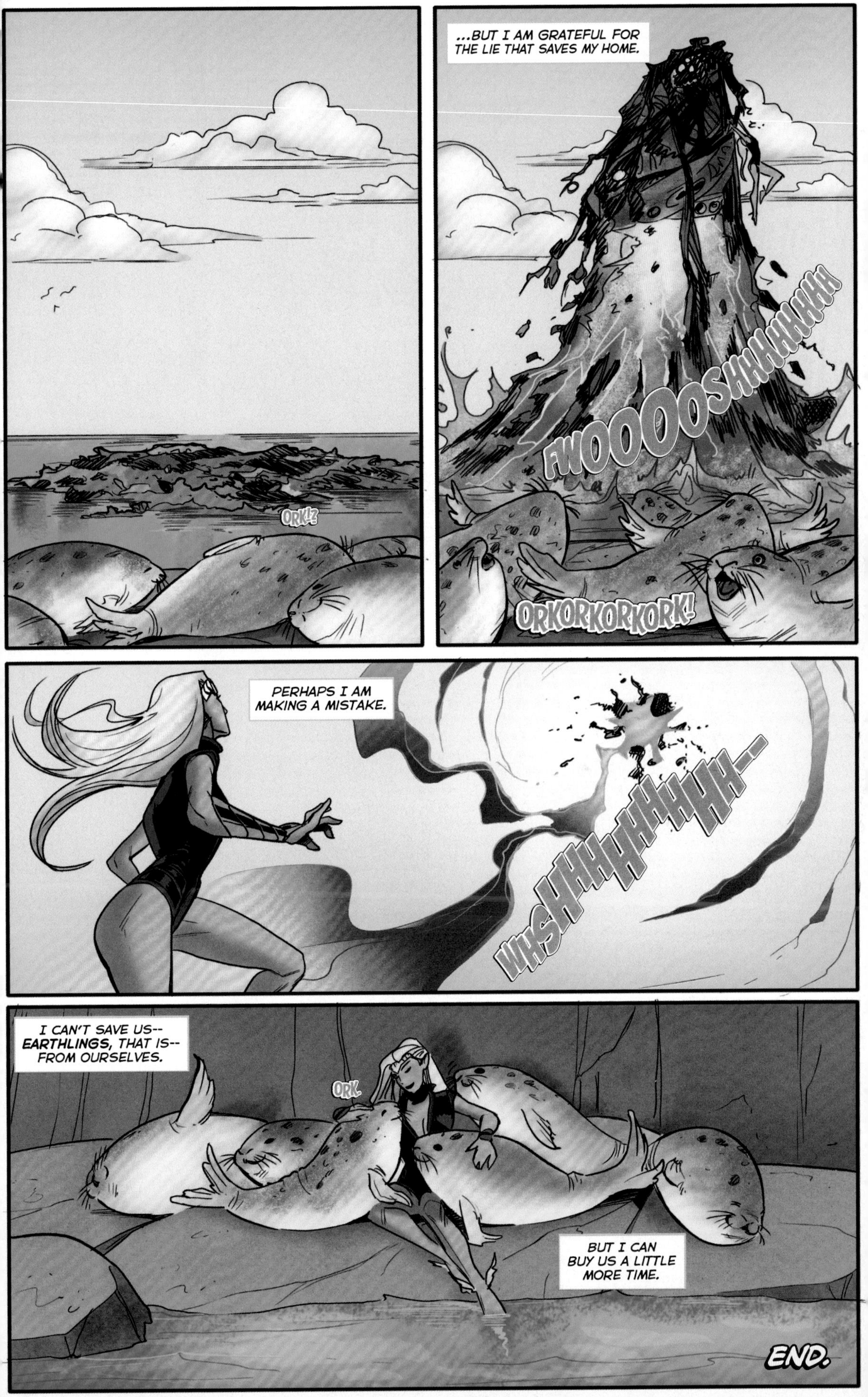
ORK!?
...BUT I AM GRATEFUL FOR THE LIE THAT SAVES MY HOME.
FWOOOOOSHHHHHHHH
ORKORKORKORK!
PERHAPS I AM MAKING A MISTAKE.
WHSHHHHHHHHH--
I CAN'T SAVE US-- EARTHLINGS, THAT IS-- FROM OURSELVES.
ORK.
BUT I CAN BUY US A LITTLE MORE TIME.
END.

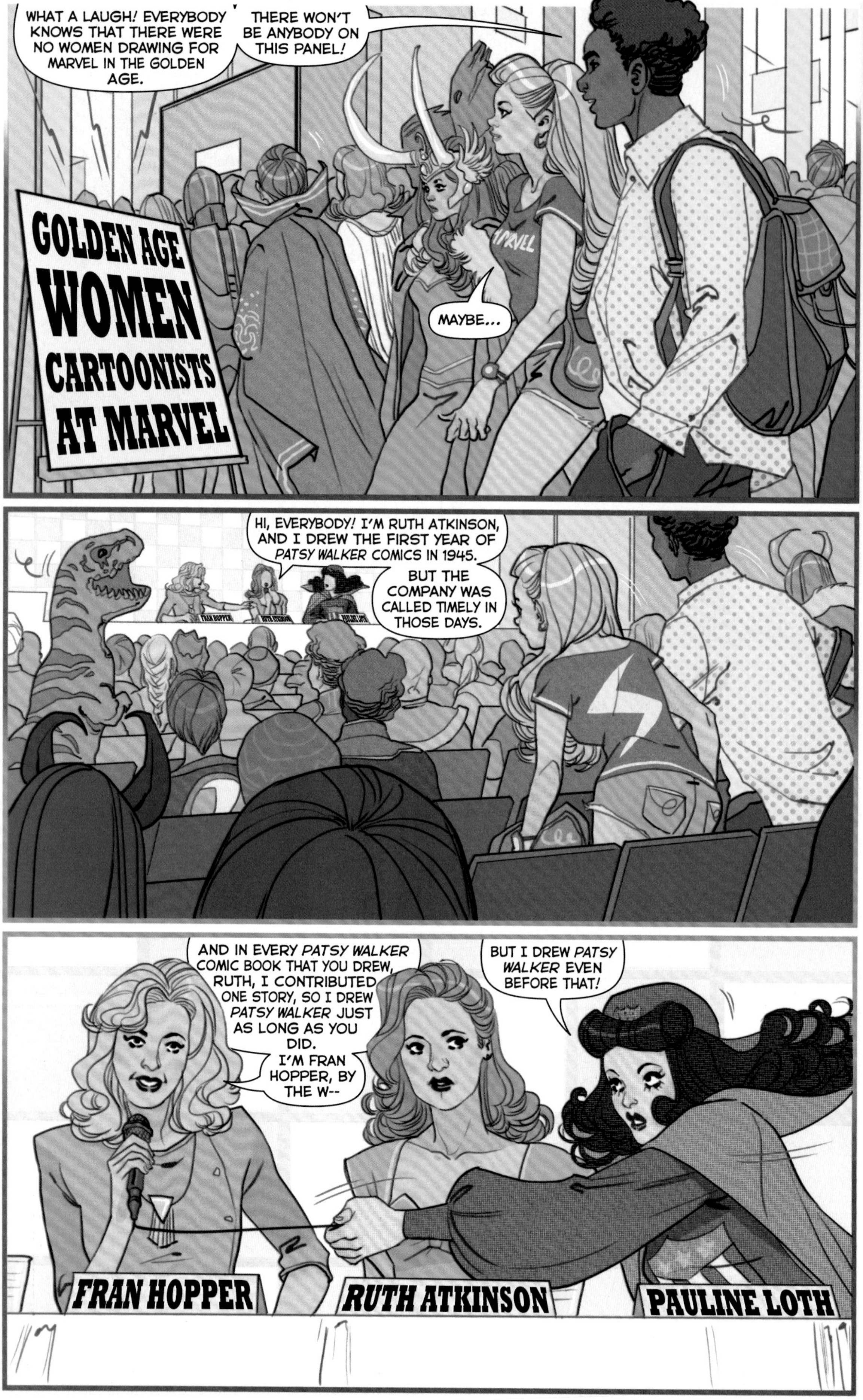

WHAT A LAUGH! EVERYBODY KNOWS THAT THERE WERE NO WOMEN DRAWING FOR MARVEL IN THE GOLDEN AGE.
THERE WON'T BE ANYBODY ON THIS PANEL!
GOLDEN AGE WOMEN CARTOONISTS AT MARVEL
MAYBE...
HI, EVERYBODY! I'M RUTH ATKINSON, AND I DREW THE FIRST YEAR OF *PATSY WALKER* COMICS IN 1945.
BUT THE COMPANY WAS CALLED TIMELY IN THOSE DAYS.
AND IN EVERY *PATSY WALKER* COMIC BOOK THAT YOU DREW, RUTH, I CONTRIBUTED ONE STORY, SO I DREW *PATSY WALKER* JUST AS LONG AS YOU DID.
I'M FRAN HOPPER, BY THE W--
BUT I DREW *PATSY WALKER* EVEN BEFORE THAT!
FRAN HOPPER
RUTH ATKINSON
PAULINE LOTH

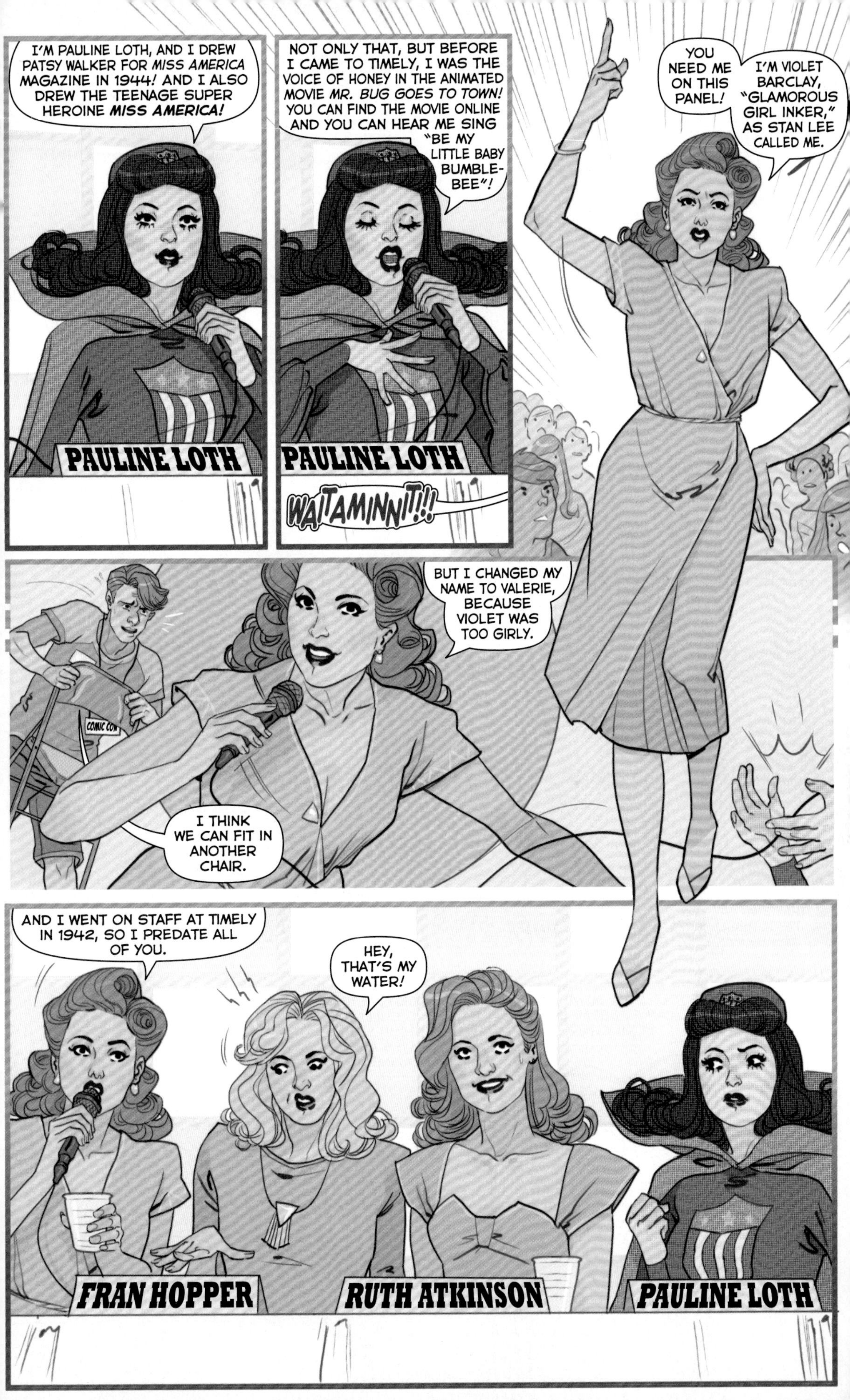

I'M PAULINE LOTH, AND I DREW PATSY WALKER FOR *MISS AMERICA* MAGAZINE IN 1944! AND I ALSO DREW THE TEENAGE SUPER HEROINE **MISS AMERICA!**
PAULINE LOTH
NOT ONLY THAT, BUT BEFORE I CAME TO TIMELY, I WAS THE VOICE OF HONEY IN THE ANIMATED MOVIE *MR. BUG GOES TO TOWN!* YOU CAN FIND THE MOVIE ONLINE AND YOU CAN HEAR ME SING
"BE MY LITTLE BABY BUMBLE-BEE"!
PAULINE LOTH
WAITAMINNIT!!!
YOU NEED ME ON THIS PANEL!
I'M VIOLET BARCLAY, "GLAMOROUS GIRL INKER," AS STAN LEE CALLED ME.
BUT I CHANGED MY NAME TO VALERIE, BECAUSE VIOLET WAS TOO GIRLY.
I THINK WE CAN FIT IN ANOTHER CHAIR.
AND I WENT ON STAFF AT TIMELY IN 1942, SO I PREDATE ALL OF YOU.
HEY, THAT'S MY WATER!
FRAN HOPPER
RUTH ATKINSON
PAULINE LOTH

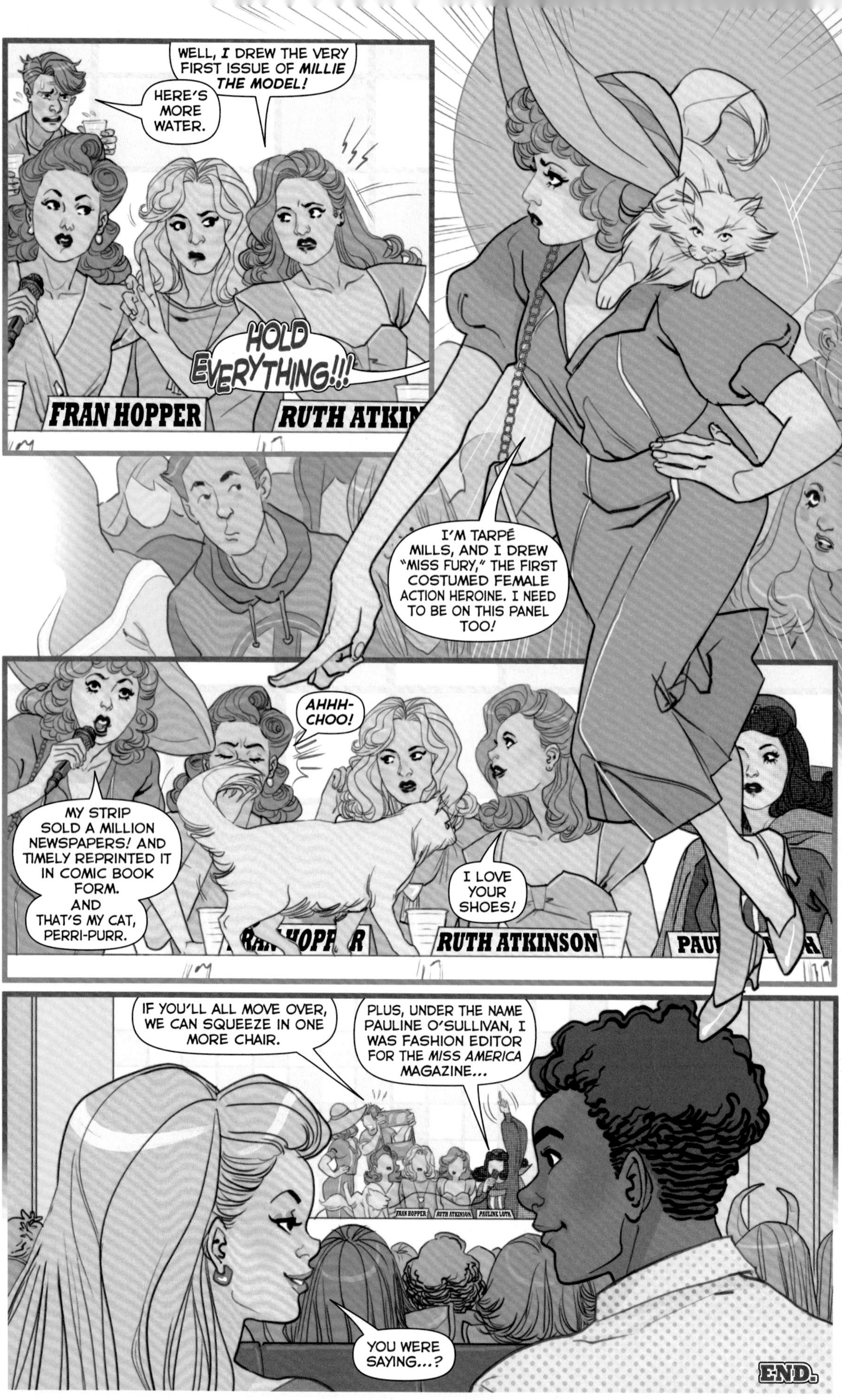
WELL, *I* DREW THE VERY FIRST ISSUE OF *MILLIE THE MODEL!*
HERE'S MORE WATER.
HOLD EVERYTHING!!!
FRAN HOPPER
RUTH ATKIN
I'M TARPÉ MILLS, AND I DREW "MISS FURY," THE FIRST COSTUMED FEMALE ACTION HEROINE. I NEED TO BE ON THIS PANEL TOO!
AHHH-CHOO!
MY STRIP SOLD A MILLION NEWSPAPERS! AND TIMELY REPRINTED IT IN COMIC BOOK FORM.
AND THAT'S MY CAT, PERRI-PURR.
I LOVE YOUR SHOES!
RUTH ATKINSON
IF YOU'LL ALL MOVE OVER, WE CAN SQUEEZE IN ONE MORE CHAIR.
PLUS, UNDER THE NAME PAULINE O'SULLIVAN, I WAS FASHION EDITOR FOR THE *MISS AMERICA* MAGAZINE...
FRAN HOPPER
RUTH ATKINSON
PAULINE LOTH
YOU WERE SAYING...?
END.

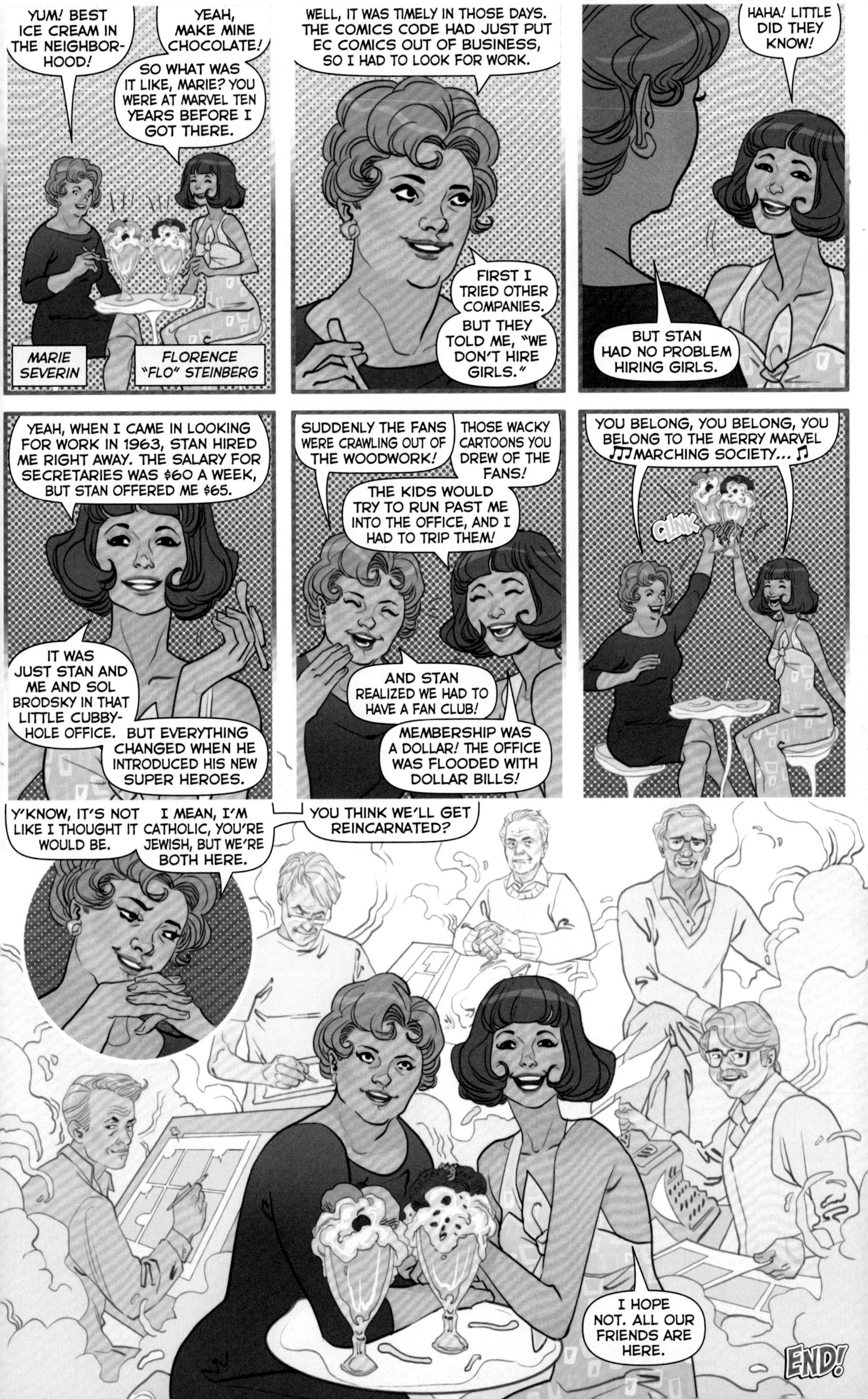
YUM! BEST ICE CREAM IN THE NEIGHBOR-HOOD!
YEAH, MAKE MINE CHOCOLATE!
SO WHAT WAS IT LIKE, MARIE? YOU WERE AT MARVEL TEN YEARS BEFORE I GOT THERE.
MARIE SEVERIN
FLORENCE "FLO" STEINBERG
WELL, IT WAS TIMELY IN THOSE DAYS. THE COMICS CODE HAD JUST PUT EC COMICS OUT OF BUSINESS, SO I HAD TO LOOK FOR WORK.
FIRST I TRIED OTHER COMPANIES.
BUT THEY TOLD ME, "WE DON'T HIRE GIRLS."
HAHA! LITTLE DID THEY KNOW!
BUT STAN HAD NO PROBLEM HIRING GIRLS.
YEAH, WHEN I CAME IN LOOKING FOR WORK IN 1963, STAN HIRED ME RIGHT AWAY. THE SALARY FOR SECRETARIES WAS $60 A WEEK, BUT STAN OFFERED ME $65.
IT WAS JUST STAN AND ME AND SOL BRODSKY IN THAT LITTLE CUBBY-HOLE OFFICE.
BUT EVERYTHING CHANGED WHEN HE INTRODUCED HIS NEW SUPER HEROES.
SUDDENLY THE FANS WERE CRAWLING OUT OF THE WOODWORK!
THOSE WACKY CARTOONS YOU DREW OF THE FANS!
THE KIDS WOULD TRY TO RUN PAST ME INTO THE OFFICE, AND I HAD TO TRIP THEM!
AND STAN REALIZED WE HAD TO HAVE A FAN CLUB!
MEMBERSHIP WAS A DOLLAR! THE OFFICE WAS FLOODED WITH DOLLAR BILLS!
YOU BELONG, YOU BELONG, YOU BELONG TO THE MERRY MARVEL ♫MARCHING SOCIETY... ♫
CLINK
Y'KNOW, IT'S NOT LIKE I THOUGHT IT WOULD BE.
I MEAN, I'M CATHOLIC, YOU'RE JEWISH, BUT WE'RE BOTH HERE.
YOU THINK WE'LL GET REINCARNATED?
I HOPE NOT. ALL OUR FRIENDS ARE HERE.
END!

WRITER SPOTLIGHT
TRINA ROBBINS

PHOTO CREDIT TO RACHELLE STEELE

DO YOU REMEMBER THE MOMENT THAT YOU FELL IN LOVE WITH COMICS?

Probably as soon as I saw my first comic. I was always very visual, so the combo of words and pictures suited me perfectly.

WHEN DID YOU KNOW THAT YOU WANTED TO BE A COMICS ARTIST/WRITER/HISTORIAN?

Well, I don't remember a time I wasn't drawing, and I was writing almost as soon as my mother taught me to read at the age of 4. When my classmates and I would do the "What do you want to be when you grow up?" thing, the other girls would want to be nurses, teachers, secretaries, but I would say that I wanted to write books and illustrate them, and that's what comics are.

WHAT WAS AN IMPORTANT LESSON ABOUT YOUR CHOSEN FIELD THAT YOU LEARNED EARLY ON THAT HAS STUCK WITH YOU THROUGHOUT YOUR CAREER?

Anyone can create comics, no matter their gender or race. All you need is talent, perseverance and a thick skin.

WHAT IS YOUR FAVORITE TOOL OF THE TRADE?

Google! Seriously, part of the fun of writing is the research involved, and I'm a stickler for research. Not just Google (but I do use it), but books, magazines, newspapers, museums, you name it.

WHAT HAS BEEN YOUR PROUDEST MOMENT IN COMICS?

I'm very proud of Strip AIDS U.S.A., the AIDS benefit book that I co-edited with Robert Triptow and Bill Sienkiewicz. I'm very proud that my 9/11 story, written by me and drawn by Anne Timmons, is in the Library of Congress.

WHAT HAS BEEN YOUR FAVORITE EXPERIENCE WITH A FAN?

That time in a thrift store when I was waiting on line to purchase that hat I'd found, and I complimented the woman in front of me on the pretty green velvet box she was buying. She asked, "Are you Trina Robbins?" and proceeded to just say some very comforting, life-affirming things to me about my work. I was going through chemo at the time (I'm cancer-free now!) and among other things was bald as an egg (thus, buying hats at thrift shops) and hadn't even realized how much I needed her words until she said them. Then she offered me the velvet box. I thanked her but told her that I already had too many tchotckes, and she said, "But I wanted to give you something," to which I replied, "You just did."

WHAT HAS BEEN YOUR FAVORITE EXPERIENCE AS A FAN?

Probably meeting and making friends with all those older Golden Age comics creators, who are now long gone. Especially making friends with Captain Marvel creator C.C. Beck, who added me to his little circle of fans that he corresponded with and once told someone that I was like the daughter he never had (gulp!).

IS THERE A MARVEL CHARACTER THAT YOU'D LOVE TO WORK WITH THAT YOU HAVEN'T ALREADY?

Patsy Walker!

FEARLESS #4

Marie and Flo are sitting in an ice cream parlor but we focus on them. We don't see who anyone else is until **Panel 8**.

We don't see any background until the last panel. Flo Steinberg and Marie Severin sit in an ice cream parlor eating ice cream from ice cream glasses with spoons. I guess with no background the only way we know it's an ice cream parlor would be the chairs and table. Maybe it would be nice to see Flo with her short poofy hair of the '60s and wearing that iconic black dress with the big white bow. Dear Artist, please vary the panels so it's not just all talking heads.

Panel 1:   **Marie (1):** Yum! Best ice cream in the neighborhood!
             Flo (2): Yeah, make mine chocolate!
             Flo (3): So what was it like, Marie? You were at Marvel ten years before I got there.

ARTIST SPOTLIGHT
MARGUERITE SAUVAGE

DO YOU REMEMBER THE MOMENT THAT YOU FELL IN LOVE WITH COMICS?

Yes, I was a kid around 9 and found my parents' library. There weren't any comics for my age, but that's the way you learn sometimes, isn't it?

WHEN DID YOU KNOW THAT YOU WANTED TO BE A COMICS ARTIST?

At age 23, when I finished my studies in law and media, I started thinking: "It's now or never. You can build up a book and look around for illustration work, or you can follow the path of office work." I started building up a book.

WHAT WAS AN IMPORTANT LESSON ABOUT YOUR CHOSEN FIELD THAT YOU LEARNED EARLY ON THAT HAS STUCK WITH YOU THROUGHOUT YOUR CAREER?

Be on time, be flexible and don't take things personally.

WHETHER IT'S A CUP OF COFFEE, A SPECIFIC TYPE OF PEN OR DESK SETUP OR EVEN AN EMOTIONAL-SUPPORT ACTION FIGURE, IS THERE AN ELEMENT IN YOUR WORKSPACE THAT YOU FEEL IS CRUCIAL TO YOUR WORK PROCESS?

Tea.

WHAT IS YOUR FAVORITE TOOL OF THE TRADE?

My Wacom Cintiq.

WHAT IS YOUR FAVORITE THING TO DRAW?

Women figures and long hair.

WHAT HAS BEEN YOUR PROUDEST MOMENT IN COMICS?

There have been many; I can't choose!

WHAT HAS BEEN YOUR FAVORITE PROJECT THAT YOU'VE WORKED ON SO FAR, AND WHY?

I'm pretty proud of working with Trina Robbins and on FEARLESS!

WHAT HAS BEEN YOUR FAVORITE EXPERIENCE WITH A FAN?

Meeting artists and writers I admire.

WHAT HAS BEEN YOUR FAVORITE MARVEL CHARACTER TO WORK WITH?

America Chavez, Storm and--gosh, there're plenty...

IS THERE A MARVEL CHARACTER THAT YOU'D LOVE TO WORK WITH THAT YOU HAVEN'T ALREADY?

There're plenty as well, from Doctor Strange to Jessica Jones.

HEY THERE, TRUE BELIEVERS!

Thanks so much for reading the **FEARLESS** anthology!

As part of Marvel's 80th Anniversary celebration, we wanted to create a book staffed entirely by women that would spotlight not only our incredible female characters but also the massively talented creators who work on them. This is also the first project that all the women currently working in editorial collaborated on. It was a true labor of love and we hope you enjoyed it!

By now, this anthology has exposed you to several amazing creators whose work you can follow out of these pages! Many of them are working on projects at Marvel now or have projects coming up in the near future. But don't stop there--women all across the industry are taking comics by storm, and there are far more of them than we could include here. Supporting their work is a great way to ensure that you get to see more of it!

As Trina Robbins and Marguerite Sauvage so beautifully illustrated in the last story of this anthology, women have had a place in comics since the very beginning, and 80 years of Marvel history would not be the same without their contributions. They belong here, and so do you, dear reader--whoever you may be!

So go forth and be fearless! Make comics, read comics, review comics and love comics! We need your voices!

Sarah, Annalise, Lauren, Kathleen, Shannon, Alanna & Lindsey

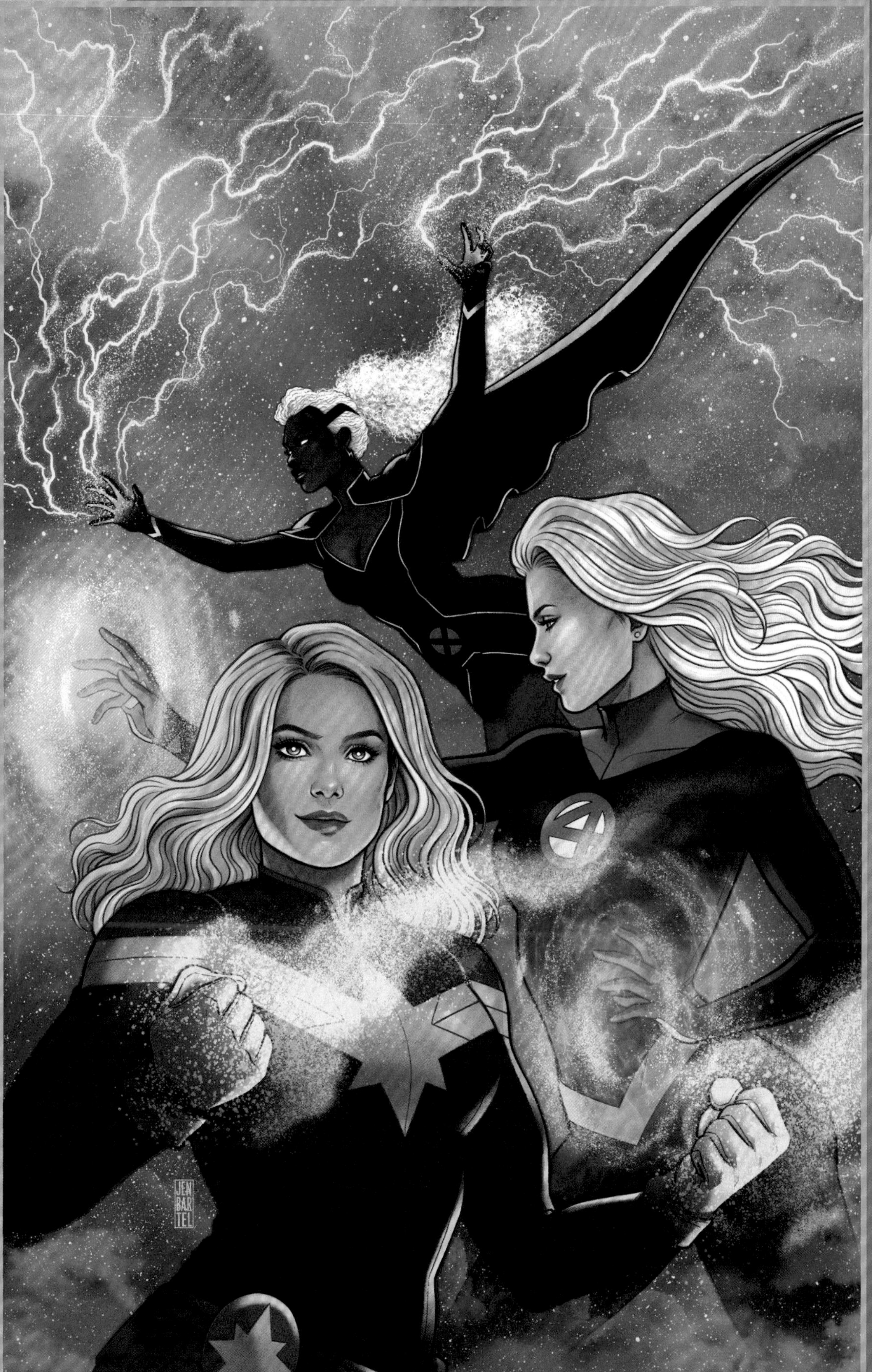
JEN BAR TEL

1 VARIANT BY **JEN BARTEL**

*1-4 COMBINED VARIANTS BY **JENNY FRISON***

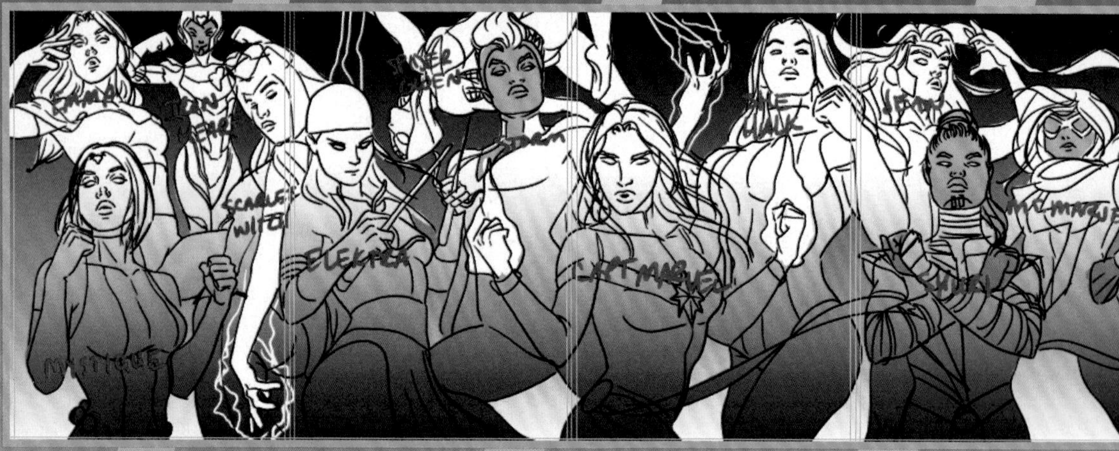
ELEKTRA
MYSTIQUE

COMBINED VARIANTS SKETCH BY ***JENNY FRISON***

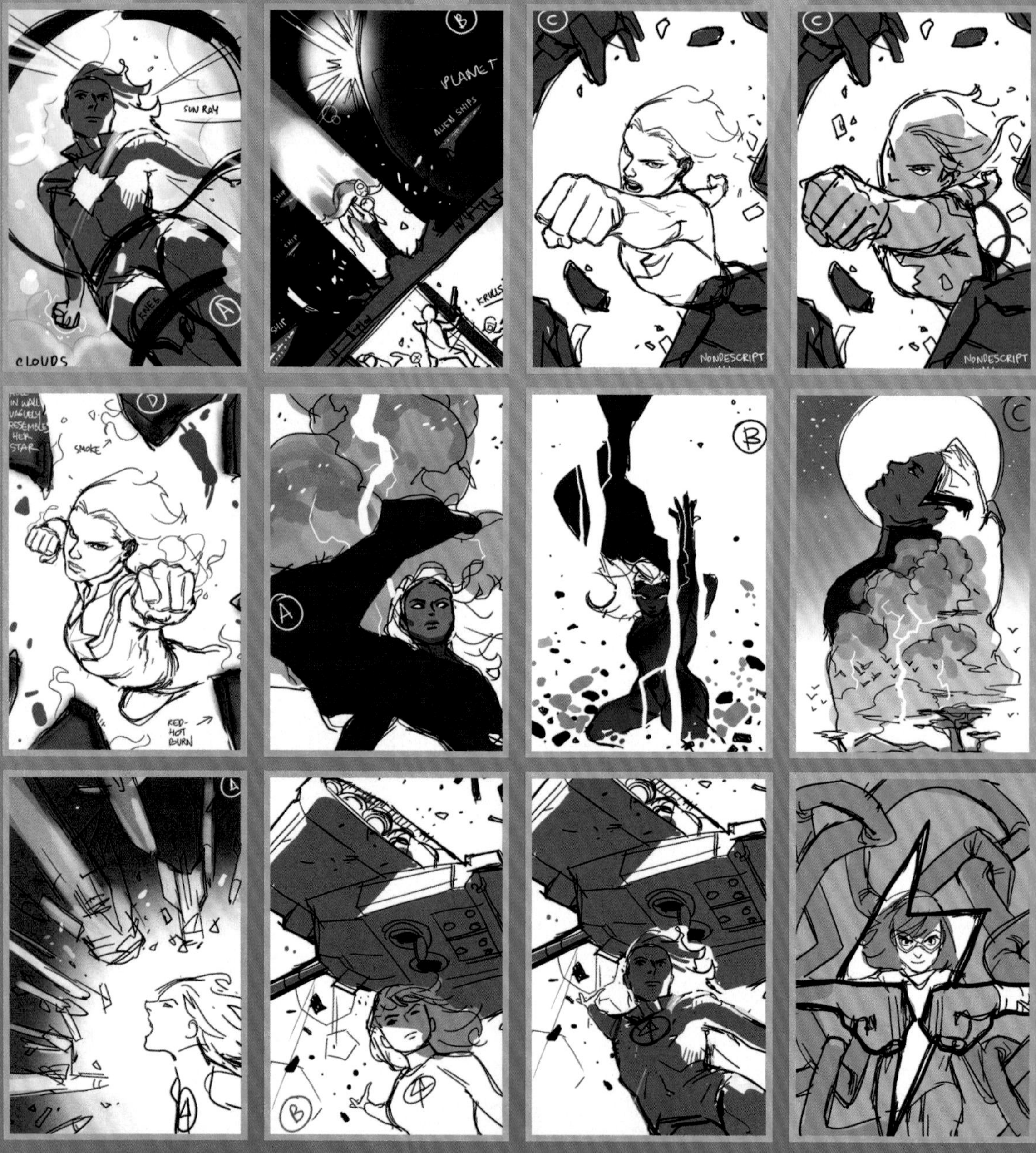
SUN RAY
CLOUDS
PLANET
ALIEN SHIPS
SHIP
NONDESCRIPT
NONDESCRIPT
SMOKE
RED-HOT BURN

1-4 COVER SKETCHES BY ***YASMINE PUTRI***

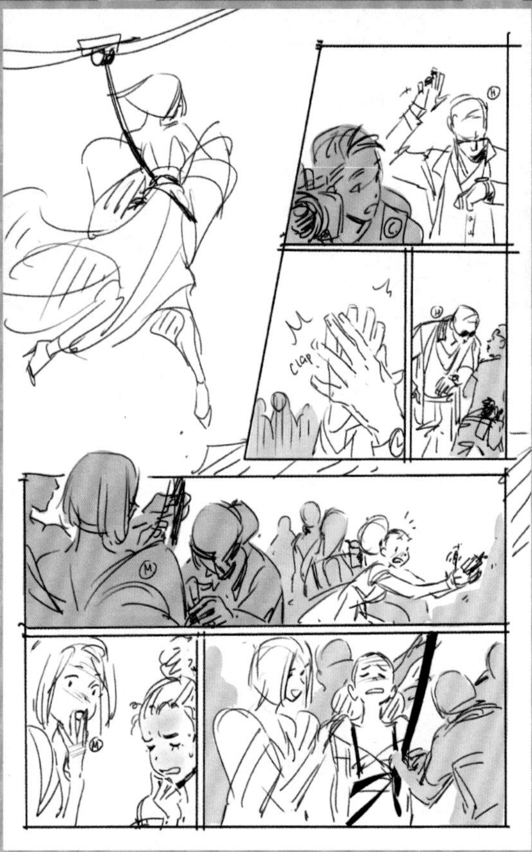
CLAP

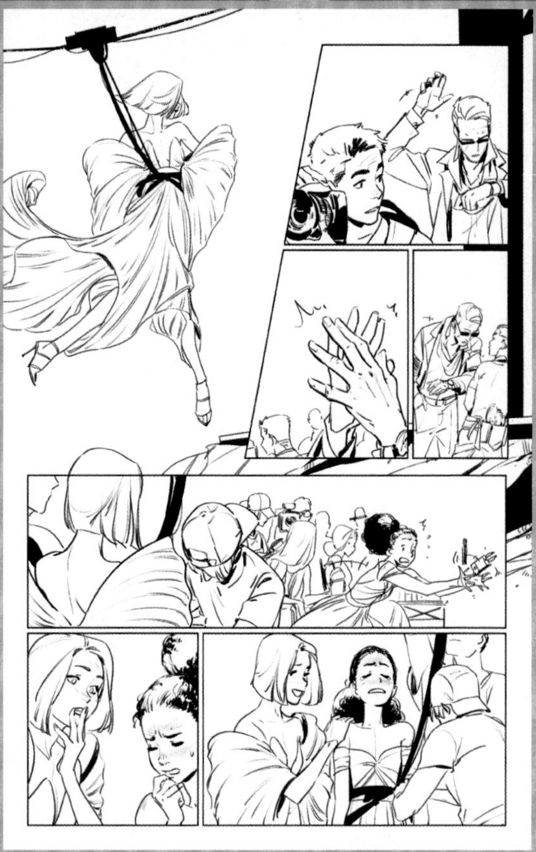

"STYLE HIGH CLUB," PAGE 8 LAYOUTS AND INKS BY **NINA VAKUEVA**

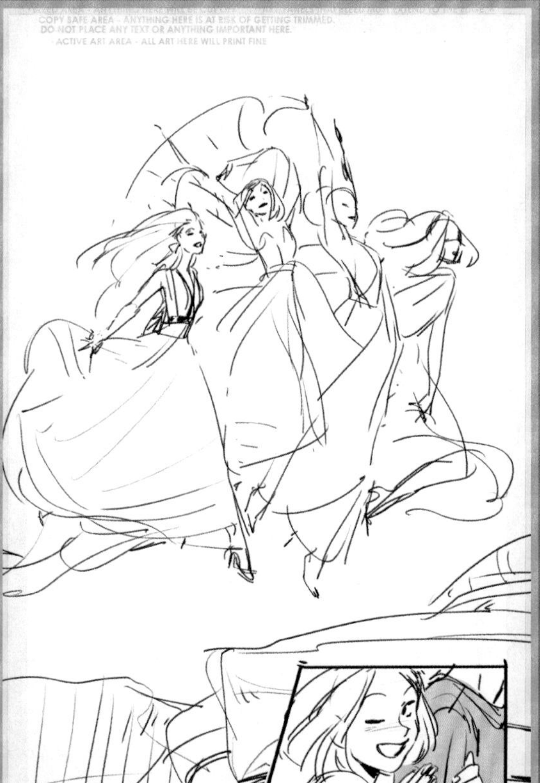
COPY SAFE AREA - ANYTHING HERE IS AT RISK OF GETTING TRIMMED.
DO NOT PLACE ANY TEXT OR ANYTHING IMPORTANT HERE.
ACTIVE ART AREA - ALL ART HERE WILL PRINT FINE

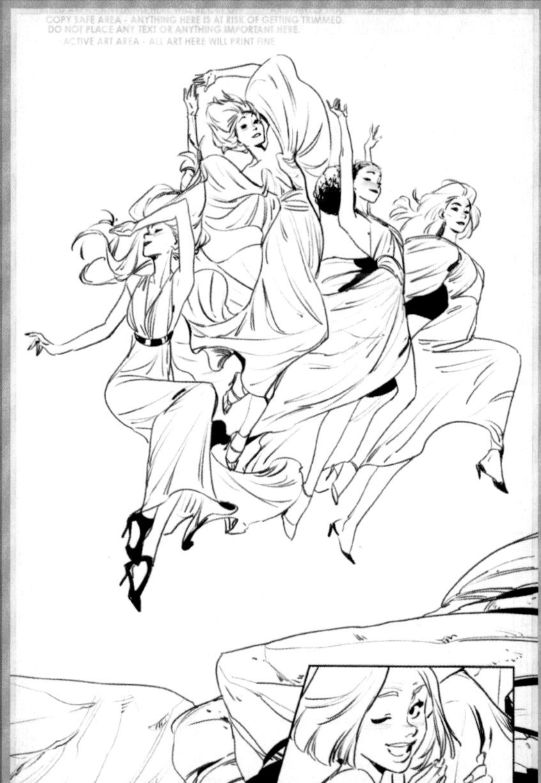
COPY SAFE AREA - ANYTHING HERE IS AT RISK OF GETTING TRIMMED.
DO NOT PLACE ANY TEXT OR ANYTHING IMPORTANT HERE.
ACTIVE ART AREA - ALL ART HERE WILL PRINT FINE

"STYLE HIGH CLUB," PAGE 12 LAYOUTS AND INKS BY **NINA VAKUEVA**

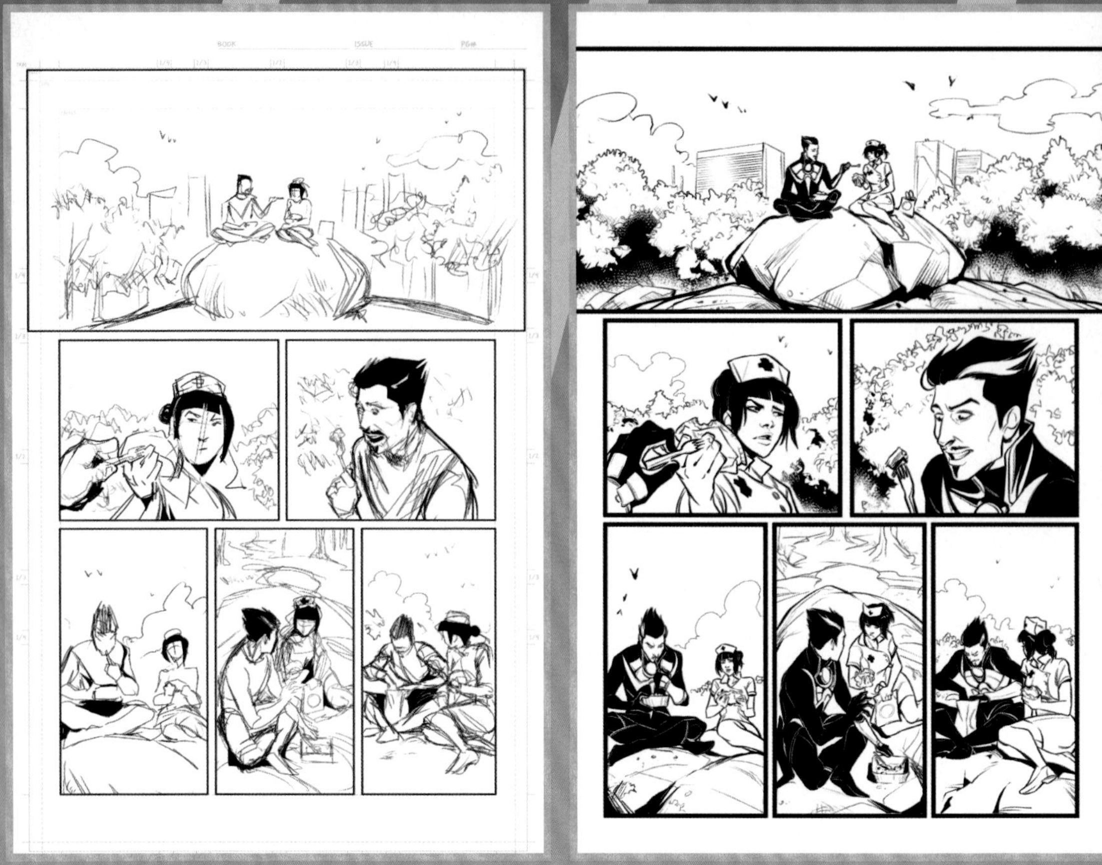

"NIGHT NURSE: A CAPE OF HER OWN," PAGE 2 LAYOUTS AND INKS BY **IOLANDA ZANFARDINO**

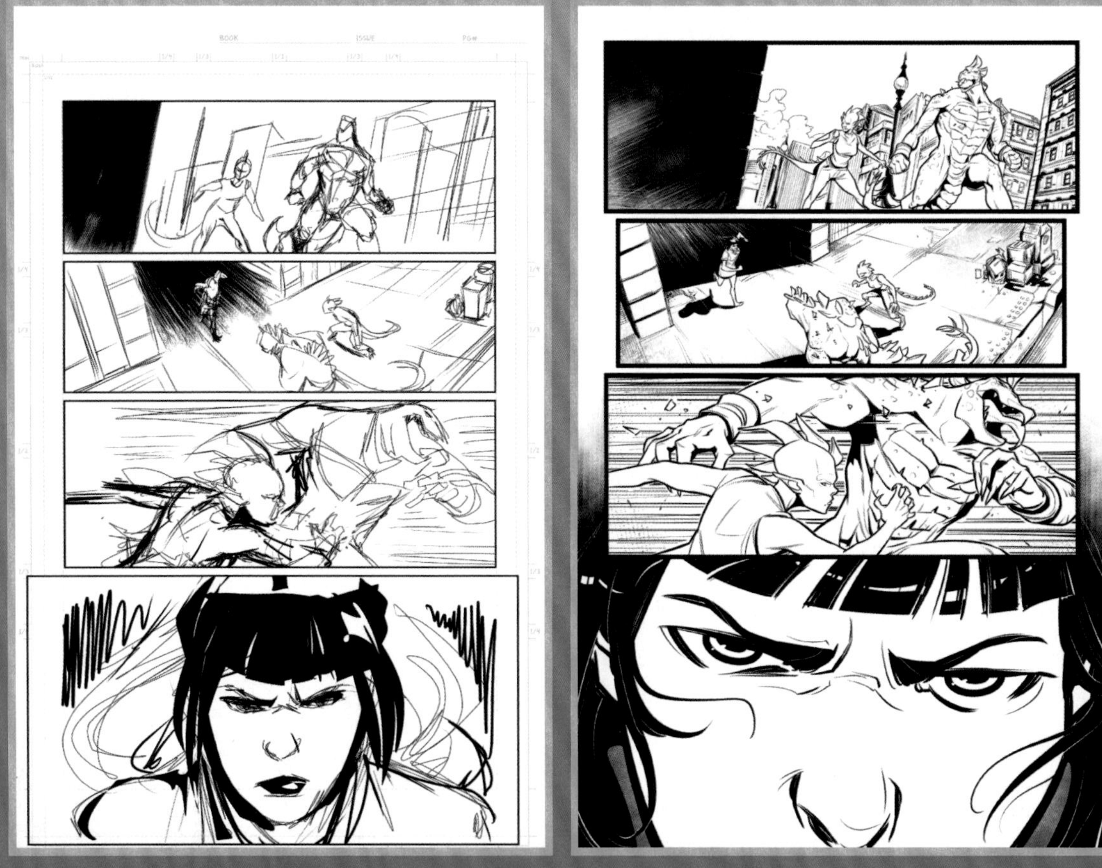

"NIGHT NURSE: A CAPE OF HER OWN," PAGE 9 LAYOUTS AND INKS BY **IOLANDA ZANFARDINO**

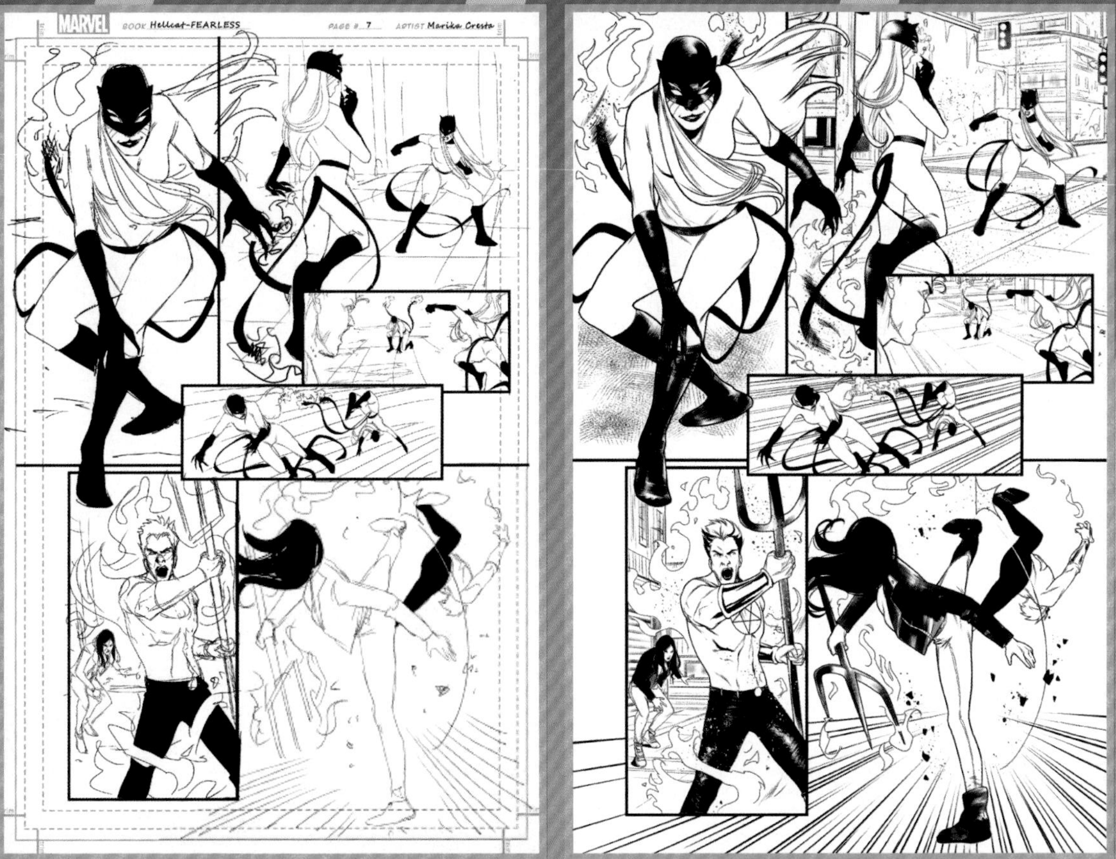
MARVEL
BOOK Hellcat-FEARLESS
PAGE # 7
ARTIST Marika Cresta

"COPYCAT," PAGE 7 LAYOUTS AND INKS BY **MARIKA CRESTA**

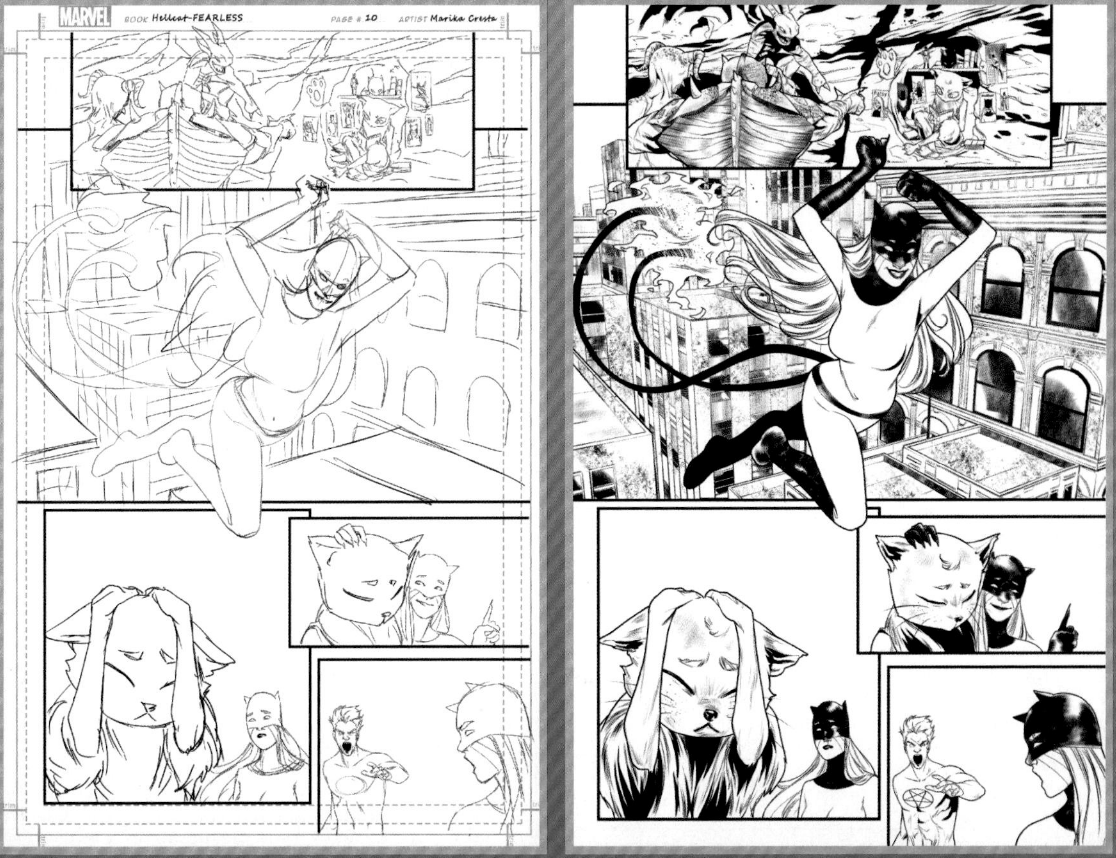
MARVEL
BOOK Hellcat-FEARLESS
PAGE # 10
ARTIST Marika Cresta

"COPYCAT," PAGE 10 LAYOUTS AND INKS BY **MARIKA CRESTA**

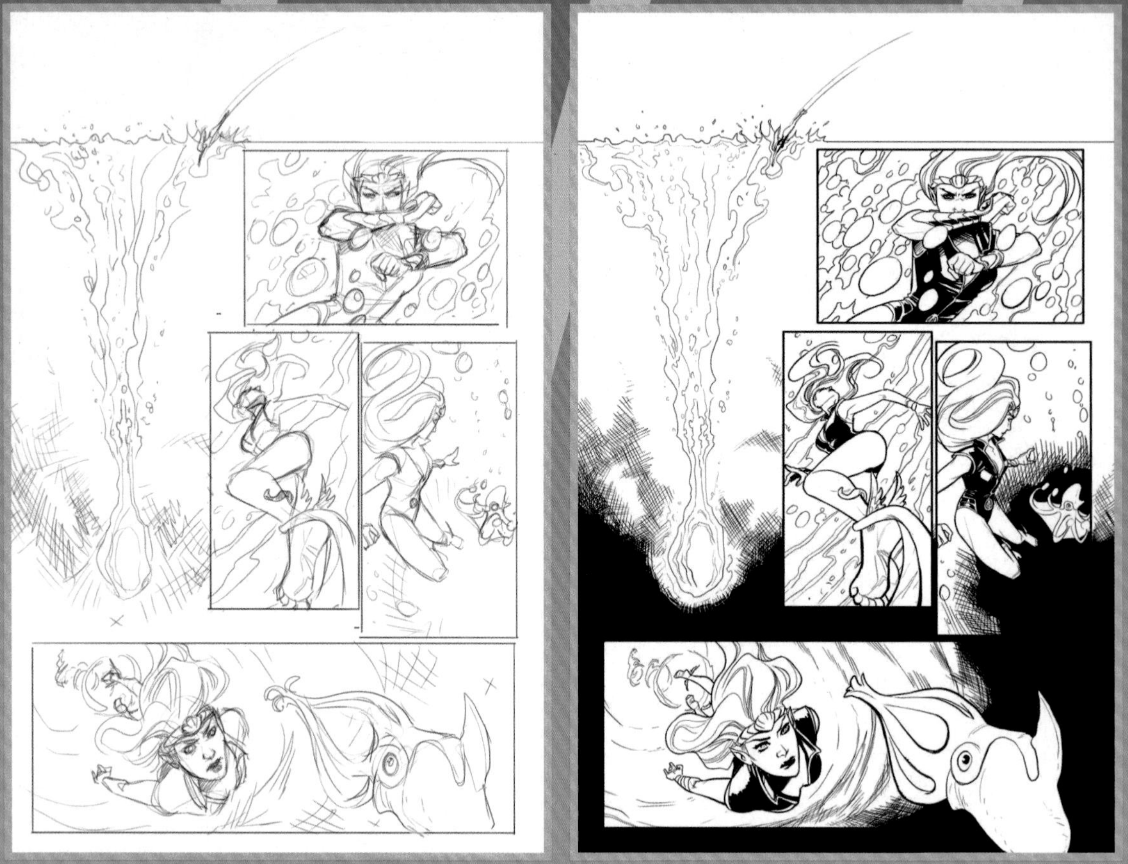

"ATMOSPHERIA," PAGE 3 LAYOUTS AND INKS BY **ROSI KÄMPE**

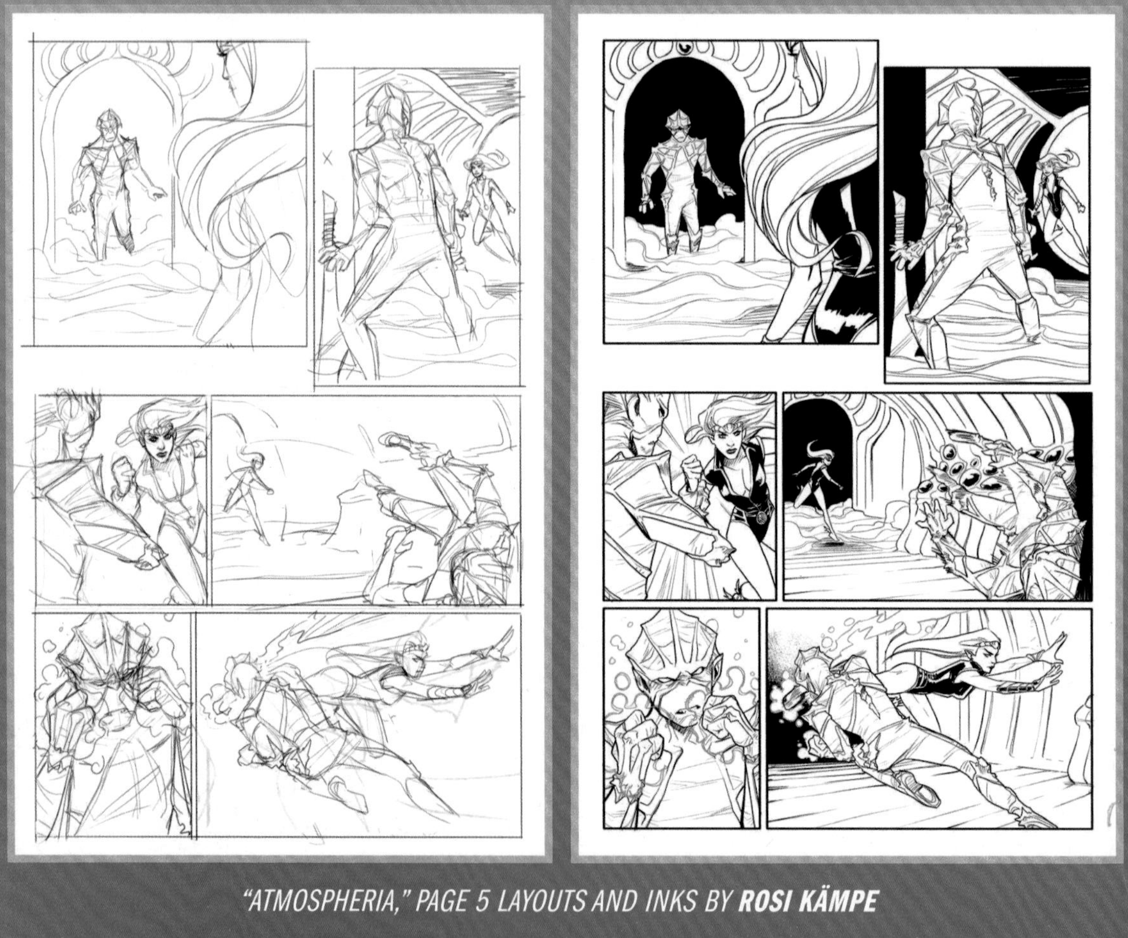

"ATMOSPHERIA," PAGE 5 LAYOUTS AND INKS BY **ROSI KÄMPE**